AN IDEALISTIC PRAGMATISM

AN IDEALISTIC PRAGMATISM

THE DEVELOPMENT OF THE PRAGMATIC ELEMENT
IN THE PHILOSOPHY OF JOSIAH ROYCE

by

MARY BRIODY MAHOWALD

MARTINUS NIJHOFF / THE HAGUE / 1972

© *1972 by Martinus Nijhoff, The Hague, Netherlands*
All rights reserved, including the right to translate or to reproduce this book or parts thereof in any form

ISBN 90 247 1184 3

PRINTED IN THE NETHERLANDS

PREFACE

When I first became acquainted with the thought of the American philosopher Josiah Royce, two factors particularly intrigued me. The first was Royce's claim that the notion of community was his main metaphysical tenet; the second was his close association with the two American pragmatists, Charles Sanders Peirce and William James. Regarding the first factor, I was struck by the fact that a philosopher who died in 1916 should emphasize a topic of such contemporary significance not only in philosophy but in so many other vital fields as well (sociology, psychology, politics, theology – to name only a few). Regarding the second, I was curious as to whether the pragmatism of Peirce and James might have influenced Royce during the course of their professional and personal contacts. Similarly, I wondered whether the idealism of Royce might have affected the thought of Peirce and James. To have appeased my curiosity in regard to all three thinkers, however, would have required (at least) three books. As a start I have now appeased it in regard to one.

In researching the writings of Royce I found my way to the Houghton Library and to the Archives of Harvard University at Cambridge, Massachusetts, where the unpublished manuscripts of Royce are preserved. (No editing job has yet been done on this bulk of material, though such would certainly be a welcome contribution to American philosophy.) Since Volumes I through 52 are for the most part the manuscripts of Royce's published books and articles, my time at Harvard was spent mostly on Volumes 53 through 98. While I found no startling divergence from Royce's published positions in the unpublished material, I was able, by researching the latter, to discover certain texts more suited to the purpose of this study. On one point in particular (the social aspect of the knowing process), I found a great deal more material in the unpublished writings than in the published works. On the whole, the access to both published and unpublished sources lent more cogency to basic evaluations of the thought of Royce.

In pursuing the topic which titles and subtitles this work I have also explored Royce's notion of community to the extent of having become greatly appreciative of the contemporary relevance of his philosophy. As a result, the present resurgence of interest in the works of Royce seems more than justified. I delight that some of the vital insights of this American thinker are being shared today to a greater extent than ever before. My hope is that they be shared throughout our country and our world not only theoretically but practically as well.

ACKNOWLEDGMENTS

My sincere thanks to the philosophy faculty of Marquette University, particularly Dr. Beatrice Zedler, Dr. Paul Byrne and Dr. Joseph O'Malley, for their interest and assistance in preparing this work. I am also indebted to Dr. John McDermott of Queens College of the City University of New York and to Rev. Frank Oppenheim, S.J., of Xavier University for their sharing of ideas in regard to the project. Finally, I am deeply grateful to many unnamed friends whose encouragement "energized" me throughout the undertaking

KEY TO ABBREVIATIONS

The following is an alphabetical listing of the abbreviations used in the Notes. Publication information is given in the first reference to each work.

CG	*The Conception of God*
CI	*The Conception of immortality*
CP	*Collected Papers of Charles Sanders Peirce*
EP	"The Eternal and the Practical"
FE	*Fugitive Essays*
HGC	*The Hope of the Great Community*
Im	"Immortality"
LMI	*Lectures on Modern Idealism*
MHS	"The Mechanical, the Historical and the Statistical"
M&R	"Mind and Reality"
OP	*Outlines of Psychology*
PC	*The Problem of Christianity*
PL	*The Philosophy of Loyalty*
Prag	*Pragmatism and Four Essay from the Meaning of Truth*
RAP	*The Religious Aspect of Philosophy*
SRI	*The Sources of Religious Insight*
War	*Ward and Insurance*
WI	*The World and the Individual*
WJO	*William James and Other Essays on the Philosophy of Life*
WVC	"What is Vital in Christianity?"

CONTENTS

Preface   V

Acknowledgments   VII

INTRODUCTION

CHAPTER I: PROPAEDEUTIC TO A STUDY OF ROYCE   3

    A. The nature of Royce's idealism   3
    B. The religious content of Royce's thought   7
    C. The empirical grounding of Royce's philosophy   10

CHAPTER II: POSSIBILITIES FOR A ROYCEAN PRAGMATISM   15

    A. The pragmatists that influenced Royce   17
    B. The notions of pragmatism that influenced Royce   20
    C. A pragmatism consistent with idealism   25

PART ONE
THE EARLY ROYCE (c. 1875-90)

CHAPTER III: HIS THEORY OF KNOWLEDGE   31

    A. Royce's early stress on the practical purposefulness of all speculation   31
    B. The usefulness of doubt and postulate in philosophizing   34
    C. The limited function of verification and the role of insight   37
    D. The relativity of truth and error   40

CHAPTER IV: HIS NOTION OF THE ABSOLUTE   43

    A. The function of belief, its origin and constitution   43
    B. The Absolute Thought, perfectly fulfilling experience   48
    C. The Universal Will, aiming at organization of experience   51
    D. The relationship of the Absolute to the problem of evil   53

Chapter V: His Conception of the Individual — 57

    A. Meaning, worth, and importance of the individual — 57
    B. A practical answer to individualism — 61
    C. The nature and significance of progress for the individual — 64

PART TWO

THE MIDDLE PERIOD (c. 1890-1906)

Chapter VI: Theory of Knowledge Pragmatically allied with Doctrine of Interpretation — 71

    A. Other theories of being as interpretations — 72
    B. The synthetic view of Royce — 75
    C. The essentially social character of the knowing process — 78

Chapter VII: Notion of the Absolute More Pragmatically Orientated — 86

    A. An explanation and definition of God in terms of Experience — 87
    B. The relation of will to the Absolute — 92
    C. The union between God and man — 96

Chapter VIII: Conception of the Individual Pragmatically Leads to Consideration of Community — 101

    A. Royce's conception of the self — 101
    B. Love as the principle of individuation — 104
    C. Freedom and responsibility of the self — 107
    D. Community as fulfilling the individual — 110

PART THREE

THE MATURE ROYCE (c. 1906-16)

Chapter IX: Knowledge by Interpretation, a Mediating Principle — 119

    A. Perception, conception, and interpretation — 119
    B. The community of interpretation — 124
    C. The role of the mediator — 128

Chapter X: God as Pragmatic Postulate — 133

- A. The Absolute, filling our need for Truth, Reality, and a Cause — 134
- B. Solving the religious paradox — 138
- C. Christianity as interpretation of man's experience — 140

Chapter XI: Community as Perfective of the Individual — 149

- A. Community in general — 151
- B. Community as end: the Beloved Community — 153
- C. Communities as means — 155

CONCLUSION

Chapter XII: The Roycean Pragmatic — 167

- A. Recapitulation — 167
- B. Critique — 171
- C. Result — 173

Bibliography — 177

Index — 183

INTRODUCTION

CHAPTER I

PROPAEDEUTIC TO A STUDY OF ROYCE

Pragmatism and idealism are sometimes considered contradictory philosophies. Such consideration is well founded if one sees pluralism as essential to pragmatism, and identifies idealism with a closed monistic system. This need not be the case, however. That pragmatism is compatible with idealism will be shown in the course of this study. The exemplar of their compatibility, through his doctrine of pragmatic idealism or absolute pragmatism, is Josiah Royce.

Nonetheless, it is not the idealism of Royce to which our attention is here directed so much as to his pragmatism. The intent is to trace the development of his philosophy in order to discern in what way and to what extent (if any) his doctrine may be considered pragmatic in character. This requires an initial investigation into the possibilities for a pragmatism in Royce. But even before examining those possibilities, it is necessary to have some understanding of Royce's philosophy in general. To that end, the following three considerations are offered as propaedeutic to a study of Royce: the nature of his idealism, the religious content of his thought, and the empirical grounding of his philosophy. These propaedeutic factors, briefly treated though they be, prepare us to appreciate the compatibility of idealism and pragmatism when these are taken in a Roycean sense.

A. *The nature of Royce's idealism*

In general Royce's idealism is much like that of the idealists who preceded him. Among the thinkers to whom he attributes a view similar to his own are Fichte, Hegel, Schopenhauer. J. S. Mill and Renouvier.[1] All idealists, remarks Royce, maintain "that the world is a phenomenal manifestation of the

---

[1] For specific references in the works of these men cited by Royce, see Josiah Royce, *The Religious Aspect of Philosophy* (New York: Houghton Mifflin Company, 1885), 362. Hereafter we abbreviate this to RAP.

life of one absolute Being, conscious, personal, all-embracing."[2] According to this position, the external world itself comprises all "the possible and actual present, past, and future content of consciousness for all beings."[3] In Royce's estimation, such a view is the most acceptable postulate that one could have about the world.[4]

Two terms require particular consideration in order to grasp Royce's description of idealism, viz., "postulate" and "possible." In regard to the former Royce uses "postulate" to refer to any workable idea that is not presently demonstrable or demonstrated. The postulate is an assumption or hypothesis which *might* subsequently be proved. In his chapter on "Idealism" in *The Religious Aspect of Philosophy* Royce treats his idealism as a postulate, suggesting thereby a relationship between his position and that of the common sense realist whom he criticizes. The realist is one who posits or postulates a world of objects that correspond in some way to his ideas of them. Neither realist nor idealist can ever verify through experience the independent reality of the external world; neither can spell out with demonstrable certainty the likeness or correspondence between external reality and states of consciousness.[5]

But Royce the idealist goes on in the very next chapter to show that his world view, even if initially merely postulated, is demonstrable through man's experience of the possibility of error.[6] The existence of an absolute infinite Thought is required to account for the partialness of human knowing and the mistakes that occur in human judging. Consequently, Royce regards his own idealism as both postulate and demonstrable theory.[7]

The notion of "possible reality" is an important one to Royce because it evokes his postulating an absolute idealism. Admittedly there are different kinds of possible beings: some are empty possibilities or pure imaginations (e.g., "I could possibly have wings and a long tail, an hundred eyes, and a mountain of gold"), and some are real possibilities (e.g., "The pages of that

---

[2] Josiah Royce, Unpublished Roycean Manuscript Folios, reserved at Widener Library Archives, Harvard University, Vol. 52, "Introduction to Paper on Problem of Job," 3. Hereafter, references to these unpublished manuscripts of Royce will be given merely by volume number, with page and title as these occur in the original text.

[3] RAP, 362.

[4] Cf. *Ibid*.

[5] Cf. RAP, 359.

[6] The argument, as Royce recounts it, runs as follows: "The substance of our whole reasoning about the nature of error amounted to the result that in and of itself alone, no single judgment is or can be an error. Only as actually included in a higher thought, that gives to the first its completed object, and compares it therewith, is the first thought an error.... The higher thought is the whole truth, of which the error is by itself an incomplete fragment. Now... there is no stopping-place short of an Infinite Thought." RAP, 431.

[7] Cf. RAP, 362.

closed book, the bones inside the body of that cat, my own brain"). Ranking the latter as "possible *experiences*," he asks "what kind of unreal reality is this potential actuality?"[8]

In answering his own question, Royce points to the motive which leads us to postulate possible experiences. This motive, he claims, is the "familiar and universal wish to apply the postulate of uniformity to our confused actual experience."[9] We expect things to happen in some sequential causal order. For example,

I see an apple fall, and no more than that. But I postulate that if I could have had experience of all the facts, I should have observed a series of material changes in the twig on which the apple hung, that would have sufficed to restore the broken uniformity and continuity of my experiences.[10]

Thus, the mind's conception of causal sequence does not create but organizes and perfects the notion of external reality as the source of possible as well as actual experience. And the assumption of "possible experiences," made to satisfy the postulate of uniformity is itself expressed through the supposition of a universal actual experience, the Absolute of the idealist.[11]

To describe more explicitly the general nature of his idealism, Royce maintains that it includes four conditions:

1. External reality is postulated, not given.
2. To a portion of our conscious states we ascribe a validity beyond the present, and this ascription of validity constitutes our whole knowledge of the external world as the counterpart of our ideas of it.
3. Our idea of any reality beyond ourselves is the expression of an effort to reduce a multiplicity of experiences, both possible and actual, to a unity.
4. External reality can only be conceived as being real for consciousness, yet the whole of the postulated reality can only be known as possible, not as actual, experience.[12]

The fourth condition points to the need for a conscious subject of all possible experiences. Therefore, as the hypothetical subject of the totality of experience, possible and actual, Royce first postulates an Absolute, then attempts to demonstrate the existence of this Absolute through his argument from the possibility of error. Except for this argument, and so far as it has thus far been described, the content of Royce's idealism accords generally with that of his idealist predecessors and contemporaries.

[8] RAP, 364, 365. (Italics mine.)
[9] RAP, 365.
[10] *Ibid.*
[11] Cf. RAP. 366.
[12] Cf. RAP. 368.

There are two points of contrast, however, and these are particularly pertinent to this study. The first involves a distinction between subjective and objective idealism.[13] The former claims that the mind can only be concerned with its own ideas. This is true, Royce maintains, if we confine our consideration to the mind itself. But if we so confine it, then sincerity and truth become identical, and truth and error are impossible. Consequently, Royce calls for an "objective idealism" through which the thought of the subject is necessarily related to a higher thought as the basis for objective truth and error. Ultimately, this higher thought is the universal thought of the Absolute.

[M]y thought and its object, both as I think this object and as it is, are together in the universal thought, of which they form elements, and in which they live and move and have their being.[14]

A yet more significant and distinguishing factor in Royce's idealism is its voluntarism, his emphasis on will. In the most important work of his mature period, *The Problem of Christianity*, Royce writes: "I have long defended a philosophy, both of human life and of the universe, which I have preferred to call an 'Absolute Voluntarism' "[15] Some form of voluntarism, he claims, is essential to any philosophy which aims to interpret and explain man's basic metaphysical interests.

For our metaphysical interests are indeed interests in directing our will, in defining our attitude toward the universe, in making articulate and practical our ideals and our resolutions.[16]

The early works of Royce support his claim that he had consistently considered philosophy an essentially practical affair. In 1885 he noted in *The Religious Aspect of Philosophy* that "we cannot pause with a simply theoretical idealism," for "[o]ur doctrine is practical too."[17]

The coupling of Royce's idealism with his interest in the practical is rooted in his notion of *idea* as the conscious embodiment of purpose.[18] The

---

[13] Cf. RAP, 378-9.
[14] RAP, 379.
[15] Josiah Royce, *The Problem of Christianity*, with Introduction by John E. Smith (Chicago: University of Chicago Press, 1968; originally published in two volumes by The Macmillan Company, 1913), 349. Hereafter, PC.
[16] *Ibid.*
[17] RAP, 434.
[18] In many places, but see, e.g., Josiah Royce, *The World and the Individual*, First Series (New York: Dover Publications, Inc., 1959; an unaltered republication of the First Edition published by The Macmillan Company, 1899), 24. Hereafter, WI I.

term "purpose" is construed as an action orientation of the consciousness.[19] Without such practical directedness there is no idea, and thus there can be no idealism. Throughout his works Royce continually stresses the voluntaristic, practical aspect of his idealism.

Such emphasis is the precise point of difference between himself and Hegel. While he acknowledges the philosophical influence of Hegel, Royce refuses to call himself Hegelian.[20] There are two main streams of thought that flow from Hegel, but only one of these suits the practical bent of Royce's philosophy.

There are in recent philosophical history two Hegels: one the uncompromising idealist, with his general and fruitful insistence upon the great, fundamental truths of idealism; the other the technical Hegel of the "Logik," whose dialectical method seems destined to remain, not a philosophy, but the idea of a philosophy. With this latter Hegel the author feels a great deal of discontent; to the other Hegel, whose insight, as we know, was by no means independent of that of Fichte and other contemporaries, but who was certainly the most many-sided and critical of the leaders of the one great common idealistic movement of the early part of the century, – to him we all owe a great debt indeed.[21]

Hegel the dialectician is too speculative and technical for the voluntaristic Royce, but Hegel the idealist represents the general basis of his own philosophizing, a basis from which Royce remains free to preserve his consistently practical directedness.

B. The religious content of Royce's thought

That Royce's philosophy is essentially a philosophy of religion is suggested first of all by the titles of his works: e.g., *The Religious Aspect of Philosophy*, *The Sources of Religious Insight*, and *The Problem of Christianity*. But where the titles themselves give no hint of this, even a cursory glance at the contents of his writings reveals his predominant interest in religion. For example, the very first lecture in the First Series of *The World and the Individual* is titled "The Religious Problems and the Theory of Being," while the last lecture of the Second Series is "The Union of God and Man." There are only two exceptions to this general trend, viz., Royce's logical works,[22] which would

---

[19] WI I, 23 ff.
[20] RAP, xi.
[21] RAP, x.
[22] See Daniel S. Robinson (ed.), *Royce's Logical Essays* (Dubuque: William C. Brown Company, 1951). Also, the text that Royce wrote for his English students at Berkeley is an early instance of his interest in logic as a tool for philosophizing; this was his *Primer of Logical Analysis for the Use of Composition Students* (San Francisco: A. L. Bancroft, 1881).

be construed as a methodology for his philosophy, and his literary works,[23] most of which were written in the early part of his career.

Roycean commentators generally attest that the religious element is essential to his philosophy. John Wright Buckham, for instance, writing just one year before Royce's death, remarks: "It is impossible to understand Professor Royce's philosophy without realizing its close relation, from the very start, to the problems of *religion*."[24] And Robert Roth, S.J., writing in 1967, goes so far as to claim the religious content of Roycean thought as the reason why his philosophy was largely rejected after the rise of naturalism.[25] All this plainly points out the importance of having some understanding of Royce's notion of religion in order to appreciate the rest of his philosophy.

Particularly noteworthy is the fact that Royce consistently maintains that his position in regard to religion is strictly philosophical, that the religious element of his philosophy is based upon considerations so general as to be applicable to any creed or doctrine.[26] "Dogma as such," he writes, "has no place within philosophy."[27] Whether or not Royce succeeded in confining his religious ideas to the realm of philosophy is open to question, and there are instances noted subsequently in which he seems to have exceeded that self-imposed restriction. But that his own intention was to remain within the scope of philosophy is clear from the texts.

In developing his religious philosophy Royce deliberately refrains from defining the term "religion." Instead he takes hold of one central idea in any man's religion and claims this as the denotative factor for "religion" in general. To show that this fundamental idea is in some sense "a given," an initiating idea rather than a reasoned conclusion or judgment, Royce again uses the term "postulate." "The central and essential postulate of whatever religion we... are to consider," he writes, "is *the postulate that man needs to be saved.*"[28]

---

[23] E.g., *The Feud of Oakfield Creek: A Novel of California Life* (Boston: Houghton Mifflin Company, 1887). Royce earned his baccalaureate in English at the University of California in 1875, and taught English there from 1878 until 1882 after receiving his doctorate from Johns Hopkins. Most of Royce's literary works belong to this earlier period, prior to his gaining sure foothold in the philosophical milieu of Harvard.

[24] "The Contribution of Professor Royce to Christian Thought," *Harvard Theological Review* 8 (1915), 1.

[25] Cf. Robert Roth, S. J., *American Religious Philosophy* (new York: Harcourt, Brace and World, Inc., 1967), 12.

[26] Cf. Josiah Royce, *The Sources of Religious Insight* (New York: Charles Scribner's Sons, 1914), 3, 4. Hereafter, SRI.

[27] Josiah Royce, *William James and Other Essays on the Philosophy of Life* (New York: The Macmillan Company, 1912), viii. Hereafter, WJO.

[28] SRI, 8, 9.

In order to clarify the meaning of this postulate, Royce subdivides its main idea:

The idea that man needs salvation depends, in fact, upon two simple ideas whereof the main idea is constituted. The first is the idea that there is some end or aim of human life which is more important than all other aims, so that, by comparison with this aim all else is secondary and subsidiary, and perhaps relatively unimportant, or even vain and empty. The other idea is this: That man as he now is, or as he naturally is, is in great danger of so missing this highest aim as to render his whole life a senseless failure by virtue of thus coming short of his true goal.[29]

Different men, according to Royce, describe their highest aim in different ways, and their various descriptions of "salvation" result in different religions.[30] While it is true that some men apparently make no effort at describing any ultimate goal because they claim it lies beyond them, yet the same individuals, insofar as they are religious, *act* in some specific direction, act towards some goal; thus their very lives describe a highest aim. Moreover, different ways of acting religiously result from diverse attempts to supplement man's felt limitation in reaching an end that exceeds his grasp. All religions, however, regardless of the means they choose, regardless of their diversity in creed or code or cult, are founded on the twofold awareness that (1) there is a highest human aim, and that (2) human nature needs help in attaining it. Hence, all religions postulate man's basic need to be saved.

Two further considerations are pertinent to a discussion of the religious content of Royce's philosophy: his treatment of religious insight and of the church. Insight in general is defined as "knowledge that makes us aware of the unity of many facts in one whole, and that at the same time brings us into intimate personal contact with these facts and with the whole wherein they are united."[31] What distinguishes religious insight from other kinds (e.g., scientific or poetic) is that its characteristic object is "religious," i.e., saving or redemptive. Royce specifies three objects of man's religious concern: an ideal, a need and a deliverer. The clarification he offers for each of the three is as follows:

First, his [man's] Ideal, that is the standard in terms of which he estimates the sense and the value of his own personal life; secondly, his Need of salvation, that is the degree to which he falls short of attaining his ideal and is sundered from it by evil fortune, or by his own paralysis of will, or by his inward baseness; thirdly, the presence or the coming or the longing for, or the communion with something which he comes to view as the power that may save him from his need, or as the

---

[29] SRI, 12. (In the original the entire text is italicized except for the first sentence.)
[30] Cf. SRI, 13 ff.
[31] SRI, 5, 6.

light that may dispel his darkness, or as the truth that shows him the way out, or as the great companion who helps him – in a word, as his Deliverer.³²

Religious insight, then, is the means through which man comes to know the objects of his religious concern. It reveals to him the way to find salvation as the harmony between one's ideal and his need.

The Deliverer referred to in the preceding passage assists man in attaining salvation through the church. By church, however, Royce does not mean any existing institution or structure. Attempting to preserve the universal applicability of his religious considerations Royce distinguishes between "visible" and "invisible" church, intending the latter as a strictly philosophical notion. The visible church is a religious organization or group of religious organizations characterized by certain traditions, history and creed, claiming divine revelation as its origin and authority.³³ Because of its specificity the visible church cannot present a universal means by which all men may be assisted towards salvation. Royce therefore stresses a wider understanding of the term in his notion of the invisible church. "[B]y the invisible church I mean the brotherhood consisting of all who, in any clime or land, live in the Spirit."³⁴ Such a church has room for all mankind in its communion. The only requirement for membership is each one's contribution to that unity of spirit which arises from the shared consciousness of a common striving towards some transcending end.

C. *The empirical grounding of Royce's philosophy*

Just as Bishop Berkeley combined idealism and empiricism in his philosophy, so also did Josiah Royce. The Roycean emphasis on experience is amply illustrated in all of his major works. In an early writing (1885), for example, he bases his proof for the Absolute on the experience of human fallibility, and his notion of moral and religious insight on man's experience of responsibility towards other men.³⁵ Later on, in *The World and the Individual* (1899), he shows the contradictoriness and/or inadequacy of the realistic, mystical and critical rationalist conceptions of being through an examination of the ways in which these theories do not square with experience. He then defends his own position on the basis of its fitting in with

---

³² SRI, 28, 29.
³³ Cf. SRI, 277.
³⁴ SRI, 280.
³⁵ See Ch. VI, XI, and XII of RAP. These considerations are developed further in Chapter III of Part One.

the totality of experience, both possible and actual, individual and universal.[36]

But the work in which the empirical grounding of Royce's philosophy is most clearly manifest is *The Sources of Religious Insight* (1912). Here he mentions seven sources of insight, six of which are ultimately derived from the first source which is individual experience. For "if there is any religious insight whatever accessible," Royce maintains, "it cannot come to us without our individual experience as its personal foundation."[37]

According to Royce there are three marks of insight: first, breadth of view (being aware of many facts); secondly, coherence and unity of view (being aware of how the facts fit together as a whole), and thirdly, closeness of personal touch (an intimate, personal contact with the oneness and manyness of reality).[38] It is the last mentioned aspect which roots all insight in experience. One can have a wide span of vision in a simple act of sight; one can "see" the coherence of reality indirectly through reason. But no one can win genuine insight without directly grasping some object of experience. Insight can only be achieved by coupling the element of personal experience with breadth of range and coherence: all three marks are necessary. Consequently, true insight is also experience, but not conversely.

Besides individual experience, the other six sources which Royce mentions in *The Sources of Religious Insight* are society, reason, will, sorrow, loyalty and church. It will be useful here to see in some measure how these factors interrelate, in order to relate them all to Royce's concept of human experience in general, and thus to the pragmatic element which may be found within his thought.

Bearing in mind that all experience is grounded in the individual one could specify the religious experience of which Royce speaks by recalling the three objects of man's religious concern (ideal, need, deliverer). These, according to Royce, are objects which individual experience as source of religious insight has always undertaken to reveal.[39] In other words, man experiences an ideal or goal that is for him personally an ultimate standard of value; he experiences his own human limitation in achieving that goal, despite his desire of reaching it; and he experiences some kind of relationship to a power greater than himself, a power capable of filling up what is wanting to him in his quest for salvation. These three objects of the religious experience of an individual form the basis for Royce's experientially rooted philosophy of religion.

[36] See WI I, Lecture II-VIII. An explication of these Roycean notions is given in Chapter VI of Part Two.
[37] SRI, 24.
[38] Cf. SRI, 6.
[39] Cf. SRI, 29.

Because of man's inevitable narrowness of view, religious insight requires a social dimension. For

> [s]ocial experience, in its religious aspects, helps the individual to win the wider outlook, helps him also to find his way out of the loneliness of guilt and of failure toward wholeness of life, and promises salvation through love.[40]

It is by pooling together the narrow views of individuals that men can approach the breadth of view required for genuine religious insight. Such "pooling" constitutes social experience. Moreover, this social aspect of human experience gives the hint or likeness, sometimes even the very "incarnation" of a life that lies beyond and above our individual human existence.[41] Through it man can grasp a reality that transcends himself.

The third source of religious insight mentioned by Royce is also a remedy for the limitedness of individual experience *quâ* individual. This source is reason, but it is reason defined in a special Roycean sense as a power which acts to synthesize (rather than analyze or abstract from) individual experiences. Reason, from this point of view, is "the sort of seeing that grasps many views in one, that surveys life as it were from above, that sees, as the wanderer views the larger landscape from a mountaintop."[42] It is the ability to get insight into wholes rather than fragments, the "process of getting connected experience on a large scale."[43]

But reason shows itself through the will, that is, through action, and in its acting the will itself becomes a source of religious insight.[44] For whenever man acts he acts because he sees something as true. His action supports the truth of some basic insight, even to the extent of labelling as "absolute" an issue that might otherwise be considered mere opinion. Since opinions themselves are mere efforts of the will to formulate the real contents of experience, when someone acts according to religious opinion the action itself evidences his formulation of some religious opinion.[45]

Of the four sources of religious insight thus far mentioned (individual and social experience, reason and will) none is adequate and all taken together are not adequate to the need for salvation. For this, man needs a Cause – a Cause to which he might respond through the spirit and experience of loyalty. The Cause, to Royce, is "some conceived, and yet also real, spiritual unity which links many individual lives in one, and which is therefore essen-

---

[40] SRI, 79. Cf. SRI, 48.
[41] SRI, 75.
[42] SRI, 86.
[43] SRI, 91.
[44] Cf. SRI, 124, 137.
[45] Cf. SRI, 158, 109.

tially superhuman."[46] It is a grace or gift which makes it possible for a man to summon his whole being to the insight which is loyalty. To the degree that one succeeds in devoting his entire self to such a Cause he succeeds in being "united in a life whose meaning is above the separate meanings of any or of all natural human beings."[47] Such union marks the culmination of religious insight.

In pursuit of this ideal, however, each individual is bound to meet obstacles, for the very existence of man's religious need presupposes the presence of evil in human life. Adversity and loyalty are, to Royce, inseparable companions: "There could not be loyalty in a world where the loyal being himself met no adversities that personally belonged to and entered his own inner life."[48] Some of these evils may and do become a source of genuine religious insight. Royce labels this source "sorrow" and defines it as

an experience of ill which is not wholly an experience of that which as you then and there believe ought to be simply driven out of existence. The insight of which sorrow is the source is an insight that tends to awaken within you a new view of what the spiritual realm is.[49]

Through the influence of this view, based on the experience of sorrow, man is creatively transformed into a new and higher way of being.

One of the chief human sorrows is our inevitably limited span of consciousness. Hence the more fruitful view of life to which sorrow points can only be achieved through *supernatural* and/or *superhuman* means. By the "super" terminology he here employs, Royce intends no technical theological interpretation.[50] He means merely those forms of consciousness which allow us to get beyond the narrow view of individual experience. It is our consciousness of community which accomplishes this function most effectively. Consequently, to Royce, the last and most important source of religious insight through experience is the community of the invisible church. Such communion as this he construes as "the crowning source of religious insight."[51] Royce thus makes "church" the highest rung on his ladder of experiential sources, a rung supported and strengthened by the experience of the individual, society, reason, will, loyalty, and suffering.

To the point of this study it is important to grasp clearly that *all* these

[46] SRI, 197. (Royce's understanding of the term "superhuman" is given subsequently in Ch. X, Part Three.)
[47] SRI, 201.
[48] SRI, 240.
[49] *Ibid.*
[50] SRI, 262. Cf. 197 and other places.
[51] SRI, 292.

sources of religious insight are grounded in the one central source of experience. In particular, the last item, the invisible church which is Christian community, is founded upon the *experience* of the early Christians, notably the Pauline Christians, rather than upon the words spoken by the historical Christ and quoted in Scripture. Such words are technically considered "revelation." But Royce wants to use the word in a much more general sense, so as to include the experience of the Christian community in his concept of revelation. Hence the only definition he will accept for revelation seems extremely tentative: "whatever intercourse there may be between the divine and the human."[52] Only with so broad a definition can we claim experience as itself a revelation. Royce consistently avoids any strict theological usage of the term in his effort to keep the discussion on a philosophical level, one that is applicable to any and every man insofar as he is "religious."

The propaedeutic intent of this chapter was to present a brief explication of three factors necessary for a proper understanding of the pragmatic element in the thought of Josiah Royce. First we noted that Royce's objective or absolute idealism deals with ideas as plans of action or conscious purposes; his voluntarism is the key to the distinction between Royce and the speculative idealists. Secondly, we saw that the content of Royce's philosophy is essentially religious, involving a persistent directedness toward practical fulfilment of a religious ideal. Finally, we observed that the philosophy of Royce is consistently grounded in experience as the source of all worthwhile and practical philosophical insight. Against this general background, we are now prepared to examine the possibilities for a Roycean pragmatism.

---

[52] SRI, 19.

CHAPTER II

POSSIBILITIES FOR A ROYCEAN PRAGMATISM

Having explored the general context of Royce's thought, some explanation and justification for the limitation of the present topic is in order. To that end this chapter aims to explicate the purpose and set guidelines for subsequent considerations. Since the meaning of the term pragmatism has been subject to a variety of historically valid interpretations, clarification of the topic is not an easy task. As early as 1908, Arthur Lovejoy recognized the difficulty of such an undertaking when he attempted to distinguish among various meanings in an article titled "The Thirteen Pragmatism."[1] Some years later F.C.S. Schiller remarked that "theoretically at least, there might be as many pragmatisms as there were pragmatists," and Giovanni Papini went so far as to claim that pragmatism is indefinable.[2] Because of general lack of agreement and/or precision in the use of the term – both by pragmatists themselves and by their commentators, the writer was at first reluctant to use it in describing the aim and topic of this thesis. In casting about for a more suitable designation, however, (e.g., "practicalism," as suggested by John E. Smith[3]), none could be found: any term chosen would require careful clarification, and the thesis would have to be developed according to the meaning indicated therein.

What reinforced the decision to use the term "pragmatic" was a recent critical study of the history of pragmatism by H.S. Thayer.[4] Thayer offers a scholarly analysis of the pragmatism of Peirce, James, Dewey, Mead and

[1] Arthur O. Lovejoy, "The Thirteen Pragmatisms," *The Journal of Philosophy* 5 (1908), 5-12, 29-39.
[2] Schiller, "William James and the Making of Pragmatism," *The Personalist* 8 (1927), 92, and Papini, "What Pragmatism is like," Popular Science Monthly 71 (1907), 351. Cf. Charles Sanders Peirce, *Collected Papers of Charles Sanders Peirce*, ed. by Charles Hartshorne and Paul Weiss, Vol. V (Cambridge: The Belknap Press of Harvard University, 1965), #495. Hereafter the last mentioned work is referred to as CP.
[3] *The Spirit of American Philosophy* (New York: Oxford University Press, Inc., 1963), 87.
[4] *Meaning and Action, A Critical History of Pragmatism* (New York: The Bobbs-Merrill Company, Inc., 1968).

C.I. Lewis, and concludes with a definition of the term as it applies to all of these thinkers. Pragmatism, he maintains, is that doctrine which "emphasizes the practical character of thought and reality." Thayer then proceeds to clarify the meaning of "practical":

What pragmatism argues as "the practical nature of thought and reality" is that, since existence is transitional, knowledge is one of the ways of effecting transitions of events, and the only reliable way of guiding them.[5]

Implied in this understanding of "the practical" are its process-context ("existence is transitional") and its insistence on the future-directedness of knowledge (knowledge effects the transitions and guides events). The essentially empirical orientation of pragmatism thus involves a necessary reference to the future.[6]

The work of Thayer lends sound support to the understanding of pragmatism according to which the present topic was chosen, researched and developed. No attempt is made here to repeat what Thayer has already done (a more thorough approach than his would require several books); but neither shall his authority be quoted as sufficient to justify the meaning of pragmatism used subsequently. What is proposed as more feasible, convincing and pertinent to the specific purpose of this study is to treat in some detail the meaning of pragmatism in Peirce and James, two leading influences upon the thought of Royce, and two of the thinkers from whom a general understanding of the nature of pragmatism has been drawn. The notion of "pragmatic element" may be grounded as well as clarified by looking first to what James and Peirce hold in common in their pragmatisms, then to Royce's understanding of a pragmatism consistent with idealism.

There are two aims which the subtitle of the present work could suggest, but which the writer does not propose to accomplish in what follows. First, although the topic is treated developmentally, this is not intended as constituting a complete exposition of the thought of Royce. Fortunately, this demanding and important task has already been undertaken by others.[7]

---

[5] *Ibid.*, 425.

[6] Thayer further specifies what pragmatism means by the practical character of reason and reality by describing three claims essentially related to that notion, viz., (1) that "*possibility* is in some sense a trait of reality," (2) "a *behavioral* interpretation and analysis of mind and thinking," and (3) "the purposive character of conceptualization." (426-9) A common element included in the three claims is their orientation towards future experience: the reality of present possibilities is dependent upon their functioning as anticipations of future experience; thought is our present guide for future behavior; and the purposiveness of our concepts is their directedness towards future results.

[7] E.g., Gabriel Marcel, *La métaphysique de Royce* (Aubier: Éditions Montaigne, 1945), and Oppenheim, Frank M., "Royce's Mature Idea of General Metaphysics," Unpublished Ph.D. dissertation, Department of Philosophy, St. Louis University, 1962.

Secondly, there is no argument here that Royce is a pragmatist to the degree of a Peirce or James or Dewey. Instead, the development of Royce's thought is traced from a pragmatic perspective, by selecting for discussion those aspects which may legitimately be labeled pragmatic. Collectively, these aspects constitute the pragmatic element of his philosophy; a Roycean pragmatism is identifiable with this element, but not with his entire system.[8] The approach then is neither pure exposition, nor argument, but an interpretation based on the texts of Royce himself. Whether a pragmatic element is actually present in his thought, and, if present, whether that element increases – these are the questions that subsequent considerations propose to answer. Their answering constitutes an interpretive study of the thought of Royce.

A. *The pragmatists that influenced Royce*

That Charles Peirce and William James, both well known pragmatists, exerted an important influence on the philosophy of Royce is evident from the biographical data, from cross references in their works, and from their correspondence, both published and unpublished. In general the relationship of Royce to Peirce may be characterized as one of deference, his relationship to James as one of friendship. It was while Royce was doing graduate work at Johns Hopkins University, that is between 1876 and 1878, that he first became acquainted with both men.[9]

Gabriel Marcel remarks that it was not until the last ten or fifteen years of Royce's life that the influence of Peirce's ideas became evident.[10] This was only possible, however, because of an earlier and continued contact between the two. It was Peirce himself who had insisted on Royce's need for logic, even after Royce had taught the subject at Berkeley, and had written a

[8] Similarly, the term pragmatism ought not to be interpreted as constituting the entire philosophy of those who are commonly called pragmatists such as Peirce and James. Certainly the pragmatic element is significantly present in their thought, but not necessarily in so predominant a manner as to define their entire contribution to philosophy.

[9] For an excellent chronology of Royce's life see Vincent Buranelli, *Josiah Royce* (New York: Twayne Publishers, Inc., 1964), 11-13. Another biographical source is Joseph Powell, Josiah Royce (New York: Washington Square Press, 1967). These are the only full biographies on Royce available at present, although another is in preparation by Rev. Frank M. Oppenheim, S.J. Buranelli wrote rather generally of Royce from a literary point of view; Powell wrote of Royce's place in American history. Oppenheim's intention is to treat more appreciatively of Royce the philosopher. For Royce's own resumé of his life see the Autobiographical Sketch which he included in an after-dinner speech at the Walton Hotel in Philadelphia on December 19, 1915, a talk published in *The Hope of the Great Community* (New York: The Macmillan Company, 1916), 122-36. Hereafter, references to the last mentioned work are abbreviated to HGC.

[10] In the Introduction to the English translation by Virginia and Gordon Ringer, *Royce's Metaphysics* (Chicago: Henry Regnery Company, 1956), xiv.

logic text for his students there.[11] In the second volume of *The Problem of Christianity*, Royce quotes what Peirce wrote to him shortly after he had sent him a copy of *The World and the Individual*: "[W]hen I read you, I do wish that you would study logic. You need it so much."[12]

Related to his logic are Peirce's doctrine of signs, his notion of interpretation, and his insistence that the search for truth ought to be a communal endeavor: points which Royce absorbed into his own idealistic system, giving credit to Peirce for their elaboration. Royce was anxious to show that it was Peirce rather than Hegel who had influenced his theory of knowledge in regard to these points. "Peirce's concept of interpretation," he maintained, "defines an extremely general process, of which the Hegelian dialectical triadic process is a very special case...."[13] Furthermore, the opinions of Peirce, "as to the nature of interpretation were in no wise influenced by Hegel, or by the tradition of German idealism."[14] In Chapter IX, which treats of the Roycean Community of Interpretation, we will see more precisely how Peirce's philosophy affected Royce's theory of knowledge.

While Royce was a student at Johns Hopkins, William James gave a talk there as a visiting professor. The two so impressed each other that their meeting marked the beginning of a deep and lasting friendship. James had encouraged Royce to make a career out of philosophy. When Royce obtained his degree and returned to California to teach English at Berkeley, their correspondence continued, and some of the content of their letters at this time involved an exchange of views of Peirce's logical essays. Finally, however, James enticed Royce out of the "wilderness" to come to Harvard to teach philosophy. Except for several trips abroad, Royce remained in that position for the remainder of his years. As a remnant of the times when either he or James was absent from Harvard and as evidence of the abundant communication between the two friends on matters both philosophical and otherwise, Ralph Barton Perry has reserved three chapters of his famous work for the James-Royce correspondence.[15] Even a cursory reading of this material gives ample basis for suspecting that the two men exerted a significant philosophical influence upon each other. While remaining a relativist and a pluralist, James nonetheless exhibited, especially in his later thought, an openness to the Absolute; Royce, while remaining an absolutist and a monist, seemed to show an increasingly pragmatic emphasis in his works.

[11] *Primer of Logical Analysis...*; cf. Ch. I, n. 22, *supra*.
[12] PC, 277.
[13] PC, 305.
[14] PC, 276.
[15] *The Thought and Character of William James*, Vol. I (Boston: Little, Brown, and Company, 1935), Ch. XLIX, L, LI.

The interaction of the two provides a fascinating chapter in the history of philosophy.

Concerning that interaction Royce's own remarks upon his relationship with James are as pertinent as they are entertaining. At a dinner given in James's home in 1910 to celebrate the completion and presentation of his portrait, Royce noted that critical people had accused James of being overly fond of cranks. So highly did he esteem his friend that Royce was quite content to place himself within the crank category.

> Well, I am one of James's cranks. He was good to me, and I love him. The result of my own early contact with James was to make me for years very much his disciple. I am still in large part under his spell. If I contend with him sometimes, I suppose that it is he also who through his own free spirit has in great measure taught me this liberty. I know that for years I used to tremble at the thought that James might perhaps some day find reason to put me in my place by some one of those wonderful lightning like epigrams, wherewith he was and is always able to characterize those opponents whose worldly position is such as to make them no longer in danger of not getting a fair hearing, and whose self-assurance has relieved him of the duty to secure for them a sympathetic attention. The time has passed, the lightning in question has often descended – never indeed on me as his friend, but often on my opinions – and has long since blasted, I hope, some at least of what is most combustible about my poor teachings.[16]

Clearly, then, Royce was glad and grateful for the criticism of his pragmatist friend.

James, on the other hand, regarded Royce as his "discovery," describing him as "a perfect little Socrates" for his wisdom and his humor.[17] The two general areas on which the two men remained in disagreement throughout their lifetime were the doctrine of the Absolute (actual for Royce, possible for James) and the role of the individual and/or community (Royce, like Peirce, stressed the community, while James emphasized the individual). One commentator goes so far as to claim that Royce, who came from a rather fundamentalist religious background, became more liberal in his conception of the Absolute, while James, from a liberal religious background, became more fundamentalist in his approach.[18] Similarly, a difference in disposition could be partly responsible for the contrasting treatment of Peirce and Royce with James in regard to community. Royce was reticent and retiring by

---

[16] *Ibid.*, 780.
[17] *Ibid.*, 797 and Vol. II, 65.
[18] Roth, 151. Cf. Ralph Barton Perry, *In the Spirit of William James* (New Haven: Yale University Press, 1938). Perry devotes the entire first chapter to a contrast between Royce and James, claiming that when "we examine the philosophical expression of these characteristic experiences, we find that each man idealized his opposite." (9)

nature, Peirce rather fiery and overbearing. Of the three, James was certainly the most gifted in the social virtues. Consequently, Perry observes that

> Peirce and Royce, who were lonely souls and more or less disqualified for social and public relations, emphasized the community, both as a reality, and as an ideal; James, the most sociable and urbane of men, – actively, eagerly, almost painfully interested in the state of his country and the world, – proclaimed the supreme value of those feelings and strivings which are unique in each individual, and whose authentic quality is immediately revealed to him alone.[19]

Thus, the biographical factors indicate that the philosophy of Royce was nourished in the course of its development both from within and from without – through his particular disposition and background as well as through his social and intellectual associations. Having seen that the thought of Royce was affected by that of Peirce and James, we are ready now to examine the general notion of pragmatism found in their philosophies.

B. The notions of pragmatism that influenced Royce

Historically, it was Charles Sanders Peirce, credited by both James and Royce as the father of pragmatism, who introduced the term "pragmatism" into philosophical circles.[20] Although some of his friends had suggested he call his system "practicalism," Peirce preferred the term pragmatic because he wanted to prevent a confusion of his meaning with Kant's use of the term in describing practical reason. In the *Metaphysics of Morals* Kant had established a distinction between "practical" and "pragmatic," applying the former term to a priori moral laws, and the latter to rules of art and technique based on and applicable to experience. Peirce realized that the two meanings were as far apart as the two poles if taken in a Kantian context. Accordingly, he chose the term pragmatism in order to indicate the essentially empirical flavor of his doctrine.[21] Had Peirce been sure that "practicalism" would be interpreted in a non-Kantian, experiential context, he might have followed the counsel of his friends. In any event, given the variety of interpreters who succeeded him, Peirce's effort to preserve precision in understanding the term would probably have failed no matter what label he selected.

---

[19] Perry, *The Thought...*, Vol. II, 266.

[20] Cf. PC, 276, and William James, *Pragmatism and Four Essay from The Meaning of Truth* (New York: The World Publishing Company, Meridian Books, 1955), p. 18. Hereafter, Prag.

[21] Cf. John Dewey, *Philosophy and Civilization* (New York: G. P. Putnam's Sons, 1931), 13 ff.

Peirce defines pragmatism as a "method of ascertaining the meanings of hard words and of abstract concepts."[22] He insists that this doctrine is neither a metaphysics nor a theory of truth. Moreover, even when so limited, pragmatism does not apply to all ideas but only to what he calls "intellectual concepts," that is, those which determine our knowledge of objective facts.[23] The "hard words" name the objective facts, and "abstract concepts" provide categories for them. Pragmatism looks to the meaning of both as types of "intellectual concepts."

The maxim according to which pragmatism clarifies ideas in order to judge their meanings was first announced as the following:

Consider what effects, that might conceivably have practical bearings, we conceive the object of our conception to have. Then, our conception of these effects is the whole of our conception of the object.[24]

Not the effects themselves, but our conception of them, Peirce insisted, is the criterion to be employed in applying the pragmatic method. Pursuing that method, the pragmatist anticipates the practical consequences of his concepts; this anticipation forms the content of his ideas. As an illustration, Peirce asks that we consider what is meant when we call a thing *hard*. Evidently, he maintains, we mean that the thing

will not be scratched by many other substances. The whole conception of this quality, as of every other, lies in its conceived effects. There is absolutely no difference between a hard thing and a soft thing so long as they are not brought to the test.[25]

The testing constitutes the empirical verification which our ideas anticipate. In other words, the pragmatism of Peirce is a prospective rather than a retrospective method; it is necessarily orientated towards future experience. The concise guide he offers for applying his pragmatic method is: "Look to the consequences."

The Peircean method is further specified as one which begins with doubt as the first impetus to thought, proceeding to the resolution of that doubt in a plan or habit of action, which Peirce calls belief. This belief, as the terminus of the thought process, is the goal of pragmatism as a method of inquiry. From the irritation of a genuine doubt one is stimulated to clarify his con-

[22] CP V, #464.
[23] Cf. CP V, #467.
[24] CP V, #402. Note that in this single maxim Peirce uses the term "conceivable" or a form thereof five times. According to Thayer, the recrudescence is "an emphatic attempt to indicate that he was concerned here with 'intellectual purport.'" (Thayer, 87)
[25] Cf. CP V, #402.

cepts according to the pragmatic maxim. The end of the thought process is achieved when the thinker/believer is ready to act.²⁶

Although it was Peirce who originally coined the term pragmatism, the usage that it subsequently acquired extended beyond his intended limitation for its meaning. As he saw James and Schiller labeling their different theories as forms of pragmatism, and as he saw the term being "abused" in literary journals, he endeavored to divorce his brand of "pragmatism" from the others by rechristening it "pragmaticism," a word he hoped "ugly enough to be safe from kidnappers."²⁷ The pragmaticism he thereafter expounded was no different from the pragmatism he had earlier introduced. "Pragmatism" remained the more general term, while "pragmaticism" specified Peirce's own interpretation of the term, i.e., as a method of inquiry.²⁸

In time, however, Peirce broadened his description of pragmaticism by relating it to absolute idealism. Because Peirce was and remained a thoroughgoing realist, such broadening is particularly significant:

[A] position which the pragmaticist holds and must hold..., namely, that the third category – the category of thought, representation, triadic relation, mediation, genuine thirdness, thirdness as such – is an essential ingredient of reality, yet does not by itself constitute reality.... The truth is that pragmaticism is closely allied to the Hegelian absolute idealism, from which, however, it is sundered by its vigorous denial that the third category suffices to make the world, or is even so much as self-sufficient.... For pragmaticism belongs essentially to the triadic class of philosophical doctrines, and is much more essentially so than Hegelianism is.²⁹

Certainly the preceding passage strongly suggests the plausibility of combining idealism and pragmatism. As a matter of fact, it was from this notion of pragmaticism in Peirce that Royce derived his theory of interpretation as a triadic theory of knowledge. A later section will treat this theory in greater detail.³⁰

That Peirce's understanding of pragmatism or pragmaticism is more restricted than that of James is generally known. Unlike Peirce, who tried to avoid the term "practical" as a proper equivalent for "pragmatic," James

---

²⁶ Cf. "How to Make Our Ideas Clear" in CP V, #388-410.
²⁷ CP V, #414.
²⁸ Cf. CP V, #413.
²⁹ CP V, #436. While Peirce generally describes himself as a realist, some of the commentators describe his thought as a metaphysical idealism; e.g., see Edward C. Moore, *American Pragmatism: Peirce, James and Dewey* (New York: Columbia University Press, 1961), 7. Peirce himself allows that his doctrine be called a "conditional idealism" as long as one means by this "that truth's independence of individual opinions is due (so far as there is any 'truth') to its being the predestined result to which sufficient inquiry *would* ultimately lead." CP V, #494.
³⁰ See Ch. IX in Part Three.

claims that the Greek *pragma*, from which the word derives, means "action, from which our words 'practice' and 'practical' come."³¹ Moreover, while Peirce viewed pragmatism merely as a method, James considered pragmatism both a method and a theory of truth. His main emphasis, in discussing the former, was to show pragmatism as a method of settling metaphysical disputes that might otherwise prove interminably unsolvable. Thus construed, the pragmatism of James is much like that of Peirce, for the Jamesian pragmatist employs his method by tracing the practical consequences of ideas through their verification in future experience. "Our conception of these effects, whether immediate or remote, is then for us the whole of our conception of the object, so far as that conception has positive significance at all."³² James admits that this principle is the same as that of Peirce. In his *Pragmatism* he shows how the method is applicable to perennial philosophical problems such as the meaning of substance, the possibility of freedom, and the "one and the many."³³

As a theory of truth the pragmatism of James conceives of truth as a verification process. "Truth," he says, "*happens* to an idea. It *becomes* true, is *made* true by events. Its verity *is* in fact an event, a process; the process namely of its verifying itself, its veri-*fication*."³⁴ In most cases of course, verifi*ability*, or the possibility of verification, is impractical. For example, we would assume that the country of Japan really exists even though we have never been there, because it works to do so. Or we might look at an object on the wall and consider it to be a clock although we have never seen the hidden works that make it one. We could actually go to Japan, or examine the inner workings of the clock in order to test the truth of our ideas about these objects, but in both cases verifiability is the preferable criterion. Our notions are already true because they work for us. Hence, "[t]ruth," according to James, lives "for the most part on a credit system. Our thoughts and beliefs 'pass,' so long as nothing challenges them, just as bank-notes pass so long as nobody refuses them."³⁵ They "work" in anticipation of future experience.

James describes the process of acquiring truths as a wedding between new facts and old theories, a marriage which is "endlessly fertile." The old theories refer to the whole body of truths already in our possession. As new experiences arise, some of them agree with our previous ideas, and some do not. "Agreement," says James, thus "turns out to be essentially an affair of

---

[31] Prag, 42.
[32] Prag, 43.
[33] Prag, Lectures 3 and 4.
[34] Prag, 133.
[35] Prag, 136-7.

leading," a leading which provides new truths for future use.[36] The leading process is a never ending one because

[t]ruths emerge from facts; but they dip forward into fact again and add to them; which facts again create or reveal new truth and so on indefinitely.[37]

The criterion as to whether the wedding between the "new" and the "old" is a true union is its effectiveness. If the marriage works then there is truth. In this regard Peirce like James uses the same test as Scripture: By their fruits you shall know them.[38] The difference between the two pragmatists on the point of verification through consequences is that Peirce emphasizes the general foreseen consequences while James emphasizes the particular. We shall see subsequently which of the two Royce better emulates in this regard.

Having considered the notion of pragmatism in Peirce and James, we are now in a position to judge what is essential to both positions. Clearly, a common feature of the two is that pragmatism is construed as a method for achieving the clarity we need to live by. It is an action-orientated approach to knowledge, a means of settling the meanings of our concepts by estimating or anticipating their practical consequences, their conceivable effects. In the understanding of both men, pragmatism is a way of philosophizing whose guiding principle can be expressed in the question: what practical difference would this idea make? (Peirce might add, "to us"; James, "to me.") The question illustrates a common and essential accent on future experience as the criterion for human judgments. Such an emphasis marks the properly pragmatic attitude for both James and Peirce. While other philosophies may also stress future experience, none claims this as its defining characteristic.[39] Since this is the emphasis that characterizes the pragmatism of both Peirce and James, it will likewise define the pragmatic element in our study of Royce. Before treating that topic developmentally, however, we ought first to examine whether Royce's own understanding of pragmatism accords with the notion derived from Peirce and James.

---

[36] Prag, 138, 141.

[37] Prag, 147.

[38] Matt. 7:16. Note the use of future tense and the emphasis on empirical verification as a criterion for knowledge.

[39] E.g., any "process" philosophy such as that of Alfred North Whitehead involves an emphasis on future experience, but that emphasis does not adequately define the specific content of that philosophy. While evolutionary thought in general presents a context which accents future experience, pragmatism is itself a *way of philosophizing* ("method" in Peirce and James) whose essential and defining emphasis is future experience.

C. A pragmatism consistent with idealism

That Royce construes his own idealism as compatible with pragmatism is clear in his writings, particularly, for example, where he describes his entire philosophy as an "absolute pragmatism."[40] In fact, he claims, all the idealists in the history of modern philosophy have been pragmatists, and their pragmatism has not blurred their absolutism in the least.

Our idealists were, one and all, in a very genuine sense what people now call pragmatists. They were also, to be sure, absolutists; and nowadays absolutism is supposed to be peculiarly abhorrent to pragmatists.[41]

As Royce sees it, the way in which these absolute idealists are true pragmatists is through their application of the dialectical method. According to this method, truth must always be related "to action, to practice, to the will." Nothing is true except insofar as its sense or purpose or meaning is expressed or carried out. Truth, to the idealists, is thus "a construction, a process, an activity, a creation, an attainment."[42] Such a notion applies with equal aptness to the thought of the pragmatist as to the idealist.

As we trace the development of Royce's philosophy we shall see points of compatibility between idealism and pragmatism in greater detail. It is pertinent here, however, to note Royce's awareness that many thinkers consider pragmatism essentially opposed to an absolutism which maintains "that the world in its wholeness has an absolute constitution in the light of which all finite truth must be interpreted."[43] Idealists, Royce claims, need not so view the world, and he himself is far from pretending to possess "any peculiar revelation as to what the content of absolute truth may be."[44] Moreover, as soon as the pragmatist claims that whatever is true is true relatively, he is as much in need as Royce of attributing to his world whatever constitution it actually possesses.

If one attempts to define a world of merely relative truth, this world, as soon as you

---

[40] E.g., PC, 279.
[41] Josiah Royce, *Lectures on Modern Idealism*, ed. by J. Loewenberg (New Haven: Yale University Press, 1919), 85. Hereafter, LMI.
[42] LMI, 86. Pertinent here are James's own interpretation of pragmatism as broad enough to encompass seemingly contradictory views, e.g., monism and pluralism (cf. Prag, 108), and his effort to show that philosophers and philosophies of the past have been pragmatic in character even if not pragmatic in intent. See, e.g., his reference to the scholastic treatment of the substance-idea in regard to the mystery of the Eucharist. (Prag, 67.) James's own understanding of pragmatism is therefore broad enough to include Royce's idealism, even though James persisted in his friendly "battle" with that idealism.
[43] LMI, 257.
[44] LMI, 256.

define it in its wholeness, becomes once more your absolute, your truth that is true.⁵⁴

Whether we be absolutists or relativists, "[i]n acknowledging truth we are indeed meeting, or endeavoring to meet a need which always expresses itself in finite form. But this need can never be satisfied by the acknowledgment of anything finite as the whole truth."⁴⁶ To Royce, therefore, the only totally fulfilling future experience is the Absolute.

As suggested earlier, Royce's idealistic philosophy involves an essential sympathy with the rational study of experience as well as with the practical ideas of life. Such sympathy indicates an emphasis on future experience. "For we all not only gather but interpret experience. And to interpret experience is to regard facts as the fulfilment of rational ideals."⁴⁷ Royce concludes that however incompatible others may judge absolute idealism and pragmatism, he personally is both pragmatist and absolutist. Believing each of these doctrines to involve the other he regards them "not only as reconcilable but as in truth reconciled."⁴⁸ In his eyes absolute pragmatism might justifiably be considered more truly pragmatic than the pragmatism of Peirce or James.

The notion of pragmatism which Royce here advocates is consistent with what is essentially pragmatic to Peirce and James. Within the Roycean context, however, the emphasis on future experience involves an essential union of thought and reality; idealism is necessary to the future directedness of his philosophizing. In contrast with James and Peirce, there are two futures about which Royce is concerned in his notion of pragmatism: one the near or temporal future which constitutes our presently projected field of action; the other the future fulfilment of experience in the Absolute. The absolute future is an indispensable dimension in a Roycean notion of pragmatism because it grounds the value and meaning of temporal future experience.

Although the understanding of pragmatism which Royce judges consistent with his idealism accords with the general definition derived from Peirce and James, there are other meanings of the term which Royce criticizes and pronounces unacceptable; e.g., an emphasis on verification by the individual, and insistence on "absolute" relativity of truth. Frequently, when Royce uses the term "pragmatism" he is considering notions such as those he criticizes, which admittedly exemplify a pragmatic attitude. Since Royce himself has several understandings for pragmatism – those which he rejects and that which he supports, an investigation of the development of a Roycean

[45] LMI, 257.
[46] LMI, 257-8.
[47] LMI, 259.
[48] LMI, 258.

pragmatism cannot be based exclusively on his use of the term. A more critical approach is to interpret Peirce's and James's notion within a properly Roycean context. While that context involves an emphasis on purpose, will, action and experience, these are all included within Royce's own system of absolute idealism.

Moreover, the empirical element involved in a properly pragmatic context is not merely the experiential grounding referred to in Chapter I in regard to Royce. Such experiential grounding abounds in classical realists as well as modern empiricists who do not thereby merit the title of pragmatist. The telling difference between a traditional and pragmatic empiricism is that the latter is an extension of the former. As Dewey noted in 1931,

Pragmatism, thus, presents itself as an extension of historical empiricism, but with this fundamental difference, that it does not insist upon antecedent phenomena but upon consequent phenomena; not upon the precedents but upon the possibilities of action. And this change in point of view is almost revolutionary in its consequences.[49]

Neither Peirce's realism, nor James's radical empiricism made of either thinker a pragmatist. Thus, the fact that Peircean, Jamesian and Roycean epistemologies are all empirically rooted is not what constitutes the pragmatic element of their thought. Its proper constitution is rather the empirical *thrust* or future directedness of their ways of philosophizing. Only this aspect of their treatment of experience may be interpreted as properly pragmatic. Consequently, the pragmatic element on which subsequent chapters focus is an emphasis on future experience. This is the understanding of pragmatism which originally provoked the topic as a problem worthy of consideration, and which gave rise to the pages which follow as a textually grounded interpretation of the thought of Royce.

On surveying the general content of Royce's thought, three rather broad themes are discernible: his theory of knowledge, his notion of the Absolute, and his conception of the individual. These specific areas have been selected for developmental consideration not only because they represent three major lines of thought in Royce but also because the lines they follow seem most clearly illustrative of the pragmatic element in his philosophy, culminating in his mature understanding of (1) interpretation as a mediating principle, (2)

---

[49] *Philosophy and Civilization*, 24. Cf. Dewey's claim in regard to James: "We must not forget here that James was an empiricist before he was a pragmatist, and repeatedly stated that pragmatism is merely empiricism pushed to its legitimate conclusions." (*loc. cit.*) Despite James's remark in the Preface to Prag (ix) that pragmatism and radical empiricism can be taken as logically independent doctrines, Thayer observes that "no sharp line divides the pragmatism from James's later ventures into radical empiricism." (133)

God as pragmatic postulate, and (3) community as perfective of the individual. In investigating the three themes the points accented in their explication are those which indicate an orientation towards future experience. Summarily, these are the points that constitute the pragmatic element in Royce's philosophy.

The dating for the three periods has been chosen at the suggestion of Rev. Frank M. Oppenheim, S.J., who observes that Royce's life reveals three major insights (ca. 1882, 1897, and 1912), which climactically determined his early, middle, and mature periods.[50] The main works which project these major insights are *The Religious Aspect of Philosophy*, *The World and the Individual*, and *The Problem of Christianity*. However, all the works of Royce accessible to the writer, both published and unpublished, have been utilized in researching his philosophy; any and all are mentioned insofar as their ideas are pertinent in the period considered. The dating is not intended as transitional or fixed; it merely provides a convenient way to divide the material while indicating the development of Royce's thought.

---

[50] *op. cit.*

PART ONE

THE EARLY ROYCE

(c. 1875-90)

CHAPTER III

HIS THEORY OF KNOWLEDGE

A philosopher's theory of knowledge is often so central as to be inseparable from the rest of his thought. That the philosophy of Royce exemplifies this interrelatedness will be evident in the course of this study. It is because his theory of knowledge is necessary to a clear understanding of his conception of the individual and his notion of the Absolute that this topic is treated first in each of our three sections. If we are to find a pragmatism at all in Royce we would expect to find it present in his epistemology.

Examining the early texts of Royce according to the understanding of "pragmatic" described in the preceding chapter, one discerns (at least) four pragmatic factors contained within his theory of knowledge:
1. an emphasis on the practical purposefulness of speculation,
2. the usefulness of doubt and postulate in philosophizing,
3. the limited function of verification and the role of insight, and
4. the relativity of truth and error.

All four points involve an orientation towards future experience. Each will now be considered within their proper textual references.

A. Royce's early stress on the practical purposefulness of all speculation

In an early fragment titled "The Critical Theory of Knowledge," Royce writes:

By Theory of Knowledge I mean an exhaustive and systematic account of the nature, the forms, the laws, the end, the validity and the scope of those mental processes that make up what is called knowing or Knowledge.[1]

Knowledge itself is described as "that which is known, or the mental process by which anything is known; i.e., either the object or the act of knowing."[2]

---
[1] Vol. 55 (1878), 2.
[2] Ibid., 1.

Many theories have been used to explain both the object and the act of knowing. Royce's own account or theory, however, links the knowing process with its object. His "Critical Theory of Knowledge" involves a "criticism of the labors of the human understanding viewed with reference to their great aim, the attainment of truth."[3]

This leads us to inquire about the nature of truth to the philosopher whose theory of knowledge purports to achieve it. And it is at this point that we must relate Royce's idealistic doctrine to the will, in a way which shows the practical purposefulness of all speculation. For "pure thought" or "speculation" is a good technical term, but one which cannot be properly applied to the thinking activity as such. Rather, the thinking process is itself volitional, so that "[k]nowledge, occurring in judgments, takes ever the form of an Act of Will."[4] While Royce claims that consciousness is the starting point of all philosophy,[5] and that experience always gives the material for our thinking,[6] he nonetheless insists that neither ego nor experience is sufficient to explain the knowing activity of man. In every judgment we take a leap beyond ourselves through the volitional act of affirmation or negation, and that leap is a leap into the realm of truth. Royce puts this quite forcefully when he asserts that

all knowledge, whether it be a datum of sense or the innate ideas, whether its contents be ordinary experience, or some transcendental knowledge of Self or of Ideas, whether an External World be its object, or an internal world of imagination, that all knowledge, as we affirm, is found, *quâ* knowledge, in the form of these elementary and inexplicable Acts of Will. The most fundamental and universal datum of reflective consciousness is that volitional activity which joins definitely our ideas, and gives them, as thoughts, a character opposed to the indefiniteness and disorder of unreflective sensation. In other words, the terms that expresses the universal datum most completely is the term Will. Not the Ego, not Experience, but the Will, shall be our principle of Philosophy. *Truth is a creation of the Will.*[7]

Here we already see the voluntarism of Josiah Royce, for whom knowledge becomes a "species of Volition" which as such is not open to further explanation. For "[t]o account for a thing or event, to explain it, is to make yet further judgments about it. And so, in the last analysis, no one can explain any act of judgment *quâ* judgment."[8] A theory of knowledge is "exhausted"

---

[3] *Ibid.*, 3.
[4] Vol. 79 (early but undated), "Of the Will as Principle in Philosophy," 53.
[5] Cf. *Ibid.*, 44.
[6] Vol. 80 (1878?), "Some Illustrations of the Structure and Growth of Human Thought," 58.
[7] Vol. 79, "Of the Will. . .," 53, 4. (My italics.)
[8] *Ibid.*, 53.

precisely at the point where one acknowledges its essential relatedness to volitional activity. Royce would hope we rest content with the realization that "[i]n and for the Will. . . all Truth finds its significance as Truth."[9]

Moreover, Royce would want us to apply his notion of truth to our conceptions of the past and to our judgments of external existence. In regard to the former, Royce maintains that our ideas of past moments are simply part of the movements of volition contained within our present judgments.

The Truth of the past, and of the time-succession that makes it up, is contained altogether in the present, and is given in and by the volition that wills the past. *The past is in the truest and deepest sense the creation of the present.*[10]

In other words, we will the past in the present by the fact that we will to act out of its context. Similarly, in regard to external existence by which Royce means the existence of matter and mind, of others and ourselves, insofar as our awareness of their existence is not included in the content of an immediate judgment. Here again Royce asserts his voluntaristic principle, maintaining that

The Truth of all External Existence is this, that it is an object of volition.[11]

To Royce, then, truth is ever, always and only accessible through our will acts.

Insofar as Royce construes knowledge as a voluntaristic activity, it is essentially teleological in character. Hence, knowledge is always purposive. "Our trains of thought mean for us work," he writes, "and work with a purpose."[12] Such a conception involves a rather broad understanding of the end of the thinking process. For example, if one were to consider the possession of purely speculative truth as the ultimate purpose of thought, he might be neglecting the element of satisfaction which arises from the awareness that one has reached the truth. Without such awareness, Royce maintains, there can be no real possession of truth. To know, one must intend the content of one's knowledge, a purpose which can only be fulfilled when the intended end as such is accomplished.

In his essay "On Purpose in Thought"[13] Royce extends his understanding

[9] *Ibid.*, 10.
[10] *Ibid.*, 58. (My italics.)
[11] *Ibid.*, 60. (My italics.)
[12] Vol. 60, "Outlines of Critical Philosophy," 7. Cf. Thayer's understanding of pragmatism as essentially involving the idea that conceptualization is always teleological or purposive (429). Thayer quotes Peirce on same from CP IV, #12.
[13] J. Loewenberg (ed.), *Fugitive Essays by Josiah Royce* (Cambridge: Harvard University Press, 1925), 219-260. Hereafter this work is referred to as FE. The essay noted was written by Royce in 1880; it occurs in Vol. 60 of the unpublished MSS.

of the end of knowledge and attainment of truth so as to include the anticipation of experience and the construction of the conception of possible experiences. Genuine knowledge, or the truth of our judgments, is evidenced in actual experience, where ideas, as anticipations of experience, provoke the knower to formulate hypotheses for future activities or possible experience. Such hypotheses are as truly knowing activities as are other judgments, since both are purposive in content. In fact, the ultimate end of the thought process is realized precisely in the act of constructing the image of possible experience, assuming through such construction a uniformity to be applied in subsequent experience.[14] The assumption is warranted, Royce claims, by the activity that follows upon it, for

the aim of thought is useful action brought about through true persuasion. The most practical thought then runs in reality towards the goal of truth.[15]

Whatever judgments bring us closer to that goal, e.g., our constructions of possible experience, make the best "runners" towards the truth, and therefore the most practical of human judgments. To Royce, then, as there are no purely speculative judgments, so speculation itself can never be divorced from its practical purposefulness.

B. The usefulness of doubt and postulate in philosophizing

Royce's treatment of "doubt" and "postulate" in his early writings reads much like an exposition of the thought of Peirce. As we noted in the preceding chapter, Peirce describes the thinking process as proceeding from the stimulus of doubt towards the satisfaction of that stimulus in belief or habit of action. Similarly, Royce sees the philosophical endeavor as beginning with the dissatisfaction of a doubt and culminating in a "postulate" or "active faith."[16]

Another likeness between the two philosophers is their insistence that it is impossible to doubt all things. For doubting, says Royce, "presupposes a

---

[14] Cf. *Ibid.*, 259.
[15] Vol. 60, "Outlines...," 14. Note the similarity here to Peirce's description of the end of the thought process as habits of action.
[16] Cf. RAP, 230, 234, 297-8: "[T]ruly philosophic doubt is of the very essence of our thought.... But it is just because we want to find a sure basis for what makes life worth living that we begin with this doubt.... A postulate is a mental way of behavior.... In general, to believe that a thing exists is to act as if it existed.... In such cases [i.e., of doubt] one voluntarily takes to himself the form of belief called a postulate.... Postulates, however, are not blind faith. Postulates are voluntary assumptions of a risk, for the sake of a higher end. Passive faith dares not face doubt. The postulate faces doubt and says: 'So long as thou canst not make thyself an absolute and certain negative, I propose to act as if thou wert worthless, although I do well see thy force.'"

certain amount of knowledge."[17] One could not doubt at all without realizing the inadequacy of his present mental condition. Uncertainty can always be grounded in the one ultimate assumption on which any theory of knowledge rests, viz., that there is knowledge. And this assumption, to Royce, is itself constitutive of knowledge.

An explanation for Royce's sympathetic appraisal of doubt lies in his keen and constant awareness of man's intellectual limitedness. In an early fragment from his Ph.D. thesis for Johns Hopkins we read:

> Of the capacity of Knowledge that we have, one thing is certain: viz., that it is limited. This appears: first, in that we experience everyday much that we could not possibly hope to predict beforehand, or precisely to remember afterwards; secondly, in that much that would be the subject of possible experience lies, as we are convinced, beyond our ken at all times; thirdly, in that in the views we form as to past and future experience, or as to the facts of experience that lie beyond our ken, we find ourselves very often convinced of error, either by fact or by argument; and so come to alter our once-formed judgments.[18]

Royce's entire theory of knowledge rests upon this experience of limitation.

But Royce is also keenly aware of the inevitable narrowness of experience alone in furnishing answers to life's great problems. The conclusion he draws from such considerations is that no man ought to content himself with stating what he knows. Rather, he maintains, "every man of character, is driven, by the force of his own life as a thinker, to add to experience hypothesis, to fact opinion, to certainty conjecture."[19] In other words, doubt ought not be construed as a condition to be lamented but as a responsibility to be met. Men *must* doubt – for their own sake as individual thinkers, as well as for the sake of the wider community of mankind. The questioning attitude which individual doubters collectively represent motivates a common quest for knowledge which may ultimately enrich others by establishing workable postulates. Such doubting, Royce writes, "is no merely a privilege, but a duty of anyone who proposes to do the least bit of genuine thinking for the good of his fellow-creatures."[20] And again, "I must doubt, in order that by doubting and working I may bring, perhaps, not myself to certainty, but mankind a little nearer to the truth."[21] Only such doubting can initiate the process of "truth-seeking," which Royce designates "a sacred task."[22]

[17] Vol. 54, "Fragments of Ph.D. Thesis and Notes Preliminary to Degree 1877-78," 38. Cf. CP V, #265.
[18] Vol. 54, "Definition and Nature of Knowledge," 13, 14.
[19] FE, 133.
[20] FE, 343.
[21] FE, 339.
[22] FE, 341.

It is consistent with his reverence for the very process of truth-seeking that Royce labels resistance to this process "sin." While noting that ascription in the following passage, we might also consider how closely the notion of Royce here resembles Peirce's understanding of pragmatism as a method of clarifying our ideas.

> Thinking is for us just the clarifying of our minds, and because clearness is necessary to the unity of thought, necessary to lessen the strife of sects and the bitterness of doubt, necessary to save our minds from hopeless, everlasting wandering, therefore to resist the clarifying process, even while we undertake it, is to sin against what is best in us, and is also to sin against humanity.[23]

To both Peirce and Royce, then, the process of truth-seeking is a neverending quest. Perfect clarity can never be achieved because of the experienced fact of human intellectual limitation.

Nonetheless, neither philosopher would disparage the effort to reach truth. As Royce advises us to "[d]oubt not because doubting is a good end, but because it is a good beginning,"[24] so he would have us continue to seek truth even while realizing we cannot wholly and absolutely obtain it. For the process itself discloses partial truths to us, which are useful in the here and now. Even in our doubting, he maintains, we have hold somewhat of truth.

> *For the truth of the matter is concealed in that doubt,* as the fire is concealed in the stony coal. You can no more reject the doubt and keep the innermost truth, than you can toss away the coal and hope to retain its fire. *This doubt is the insight partially attained.*[25]

The doubt is a first step towards possession of the truth; without it one can never have the joy of truly knowing.

To show the practical usefulness of doubting, Royce emphasizes the positive import of postulates, assumptions or hypotheses.[26] These are mental ways of behavior or forms of belief by which men live.[27] Certainly, Royce claims, it would be better if we knew in advance that our conclusions were indubitably correct, but this is the situation only very rarely. Consequently, the most practical thing we can do is to take the risk of postulating, i.e., to live according to an active faith. As a matter of fact we do this anyway – perhaps without realizing it. For example, "[w]e all postulate that our lives

[23] RAP, 5.
[24] FE, 335.
[25] RAP, 231. (Italics are in the text.)
[26] Royce uses the three terms synonymously, but the one he seems to prefer (since he uses it more than the other two) is "postulate."
[27] Cf. RAP, 297.

are worth the trouble" merely by refusing to "end it all."[28] Or, we assume the existence of the world about us, and then proceed to follow the laws which we hypothesize concerning the way it works.[29] If we have the right to postulate in ordinary life and in scientific endeavor, then we have just as much right to postulate in other areas, such as that of religion.[30]

Not that postulates should be asserted haphazardly. On the contrary, although anything not contradictory is a possible subject of postulates, no postulate is to be assumed except after careful criticism, and only because we cannot do better.[31]

> It is not then that postulates occur here and there in our thoughts, but that, without postulates, both practical life and the commonest results of theory, from the simplest impressions to the most valuable beliefs, would be for most if not all of us utterly impossible..... Where there is a deeper basis, that involves more than mere risk, let us find it if we can. But where we have nothing better than active faith, let us discover the fact, and see clearly just why it is worth while to act in this way.[32]

Royce stresses the contrast between his notion of postulate and "blind faith." "With blind faith," he maintains, "little good is done in the world." On the other hand,

> without active faith, expressed in postulates, very little practical good can be done from day to day. Blind faith is the ostrich behind the bush. The postulate stands out like the lion against the hunters. The wise shall live by postulates.[33]

In this respect then we must all possess some wisdom, for "postulates, theoretically uncertain, but practically worth the risk, are at the foundation of our whole lives."[34] If we live at all, Royce would say, we live with faith. And this is well and good because – it works.

C. The limited function of verification and the role of insight

We have already seen through the Roycean texts that his theory of knowledge involves a practical orientation.[35] This is the case both prospectively – through Royce's emphasis on purposeful action, and retrospectively – in his

---

[28] RAP, 299.
[29] Cf. RAP, 292.
[30] Cf. RAP, 331.
[31] Cf. RAP, 300.
[32] RAP, 324.
[33] RAP, 299.
[34] RAP, 331.
[35] Cf. section A *supra*.

treatment of verification. Like his pragmatist contemporaries, Royce endorses the verification process as an empirical means of testing the truth of our assertions through the consequences that follow upon them. Besides maintaining with James that verifiability is more practical than verification in most situations, Royce also asserts that verification is at times impractical and/or impossible. Basing his claim on experience, Royce argues that verifiability is an insufficient truth criterion because certain of our judgments are by nature unverifiable. Since even these judgments are legitimately subject to the imputation of truth or falsity, how, he asks, might such imputation be explained or justified?

In attempting to answer the question adequately, Royce first defines verification as "the act of satisfying by an actual experience the expectation of experience that has been expressed in assertion."[36] He then proceeds to classify all judgments or assertions as follows:

Assertions are
1. About the Present, true without verification, because themselves the means of verification.
2. About the Future, by nature verifiable.
3. About the Past, by nature unverifiable.
4. About the Possible
   a. About the possible in the past, by nature unverifiable.
   b. About the possible in the future, by nature sometimes verifiable and sometimes not.
   c. About the possible without reference to time. Sometimes verifiable.[37]

Regarding the first type, the act of verification and the act of judgment constitute the same assertion. Their coincidence is the basis for their truth. Regarding judgments about the future, these comprise only assertions that may ultimately be submitted to a rigid test, and verified or cast aside. The truth of these statements cannot be known prior to their verification. In regard to judgments about the past, since these can never conceivably be submitted to actual verification through experience, their truth can never be ascertained as absolute or indubitable. This is not to say that there is no truth contained within such statements but merely to posit that neither verification nor verifiability is a sufficient criterion in determining it. The same is true with reference to judgments about what was possible in the past. Regarding the last two types of judgments about the possible, these may in

[36] Vol. 60, "The Work of Thought," 12. Cf. the classification which follows with *Ibid*.

[37] *Ibid*. Arrangement as well as wording are taken directly from the manuscript. So neat a classification is rather unusual in Royce's writings, but the "neatness" does not necessarily facilitate clarity of comprehension.

some cases be verified by actual experience but need never be. Royce looks elsewhere, then, as we shall subsequently see, to obtain a final determinant of the truth of judgments.

In looking elsewhere our idealist hits upon the notion of insight which we have already indicated, though briefly, in Chapter I. To Royce, insight arises out of experience for the sake of experience. Although this holds true for insight in general, he mentions the moral insight and religious insight as particular examples. Note for instance his injunction in *The Religious Aspect of Philosophy:*

Get and keep the moral insight as an experience, and do all that thou canst to extend among men this experience. . . .. Act out in each case what the moral insight bids thee do.[38]

From what type of experience does the moral insight arise? Royce maintains that it originates in the experience of certain conflicting wills that actually exist in the world. By considering these wills as motivations towards separate ideals, one comes to realize the true inner nature of all the conflicting wills in the world. Such an awareness or realization is what constitutes the moral insight as the ultimate ideal towards which all others point. In practice all lesser ideals are doubted; from their doubting, insight into a universal moral principle can emerge. In this manner the experience of doubt can give way to an insightful surety in regard to future behavior.

Nonetheless, no one can achieve the moral insight of which Royce speaks unless he possesses the will to harmonize as far as possible the conflicting wills at work in the world. In other words, an openness to others' views, and to mediation of apparently divergent views, is prerequisite to obtaining that broader knowledge which is the insight. "If the moral insight be concerned," for example,

directly with two conflicting wills, my neighbor's and my own, then this insight involves the will to act as if my neighbor and myself were one being that possessed at once the aims of both of us.

Or,

If the moral insight be concerned with conflicting general aims, such as could express themselves in systems of conduct, then the moral insight involves the will to act, so far as may be, as if one included in one's own being the life of all those whose conflicting aims one realizes.[39]

---

[38] 72. (Italics omitted.)
[39] Both from RAP, 168.

Consequently, there are two attitudes which impede the attainment of insight: dogmatism and insularity. The former closes the door to all but a single possibility; the latter refuses to open the door. Both stand as obstacles to the universality which genuine insight requires.[40]

To Royce, the achievement of religious insight is only possible through the experience of moral insight. For "the moral insight in us must lead us to aim at progress in goodness,"[41] and in this progress one experiences a transcending of evil which is only explicable in terms of that ultimate and infinite Good which is the object of religious insight, as well as the Ideal of all moral and religious living. In the moment of religious insight one glimpses the Wholeness in which human limitation may find fulfilment, where the inevitable fragmentation of human experience can not only be completed but perfectly unified once and for all. To Royce, such an insight into a future totally fulfilled experience – far from standing apart from practical life – gives meaning and direction to each detail of ordinary living.

D. *The relativity of truth and error*

The truth theory of a pragmatist is frequently called a relativism. What the term connotes is that the nature of truth is not fixed but changeable. With James, for example, "[t]ruth *happens* to an idea;"[42] the happening implies the changefulness. With Royce too, truth happens to an idea, but the happening implies something expressed more clearly as growth than as change. Like the spread of grease-spots to which James compares the growth of human knowledge,[43] truth to Royce involves an unlimitedly fulfilling process. Truth "changes" for our idealist, not in the sense that it alters, but in the sense that it increases or grows. Truth is relative in that it is inevitably partial or limited, incomplete-while-completing itself.

Royce relates the relativity of truth to the relativity of knowledge through a notion of the latter as a process of comparison. "By relativity, in this sense," he writes (i.e., the relativity of all human knowledge),

is meant briefly this phenomenon of knowledge, that whenever we know, we always know by and through comparison with some former knowledge.[44]

---

[40] Cf. RAP, 168 and 211.
[41] RAP, 467.
[42] Prag, 133.
[43] Cf. Prag, 112, 113.
[44] Vol. 58, "Berkeley Lectures on Logic," Lecture II, 39. Cf. James's notion of pragmatism as a "theory [which] must mediate between all previous truths and certain new experiences." (Prag, 142)

Rather platonically he remarks that "Cognition is invariably Recognition."[45] Thus to know is to relate new and always partial truths to our previous fund of knowledge.

Royce bases his understanding of the nature of truth on his argument from the possibility of error. Briefly, the argument runs as follows: Error as a reality cannot be denied because its existence is a matter of experience; it is a given. But error as a possibility can only be adequately explained through the actual existence of an absolute truth against which judgments can be measured as to their relative truth or falsity. Therefore, writes Royce, "*[t]he conditions that determine the logical possibility of error must themselves be absolute truth.*"[46] Even in "our wildest doubt," we must assume the actual existence of those conditions that make error possible, viz., the existence of an absolute.[47]

None of the explanations previously offered by philosophers for the possibility of error can sustain the Roycean criticism. One by one he represents and repudiates views other than his own. The common sense theory, for example, which asserts that error or falsity[48] occurs through a lack of correspondence between thought and thing, cannot explain the truth status of statements about the past or future. On the other hand, if we claim that either the individual or the consensus of a group is the standard by which to judge the presence or absence of truth, we have no real basis for maintaining that a judgment is final for other than its unique and unrepeatable situation. Neither is a theory of consistency sufficient for explaining the possibility error – except in regard to statements that have logical import only. All of these theories are justifiably utilized in explaining certain types of errors, but none can explain all types. An adequate explanation must be general enough to apply in every case.

Obviously, Royce construes his explanation as adequate. After presenting his theory first as a "new hypothesis" whose postulation is motivated by his recognition of the defects in other theories, he attempts to show that the theory is not merely a hypothetical assertion but that it is existential in its impact. Accordingly,

[i]f anything is possible, then, when we say so, we postulate something as actually existent in order to constitute this possibility. The conditions of possible error must be actual.[49]

---

[45] Vol. 58, "Berkeley Lectures on Logic," Lecture II, 39.
[46] RAP, 385.
[47] *Ibid.*
[48] To clarify and justify usage of the two terms as correlative, falsity (to Royce) = the assertion of an error.
[49] RAP, 429-30.

Infinite Thought, or absolute Truth, as the condition for the possibility of error must therefore exist. "Save for Thought, there is no truth, no error. Save for inclusive Thought, there is no truth, no error, in separate thoughts."[50] "*All reality must* [therefore] *be present to the Unity of the Infinite Thought*"[51] which is the Absolute. This we cannot doubt, since all our doubting presupposes it.

Hence Royce rejects, and rather forcefully, the doctrine of total relativity of truth, at the same time as he insists, just as forcefully, on the relativity of truth and error. Error exists as relative to absolute Truth. The absolute Truth exists but not as ever wholly ascertained by man whose intellectual limitation Royce is so keenly aware of. In other words, all truth as known is relative, but only by positing the existence of an Absolute can this theory of relativity work. In the workability of his theory Royce regards his absolute idealism as more pragmatic than any theory of total relativity.

It is evident from the preceding examination of the Royce texts that the four points mentioned at the beginning of this chapter are present in his early theory of knowledge. The philosopher's voluntarism interprets speculative effort as essentially inseparable from purposeful action. His experientially rooted conviction of man's intellectual limitation leads him to stress the usefulness of postulates for philosophizing in terms of future experience. Similarly, his recognition that verification cannot always be applied as a truth test suggests that we measure our judgments against a more workable guide, i.e., a universal or Absolute – a standard which explains relativity of truth and the possibility of error. All of these factors point to the presence of a pragmatic element in the thought of Royce, since all describe the practical thrust of even his early philosophizing.

---

[50] RAP, 432.
[51] RAP, 433.

CHAPTER IV

HIS NOTION OF THE ABSOLUTE

A very likely reason for the tendency to regard idealism and pragmatism as incompatible is the "absolutism" which the former generally espouses. The pragmatist frequently finds any notion of an Absolute unacceptable because it supposedly closes the door to other possibilities. Instead of any absolute monistic system, the typical pragmatist wants a healthy pluralism, which might provide him with a never-ending fund of workable, practical theories. No system, least of all an absolutistic system, could (supposedly) do this. A treatment of Royce's notion of the Absolute is therefore much in order at this point, for Royce definitely retains his doctrine of the Absolute along with the pragmatic element that we find developing in his philosophy. It is the aim of this chapter to discover how he does this.

Prior to a consideration of the Absolute itself, however, we will examine Royce's conception of belief and how beliefs are made. For here, also, we may detect the pragmatic thrust of his thought, in ideas subsequently applicable to the Absolute of his idealism.

A. The function of belief, its origin and constitution

Royce once recalled a conversation with a friend on the subject of belief. Disclaiming all responsibility for his beliefs on some important topics, the friend remarked:

"I try to conquer prejudice; but having done this, I can do no more. My belief, whatever it is, forms itself in me. I look on. My will has nothing to do with the matter...."[1]

Since Royce had much admired some of his friend's beliefs, he was so disappointed that he refused to be held responsible for them. Furthermore, he rejected the friend's refusal: "Despite his disclaimer, I thought, and yet

[1] FE, 345.

think, that he has made his beliefs very much for himself, and that these beliefs do him honor. . .."[2]

Not that Royce denies the influence of many other factors in the formation and formulation of belief – education, environment and temperament, to name but a few. But just as the will is inseparable from the act of knowledge, it is equally inseparable from the act of belief. Insofar as these acts are necessarily the expression of our will, "nobody can justly disclaim responsibility for his creed."[3]

As Royce explains his case for the responsibility of believers as believers, he seems to blur a distinction between knowing and believing which he elsewhere maintains.[4] In an early essay, he describes the process through which all knowledge is reached as involving attention, recognition and construction.[5] All three are activities of the will as well as intellect, all three following upon the reception of sense impressions. Attention is that act through which we consciously focus upon a certain impression among the many received. In the act of recognition the new datum is associated with past data, and modified accordingly. The modification is always directed towards simplicity and definiteness of consciousness. For example,

in listening to an indistinct speaker we often supply what is lacking in the sounds he makes, and seem to hear whole words when we really hear but fragments of words.[6]

Or

Mistake a few brown leaves in some dark corner of a garden for some little animal, and the leaves take on for the moment the distinctive familiar color of the animal; and when you discover your blunder, you can catch the colors in the very act of fading into their dull, dry-lead insignificance.[7]

Such experiences as Royce thus describes illustrate the constituting aspect of the knowing (and believing) process. It is this aspect which embodies man's natural tendency to unify and clarify the multiple and vague data of his consciousness. Although the knower is subject to error in his act of constituting, here is also the point at which he can make a real contribution to the

[2] *Ibid.*
[3] FE, 346.
[4] E.g., Vol. 54, "Fragments of Ph.D. Thesis...," I.a.45: "how wide the gulf is between believing that we know and knowing."
[5] Cf. FE, 360.
[6] FE, 358-9.
[7] FE, 359.
[8] FE, 363.

universal fund of human knowledge. "The most significant knowledge," Royce claims, "is in some sense an original product of the man who knows."[8] But this knowledge does not stay with the individual knower: it enriches others through its universal applicability to future experience.

If we bear in mind that Royce incorporates the preceding description of the knowing process under the title "How Beliefs Are Made," it would certainly seem that he intends us to relate that process with the origin of belief. Perhaps he would have us understand that the judgment which terminates the process in the act of constituting is a statement of belief rather than of knowledge. Obviously this is very similar to the theory of Peirce already mentioned.[9]

The term "belief" has yet a wider connotation when Royce employs it to describe his theory of truth:

The Theory of Truth finds its subject-matter and its problem given wherever there may be found, in any mind, the possession of any consciously true belief, or the attainment of or power to impart such belief in any rational conscious way.[10]

Belief thus forms the end ("possession" or "attainment" of belief), the means ("power to impart such belief"), and the matter ("its subject-matter and its problem") in Royce's theory.

Whether we interpret belief in the narrower or in the broader sense employed by Royce, it is clear that his notions of truth, knowledge and belief are so intertwined as to be inseparable. While he does not concern himself to stick with a fixed usage, it is consistent with his overall thought to construe *T*ruth as the ultimate category in which knowledge and belief are contained: knowledge is the process leading to the acquisition of partial *t*ruths, beliefs supplementing their partialness.[11]

The pragmatic point involved here is that our beliefs work in that very wide area where we cannot achieve absolute certainty. According to Royce that area includes such commonplace conceptions as our judgments about the everyday world, as well as our more lofty assertions about God and religion. All statements, he maintains, employ language to convey a belief. "The assertion or judgment is the belief as it is in the mind."[12]

---

[9] Cf. Chapter II, section B, *supra*.

[10] Vol. 55, "The Critical Theory of Knowledge," 5.

[11] Use of capitals follows the general usage of Royce, although he himself is not utterly consistent on the point. Whatever substantives refer to the Absolute or God are capitalized, but personal pronouns referring to the same are not. Substantives which indicate man's partial involvement in the Absolute are never capitalized.

[12] *Primer of Logical Analysis...*, MS Copy, preserved at Houghton Library of Harvard University, 18.

But why are such faith assertions necessary even among our ordinary judgments? Royce would answer this question with the claim that man *needs* to believe. We all wish that the content of our assertions conform to "the real nature of things." This universal wish, however,

> is precisely the same as to wish for stability of belief and for power over the opinions of others. There is no difference. . . . Who seeks for what he chooses to call conformity with the real, seeks in fact but for satisfaction and security of belief.[13]

Even if one were to criticize the more ordinary beliefs upon which he acts, he must ultimately admit to conviction or belief as the starting point for all his claims to knowledge.

> Let me go on as long as I please; my conviction of the convincing nature of my conviction of the validity of a first conviction will never itself be more than a conviction. The superior reality to which I am to conform either means simply the ideal of stability of belief, or it means nothing that I can ever claim.[14]

Nonetheless, in insisting upon the need of men to believe, Royce does not want to imply that belief – even religious belief – requires an emotional content or concomitant, or even that it is enhanced by such. "[I]t is a noticeable fact," he observes,

> that the supernatural may be believed in without the existence of any pious emotion, just as, on the other hand, the deepest piety, in a person of a strong religious temperament, may be found existing almost without any belief in the supernatural.[15]

Rather, belief occurs in the somewhat staid and stolid area where one recognizes that he does not and cannot know absolute answers to fundamental questions. In these darker areas which are much of life, he lives with faith. A believing life constitutes the actualized clarification of his concepts. At best one lives therein with confidence, sometimes with the added joy of being able to communicate that confidence to others.[16]

Nowhere does Royce suggest that our believing is to go unchallenged or uncriticized. For one so appreciative of the speculative endeavor such an

---

[13] Vol. 55, "1878 Notes," 8.

[14] *Ibid.*, 10. Cf. Aristotle's "basic premises" as he describes these in *Posterior Analytics* I, 2.

[15] Josiah Royce, "The Intention of the Prometheus Bound of Aeschylus, being an Investigation in the Dept. of Greek Theology (B.A. Thesis, University of California, 1875)," *Bulletin of the University of California*, June, 1875, 17. (In the original text the word after "believed" is *is*, but since the context suggests that this is a typographical or printer's error, this is changed to *in* to make for more fluent reading.)

[16] Cf. Vol. 79, "Reality and Consciousness," 8.

attitude would be inconsistent. Instead, realizing the inevitable relativity of every belief to the particular consciousness and particular moment in which it is believed, he discusses several possible tests of faith.[17] The first, the test of persistence, is a purely psychological means of judging the sincerity and intensity of a belief; it cannot say anything of the truth status of the content asserted in belief. On the other hand, the test of consistency, while theoretically adequate, is practically limited by the fact that all we are finally doing in examining a belief for consistency is to compare it with other beliefs. In other words, investigation can never lead us beyond the consciousness that we believe something to be true. It cannot offer indubitable verification in regard to faith assertions.

Another test, one which the classical pragmatists would readily support, is the criterion of satisfaction. Royce maintains, however, that

there is an incongruity in accepting a faith as true simply because you happen to feel it agreeable or satisfying to even your highest interests, for other men have felt other opposing faiths equally satisfying.[18]

Nevertheless, Royce uses the notion of satisfaction to arrive at a criterion which to him is yet more satisfying. After asking what a faith must be in order to satisfy all men, he describes his own ideal of absolute Truth as the only satisfactory criterion for the faith of an individual believer or for any group of believers. The universal creed he thus endorses

would be of a nature to demand acceptance from all men. It would be the one faith opposed to the many opinions, and certain to conquer them. It would be the one reality that could wait for ages for a discoverer.[19]

In a sense, Royce has claimed to be the discoverer of that one reality through his ideal of truth which is the Absolute. Once this is discovered, the practical aim of all truth-seeking, whether through knowledge or belief, is apparent: "to harmonize the conflicting opinions of men, to substitute for the narrowness and instability of personal views the broadness of view that should characterize the free man."[20] In forceful terms we are reminded of our responsibility to believe selflessly as well as critically:

You may not, you dare not, if it is your vocation, to think at all – you dare not accept a faith simply for the satisfaction it gives you. You dare not, I say, because

---

[17] Cf. *Ibid.*, 3-5.
[18] FE, 336-7.
[19] FE, 337.
[20] *Ibid.*

as a thinker your true aim is not to please yourself, but to work for the harmonizing of the views of mankind, to do your part in a perfectly unselfish task. This is the one great argument against all uncritical faith.[21]

Only such a creed, Royce maintains, would be universally acceptable and useful in satisfying the real intellectual needs of men. Only such a creed is applicable to the totality of human experience, in anticipation of which we take the risk of faith. To such a creed Royce bids each of us give our lived assent: "We are responsible for our own creed, and must make it by our own hard work."[22]

B. The Absolute Thought, perfectly fulfilling experience

Royce uses many designations in speaking of the Absolute which is at once the source and goal of all man's knowledge and belief. In this section we will generally lump together those designations which have to do with intellect – such as *Thought, Truth, Consciousness,* and *Knower,* and leave to the next section those designations which are more related to the will – such as *End,* or *Will,* or *Power.* In the first case, we look to Royce's notion of the Absolute which perfectly fulfills experience; in the second we consider the Absolute as the organizer of that experience.

Within the diverse designations Royce employs, he uses descriptive terms which serve to point up certain aspects of his Absolute. For example, the term *absolute* itself (whether used adjectively or as a substantive) conveys the note of finality or unchangeableness as opposed to relativity.[23] On the other hand, the term *infinite* indicates that our own (finite) comprehension of the Absolute is inevitably limited. The terms *all-embracing* or *inclusive* which Royce sometimes uses suggest the relation between the Absolute and ourselves: we, with all our thoughts and will acts, are inevitably fragmented particles whom the Whole unites. Besides the diversity of adjectives with which Royce describes the Absolute, he uses other noun designations such as *Life, Reality,* and *God,* although none of these occur so frequently in his early or middle works as "Absolute." Finally, the term *Experience,* one particularly pertinent to our interest in Royce's pragmatism, is employed in reference to the Absolute.

[21] FE, 337-8.
[22] FE, 363. Cf. 338.
[23] In RAP Royce makes an interesting point of identifying "absolute" and "real" in applying these terms to the distinction between truth and error: "[W]hen we here talk of an 'absolute' distinction between truth and error, we mean merely a 'real' distinction between truth and error. And this real distinction the fiercest partisan of relativity admits; for does he not after all argue for relativity against 'absolutists,' holding that he is really right, and they really wrong." (376)

It has already been suggested – though briefly – that Royce arrives at his notion of the Absolute after having rejected both experience and the self as inadequate principles of philosophy. As problems rather than principles, these notions require explanation themselves before they can effectively be utilized in further philosophizing.[24] In seeking such explanation, Royce finds that "even in the most exact human thought there is an element which transcends experience."[25] As our present experience opens out towards the future, it says to us:

> There is something beyond our experience, *viz.*, another experience: that is the first postulate. Experiences form an uniform and regular whole of laws of sequence. That is the other postulate, subordinate to the first.[26]

Initially, Royce maintains, the subordinate postulate helps us to form an idea of a material world beyond our individual consciousness. If we reflect more critically upon this idea, however, we are compelled to admit that the facts assumed as existent beyond the range of our individual consciousness are no more than "possible experiences."[27] Further, if we try to express the nature of our assumption of "possible experiences" we must take account of the fact that they are assumed to satisfy the postulate of uniformity, to fill the gaps in our actual experiences. We are thus led to the conception of one uniform and absolute future experience in which all facts would be connected as uniformly subject to fixed law. But we can yet only label our conception of this absolute experience as "possible."[28]

To move from the possible to the actual conception of absolute experience, Royce needs "a hero," i.e., a hypothetical subject for all the possible experiences. All that is necessary is to *hypothesize* the existence of this subject, since "to assume a consciousness for which the 'possible experiences' are present facts, is to do no more than our theory seems to need."[29] Other hypotheses, he claims, assume more than is demanded for the theoretical conception of reality. His assumption is the best available because it combines simplicity with adequacy. Admittedly, were we to demonstrate the actual existence of the subject of all possible experience, this would be the preferable procedure. But we know that this cannot be done. Therefore, to

---

[24] Cf. Vol. 79, "Of the Will...," 9, 27, 41-2.
[25] Vol. 80, "Some Illustrations...," 47.
[26] Josiah Royce, "Mind and Reality," *Mind* 7 (1882), 51. Hereafter, M&R.
[27] Cf. *Ibid.* and with Thayer's description of pragmatism as necessarily involving the notion of possibilities as traits of reality (426).
[28] Cf. M&R, 51-2. Note use of subjunctive in text: "This absolute experience, to which all facts would exhibit themselves in their connexion as uniformly subject to fixed law, is conceived as 'possible.'"
[29] M&R, 53.

make our theory of reality and knowledge as simply reasonable and practically workable as possible,

> we shall suggest what of course never can be proven, that all the conceived "possible experiences" are actual in a Consciousness of which we suppose nothing but that it knows these experiences, or knows facts corresponding in number and in other relations to these experiences. This Consciousness is the Universal Consciousness.[30]

According to Royce, having thus hypothesized the actual existence of the Universal Consciousness, we have increased our own capacity for obtaining and applying knowledge usefully. Knowledge of possible experiences, he asserts, is useful in regard to future experience. While by nature we tend to be in agreement with the Universal Consciousness, our actual progress towards more definite and extended agreement requires that we postulate its existence. Further growth in truth as agreement with the Universal Consciousness is consequently "both possible and practically useful."[31]

While Royce talks about the Absolute as existing he does not here claim its existence to have been demonstrated. Neither does he hold that man – either individually or collectively – can ever wholly comprehend the Absolute Truth or Thought. The closest we might come to possession of that Truth, he maintains, would be the "perfect agreement of all rational beings with one another."[32] Even this is an ideal not-yet-realized, but were it otherwise, the realization would still not constitute the Absolute. Thus, our thought growth is a relative progress in the direction of more general, more definite, more fully conscious, more deliberate assertions. The clarification of our conceptions is accomplished through our lived experience. An absolute vision of truth, free from all taint of postulates or of imperfect efforts towards direct knowledge: this we can never expect to obtain.[33] Although all our own thoughts partake of the divine (so much as to suggest a pantheism that Royce denies[34]), as knowers we can never exhaust the Absolute Thought that perfectly fulfills and gives meaning to our experiences. "As absolute,

---

[30] *Ibid.*
[31] M&R, 37.
[32] FE, 346. Moreover, as Royce points out in an early article, even intuition cannot furnish us with proof positive in regard to the existence of the Absolute. Cf. Vol. 60, "Reality and Consciousness," 43, 44: "We do not look for any intuition of the Absolute, for any revelation internally of a reality that is at the same time and in the same sense external; we seek only for the simplest and most consistent expression of the assumptions of our thoughts, hoping not to make them appear to be anything but assumptions. To do otherwise is to make gods with our own hands for the sake of worshipping them."
[33] Cf. Vol. 79, "Reality and Consciousness," 6.
[34] E.g. M&R, 39: "Our hypothesis is not pantheistic or theistic."
[35] Vol. 60, "Reality and Consciousness," 38.

this reality is then unknowable; it is not absolute. Before this inscrutable mystery we stand amazed...."[35]

C. *The Universal Will, aiming at organization of experience*

Before considering how Royce puts his Absolute to work as the organizer of experience, we ought first to see how he arrives at the notion of Universal Will, and what this means to him. As might be suspected from one whose theory of knowledge is essentially voluntaristic, Royce does not wish to limit the Absolute to the realm of speculative knowledge, truth or thought. Postulating the existence of a Universal Consciousness completes our conception of an absolute experience, but this says nothing that would have the Universal Consciousness "be transformed into what he now is not, an active Spirit."[36]

To effect the transformation is not terribly difficult if we begin by recalling that

[t]he Infinite Thought must, knowing all truth, include also a knowledge of all wills, and of their conflict. For him all this conflict, and all the other facts of the moral world take place. He then must know the outcome of the conflict, that Moral Insight.[37]

According to Royce, the different aims represented by conflicting wills must all be the expression of somebody's will. That somebody is, of course, the Absolute.[38] The real doubt which occurs in the situation which involves a conflict of wills (all cannot be equally right, nor all equally wrong) can only be explained by positing the existence of a Universal Will against which our relative wills are measured. Moral insight affords us a glimpse of that Will which Royce wants for his Absolute Thought. "In the Divine Thought," he writes, "is perfectly and finally realized the Moral Insight and the Universal Will."[39]

As all insight is grounded in experience, unless a man experiences the reality of the conflict of wills in the world (even though that experience may sometimes be bitter),[40] he is apt to miss the moral insight which establishes the existence of the Universal Will. Having experienced the conflict as well as the insight, however, he recognizes the need for harmony among the human wills, and he sees the Absolute as that Universal Will towards which all

---

[36] M&R, 54.
[37] RAP, 433.
[38] Cf. RAP, 134.
[39] RAP, 442.
[40] Cf. RAP, 176.

other wills ought to be directed if the harmony is to be achieved. He also experiences the importance of a communal effort to achieve "the highest good" which is the harmony of human wills.[41]

The highest good then is not to be got by any one of us or by any clique of us separately. Either the highest good is for humanity unattainable, or the humanity of the future must get it *in common*. Therefore, the sense of community, the power to work together, with clear insight into our reasons for so working, is the *first* need of humanity.[42]

Based on his double awareness of individual limitation and a universal ideal, we here see an early indication of Royce's "sense of community." By and large, however, the references to community are few and far between in the early Royce.

From experience then one learns the means to be applied towards the End of action which is essentially Ideal. "For behold, made practical, brought down from its lonesome height, my Ideal very simply means the Will to direct my acts *towards* the attainment of universal Harmony."[43] Such a universal ideal is quite demanding in the here and now, requiring that everywhere and always we give preference to the wider need and good of men rather than our own.[44] Royce spells out this demand yet more positively when he says that the ideal task of the community in which the moral insight is attained is: *Organize all Life*. This means, he explains, that the members of such a community are to be future orientated: they are to

find work for the life of the coming moral humanity which shall be so comprehensive and definite that each moment of every man's life in that perfect state, however rich and manifold men's lives may then be, can be and will be spent in the accomplishment of that one highest impersonal work. If such work is found and accepted, the goal of human progress will be in so far reached.[45]

Such a life orientation requires a twofold faith or belief; first, in a power that secures the moral ordering of the universe, and secondly, a faith in oneself – that he is capable of living in conformity with such ordering.[46] The will of a

---

[41] Note that diversity is essential to real harmony; else it reduces to unison or uniformity.
[42] RAP, 175. (Italics in text.)
[43] RAP, 140-1.
[44] Cf. RAP, 201.
[45] RAP, 211.
[46] Recalling that Royce's philosophy is essentially a philosophy of religion, consider the following: "The essence of Religion is therefore faith in the actual power of just and charitable deeds to render him happy who lives in constant performance of them, and faith consequently in a Power that secures the moral ordering of the universe. Whatever sect

man can organize his life's experiences only if he recognizes, accepts, and utilizes his own power and the Power of the Absolute.

While the goal described by Royce smacks of an impersonalism that might impede individuality, he nonetheless maintains that in the midst of pursuing this Universal Ideal which unites the separate selves we must be very careful of every soul, and of every individual tendency that may be moulded into the service of the Universal Will. "The moral insight," he remarks, "desires that no hair fall from the head of any living creature unnecessarily."[47] For

[t]he One Will is not a one-sided will. . . . [I]ts warfare is aimed at the intolerance of the separate selves, its yoke is the yoke of complete organic freedom, its pride is in the perfect development of all life.[48]

Consequently, when we serve this Universal Will

we must sternly cut off all that life in ourselves or in others that cannot ultimately conform to the universal will; but we have nothing but love for every form of sentient existence that can in any measure express this Will.[49]

In other words, the divine Will as absolute remains both primary and final in regard to our relative ideals and wills, but that same divine Will as universal and all-inclusive accommodates itself as far as is "divinely" possible with the divine respect of which only God is capable in regard to each and all of our particular hopes and wants.

D. *The relationship of the Absolute to the problem of evil*

As Universal Thought and Will, the Absolute of Royce is essentially related to the problem of evil. The relating is a clear instance of emphasis on future experience. By providing solid rational grounding for moral principles, Royce maintains, his theoretical absolutism offers the only adequate philosophical basis for living a practical moral life. Without attempting a thorough explication of his moral philosophy, it is pertinent here to describe at least briefly how Royce relates his idea of the Absolute to the problem of evil, thereby indicating the practical thrust of his thought.[50]

supports these principles, is a religious sect, whatever its other articles of faith. Whatever sect opposes them is truly atheistic, however outspoken its confessional orthodoxy." (Vol. 55, "Fragment about Dec. 1877," 46)

[47] RAP, 217.
[48] RAP, 217-8.
[49] RAP, 218.
[50] For an excellent treatment of Royce's moral philosophy, see Peter Fuss, *The Moral Philosophy of Josiah Royce* (Cambridge: Harvard University Press, 1965).

While the reality of evil is generally admitted as a fact of experience, several theories have been proposed in the past to explain its origin and nature. Royce claims that his explanation of the problem fills the gaps in other views that have been expounded.[51] For example, to those who define evil as a mere illusion which arises from the partialness of our perspective, he replies that this leaves unexplained the positive element which evil manifestly involves. Secondly, Royce mentions the view of evil as a means to goodness. Such a position, he says, requires that evil be attained prior to the attainment of good, and therefore as separate from the good. But to separate the evil from goodness would be to separate it from being entirely. Since we know that evil does exist as a fact of our experience it must exist not as mere means but as end also, i.e., as comprised by the Absolute Good which is the end of all. In presenting his own theory, Royce retains aspects of both of the theories which he otherwise regards as inadequate.

The evil we experience, our idealist maintains, is of two general types: external seeming evil such as death, pain, or weakness of character, and the internal actual evil which is the bad will itself. Because of our limited knowledge we can never verify whether external evils are actually so or not. They might instead be blessings in disguise or expressions of some wicked diabolical will. On the other hand,

> with regard to the only evil that we know as in inward experience, and so as a certain reality, namely, the Evil Will, we know both the existence of that, and its true relation to universal goodness, because and only because we experience both of them first through the moral insight, and then in the good act.[52]

Whether our own acts are good or evil, they are neither except in relationship to the Absolute Good to which the moral insight gives us access. Rather optimistically, Royce asserts that

> [t]he evil will as such may either be conquered in our personal experience, and then we are ourselves good; or it may be conquered not in our thought considered as a separate thought, but in the total thought to which ours is so related, as our single evil and good thoughts are related to the whole of us.[53]

Given this absolutistic system, not only is evil compatible with good, but evil is necessary to the very existence of good, whether in man or in God. For

---

[51] Cf. RAP, 455. Also, cf. RAP, 252-283. Royce here refutes theistic positions other than his own; e.g., a monism not founded on experience, dualism – which is ultimately self-contradictory, and the "halting half Theism of the empirical Design Argument." (279)
[52] RAP, 455.
[53] Ibid.

in experiencing the good one experiences the victory of the moral insight over the bad will. In other words, we experience

in one indivisible moment both the partial evil of the selfish impulse and the universal good of the moral victory, which has its existence only in the overwhelming of the evil. . . . Only through this inner victory over the evil that is experienced as a conquered tendency does the good will have its being.[54]

Evil then is a positive entity in the sense that it makes possible the existence of all good, both relative and absolute. If any good at all is useful or practical then evil is also, insofar as it is essential to the being of the good.

As evil exists always and essentially as the concomitant of an existential good, there can be no absolute evil. We can theorize about what an absolute evil would be, but we cannot rationally justify its existence in the practical order. Linking the notion of an Absolute Evil with that of an absolutely Evil Will, Royce writes:

Because thy evil intent, which, in its separateness, *would be* unmixed evil, thy selfish will, thy struggle against the moral insight, this evil will of thine is no lonesome fact in the world, but is an element in the organic life of God.[55]

Thus God exists as the all-inclusive one, as one who embraces all of good and evil (the latter as condition for the good) within his being as Absolute Thought and Universal Will. His divine life is perfect precisely because it comprises not only the knowledge of our finite wicked wills but the insight into their truth as moments in the real universal will.[56]

A name for the Absolute through which Royce sometimes describes the relation between it and good and evil is *Judge*. Insofar as there is any objective truth in our moral conceptions, this truth must be known to the all-embracing Thought, who as Universal Will, also acts as an absolute Judge who perfectly estimates the world.[57] Within his jurisdiction all of particular reality is encompassed.

All of you then is known and justly estimated by the absolute thought that embraces all possible truth, and for whom are all relations, present, past, and future of all possible beings, acts, and thoughts in all places.[58]

---

[54] RAP, 453, 452. Cf. 455, where the pantheistic strain of Royce's thought is even more manifest: "As the evil impulse is to the good man so is the evil will of the wicked man to the life of God, in which he is an element."
[55] RAP, 454. (Italics in text.) Note the future subjunctive and cf. Peirce's fondness for same.
[56] Cf. *Ibid*.
[57] Cf. RAP, 382.
[58] RAP, 381.

Both possible and actual truth are judged by this all-knowing One, in whose presence all our lives are manifest, and from whom our lives derive their meaning, truth and usefulness.

So much for Royce's early notion of the Absolute. We have seen in this chapter that even at this stage Royce insisted that our believing involves a willful orientation towards future acting. By indicating textual references to the Absolute as Thought, as Will and as Judge, we have observed that Royce's conception of the Absolute is no impractical abstraction. The conception arises from our concrete experiences of human intellectual limitation, conflicts of wills, and the presence of evil in the world. From these experiential origins Royce paints a picture of an Absolute who is very much involved with the workings of our universe, and particularly with the practical life of man, as one who is responsible for ordering all of his experiences towards their final future fulfilment.

Probably, his theory of the Absolute is the most useful notion in the early writings of Royce. Without it his philosophy would be practically groundless and aimless. With it, his idealistic system works in the sense that it touches the real man precisely where he lives, i.e., in the inbetween area between the grounding and the aim.

CHAPTER V

HIS CONCEPTION OF THE INDIVIDUAL

One would suspect that the absolutism of any absolute idealist would result in the diminishment of his appreciation for and treatment of the individual. Having examined Royce's early notion of the Absolute, having noted the ultimacy and all-inclusiveness which he ascribes thereto, we might well wonder whether his philosophy is at all accommodating to single existents or individuals as such, or whether individuality must be finally dissolved in the vastness of the Absolute. The present chapter is an effort to appease that wonder. In appeasing it, we may also detect whatever if any pragmatic elements are contained within Royce's early conception of the individual.

A. Meaning, worth, and importance of the individual

Regarding the actual origin of conscious individuals, Royce writes:

When the earth became filled with life, there appeared in the universal consciousness the data known as organisms. And at the same time, there arose individual conscious beings, whose states were more or less imperfect copies of the universal consciousness in certain of its facts.[1]

Each resultant individual, Royce maintains, is a different series of conscious states, existing in a fixed relation to the universal consciousness.[2] The uniqueness of the individual is constituted by the relationship it (and no other) bears to the Absolute.

Two factors precede the individual's awareness of personal identity or self-consciousness, viz., existence of oneself and others, and consciousness of other existents including other selves or consciousnesses.[3] The primary datum, therefore, is that there really are existents in this world, whether we

---
[1] M&R, 40.
[2] M&R, 41.
[3] Cf. Vol. 79, "Of the Will...," 19-20.

are conscious of them or not. Secondly, there is the datum of feeling which is the experience of other existents, including my body insofar as this is construed as an object of experience. From the experience of the various facts of consciousness the notion of personal identity or the sense of self arises, for

> Feeling is only possible as feeling in a Self. Self-consciousness is the non-sensuous accompaniment of sense, that which is in all data of Feeling, but not one of them.[4]

As soon as one is at all aware of feeling or experiencing an object, he becomes aware also that he is the subject of the experience. Personal identity is thus "a matter of mediate reasoning, a conclusion from the facts of consciousness."[5] In the early writings, Royce makes no claim that the establishment of self-consciousness requires recognition of other individuals as other consciousnesses, but merely as other. Once achieved through our awareness of others, the sense of self or knowledge "that one's own personality is a substantial fact beyond the possibility of doubt, forms with most of us a fundamental and unquestioned truth."[6]

The reason that the sense of self can be given mediately through diverse conscious acts is because the self is present in many of our moments of consciousness. Whenever the acts of consciousness are "distinct and organized," the self must be present as the organizing principle. Consequently, all such acts are

> found to be coexistent with more or less Self-consciousness. And the two, the Self-element and the not-Self element are united as are other elements in themselves various, in single acts of consciousness. Many moments there are in every complex and distinct act of Knowledge; and one of these moments is Self.[7]

Hence, by experiencing the momentary unities of the self's presence in a series of distinct and organized conscious acts, one arrives at the sense of self which is personal identity.

Having given his account of the origin of self-consciousness, Royce goes on to explain that our awareness of the existence of other consciousnesses as conscious is grounded in our experience of ourselves as conscious. In other words, we judge that other beings are conscious because we observe that their actions are similar to those which arise from our own conscious experiences. It is in the consciousness of individuals, therefore, that we find "the elements that shall develop into all the complicated social phenomena."[8]

---

[4] *Ibid.*, 20.
[5] *Ibid.*, 19.
[6] Vol. 58, "Berkeley Lectures 1878," Lecture VI, 5.
[7] Vol. 79, "Of the Will...," 27; cf. "Reality and Consciousness," 27-8.
[8] Vol. 55, "The Historical Method in Sociology," 18.

According to Royce, such phenomena are explicable only through the presence of two factors within individual consciousness, viz., a consciousness of other minds as existent, and a desire to conceive the relations of the self to others in the most simple manner possible. From these fundamental elements emerge all the different forms of self-to-other relationships, such as the relation of the individual to the law, to social conventions, to humanity in general, and to divinity.[9]

The fact that the diversity of possible self-to-other relationships offers no definite grounding for communication among the various selves is a problem to our idealist, as to any idealist. Royce admits that the problem is not wholly answerable: communication with other minds or even with one's own past can only be accomplished indirectly through conversation and through memory.

In truth the barrier between one mind and another can never conceivably be broken down. One mind can never hope to see directly into another by any sort of intuition. And equally insurmountable is the barrier between one's own present and one's past. To overtop the first barrier we seek by means of conversation with one another. To communicate with our own past we make use of our memory. But methods are indirect.[10]

Here Royce does not lay so much stress on the importance of communication among the selves, indirect though it inevitably be, as he does in later writings. Nonetheless he claims that some type of communication is necessary to self-development, as "a means of measuring our progress in reaching the goal."[11] Since we can never have perfect knowledge of the Absolute Good towards which we strive as individuals, our only way of discerning our "grade of self-attainment or self-perfection" is through a comparison of our state at any one time with our previous state of development, or with a higher stage of development, i.e., another person.[12]

Like William James, Royce recognizes that the thought of an individual is influenced by his temperament.[13] Unlike James, however, Royce places the whole weight for the value and usefulness of that thought within the context of his all-inclusive Absolute. Individuals are truly esteemed, but only insofar

---

[9] Cf. *Ibid.*
[10] Vol. 60, "Thought-Purposes," 20.
[11] FE, 45.
[12] Cf. FE, 145.
[13] Cf. Royce: "It is true that the thought of the individual philosopher depends upon his temperament, his training, his actual knowledge of previous thinkers." (Vol. 59, "Berkeley Lectures 1879," Lecture I, 16) In James, a similar attitude is evident in the following: "The history of philosophy is to a great extent that of a certain clash of human temperaments." (Prag, 19)

as they act as useful "instruments," collectively contributing towards filling up what is wanting in the Universal Thought and Will.[14] In seeking their development as individuals, they overcome the evil of their own separateness, while acquiring for themselves a share in the worth of the universal life. Since their whole reality is constituted through this sharing, they are no mere fragmentary "dreams" in the mind of the Absolute, but living "drops" in the ocean of his truth. Thus, individuals, as such, do not become

"things in the dream" of any other person than themselves, but their whole reality, just exactly as it is in them, will be found to be but a fragment of a higher reality. This reality will be no Power, nor will it produce the individuals by dreaming of them, but it will complete the existence that in them, as separate beings, has no rational completeness.... The world of life is then what we desired it to be, an organic total; and the individual selves are drops in the ocean of the absolute truth.[15]

Admittedly, the "drops" which are the individuals of Royce are practical in their very being and meaning, since they comprise the very being and meaning of the Absolute. Without the individuals, therefore, there can be no useful life or purpose. Despite their usefulness, however, it is difficult to see how the various drops retain any real individuality or uniqueness within the absolutistic context which Royce prescribes for them.

In a passage written in 1886, Royce reinforces our opinion that the uniqueness of personality is lost in his conception of the Absolute. Along with its ethical orientation, the same text is the most clear indication of pantheism in the early Royce:

Now a finite personality is merely a self-determined and free limitation of the one great universal Self.... To enjoy his own infinite wealth, the Divine One becomes flesh in myriad self-conscious forms.... A finite mind is simply the Infinite engaged in a particular reflection upon a select portion of his own majesty. He is the game, and accordingly he appears phenomenally both as the players, who are the individuals and as the rules of the game, which are the laws of nature, and finally as the hits, bases, runs, fouls, and outs, which are the facts of the physical and psychophysical world. Whoever knows him not, loitres about the outskirts of the field, a curious and helpless observer, nothing here and there a running and a shouting, a stroke and a catch, a jumping on a sprawling player, but never making out the true sense, the inner rationality, the self-surrendering freedom, the self-determined necessity, which mark the whole blessed business.[16]

---

[14] Cf. Vol. 55, "Papers written 1877-78," MS of *The Spirit of Modern Philosophy*, 3: "The individual is but an instrument. The human intellect is but a stepping-stone of progress." Also, cf. RAP, 216: "Thou and I, neighbor, have in this world no rights as individuals. We are instruments."

[15] RAP, 380, 381, 441.

[16] Vol. 85, "About 1886-7? Unfinished: A Speculation as to the Nature of Mind," 15-17.

In short, the whole blessed business which is the Absolute of Royce is the basis for the worth and importance of the individual.

B. A practical answer to individualism

Probably a main reason for Royce's early tendency to let his absolutism stifle individuality is his abhorrence for mere individualism. Although he does not yet make a clear distinction between individuality and individualism we can see the roots of that later distinction if we compare his sparse but respectful references to the separate selves with his discussion of the forms of individualism in *The Religious Aspect of Philosophy*.[17] Individualism itself is construed as an evil in all of its phases. Nevertheless, Royce points out the practical significance of his rather pessimistic regard for the individual as such by using the consideration of individualism as a support for his moral absolutism.

Individualism in general is defined as "the doctrine that tries to understand everything from the standpoint of the individual man."[18] Such a doctrine has definite empirical roots, since we all experience the "tendency to hold that the ideal of life is the separate happy man." According to Royce, this tendency is even more natural and normal in "unreflecting strong natures, to whom happiness has been in a fair human measure already given."[19]

The first and crudest form of individualism is that of the man for whom all the world is classified as "either his or not his, as to a cow all is either cow feed or not cow feed."[20] A supposed friend of Royce evinced this attitude in remarking: "My notion of a good life is that you ought to help your friends and whack your enemies."[21] As a rule this type of individualism is so blatantly selfish that it becomes embarrassing; therefore it next assumes a less obvious form, viz., that of total dedication to inner self-development. Those so dedicated seek what the world refuses them in outer self-realization, through an attitude of rather cynical introspection.[22] Frequently this second type of individualism follows upon an experience of frustration or failure in pursuit of one's ideal or in personal relationships.

The third form is sentimental individualism. Here we often find a great deal of inadvertent rationalizing involved in a rather romantic effort to achieve contentment for oneself.

---

[17] Concerning the later distinction see Part Three, Ch. XI.
[18] Vol. 57, "1878 Lectures on Romanticism," Lecture I, 9.
[19] RAP, 201.
[20] *Ibid.*
[21] RAP, 202.
[22] Cf. RAP, 203.

The sentimental self admits that the world cannot understand it, and will not receive it, but it insists that this neglect comes because the world does not appreciate the strength and beauty of the inner emotional life.[23]

As their response to the supposed insensitivity of others, such selves pursue a kind of individualistic hedonism as their ideal.

Another somewhat romantic type of individualism is the fourth form which Royce calls the Heresy of Prometheus or Titanism. This phase, he remarks, is less dangerous to genuine morality and far higher in the scale of worth than the other three. At the same time it is probably the most subtle form of individualism, containing within it the seeds of destruction of the individual. Although we might expect to find this attitude but rarely, and only in heroes, the Titanism described by Royce

is the ideal of many a quiet, matter of fact man, who has little happiness, but much spirit and energy, who is too busy and too healthy to be sentimental, who knows little of poetry, who has never heard the name of Prometheus, but who knows what it is to hold his own in the fight with the world. . ... There is no judge above him save God or his conscience.[24]

His ideal of perfection and the self he thinks himself to be is lonely, active and indomitable. But the ideal, says Royce, is an illusion. As lonely as he might wish to be, his self-estimation depends entirely upon the respect he excites from others. Were they to stop talking about him or ignore him utterly, his inner heroism would soon vanish. "He exists as a hero, in fact, only because he is in organic relation to the world about him."[25] Like it or not, he cannot truly be Prometheus – alone. For

just what the Heresy of Prometheus asserts to be the perfect, namely the complete and all-sided development of life, just that can belong only to the general, not to the individual life.[26]

Hence, Titanism always contradicts itself. In his effort to live heroically in isolation, the Titan inevitably blocks his own progress.

As a matter of fact all the phases of individualism contain inherent contradictions or tensions. While the ideals they represent are generally acceptable and good (e.g., self-realization, fulfilment, or happiness), the means they undertake (e.g., excessive introspection, and closing oneself off to other people and possibilities) cannot ever lead to the desired end. A clear

---

[23] RAP, 204.
[24] RAP, 206.
[25] RAP, 210.
[26] *Ibid.*

proof of this unavoidable inadequacy of individualism is "the old empirical truth that individual happiness is never very nearly approached by anyone, so long as he is thinking about it."[27]

In the apparent contradiction which we all experience in trying to realize the ideal of individualism lies a positive and practical significance. Our consciousness of the limitation of individual life as such provokes us to posit the existence of an Absolute who will strengthen, supplement, and fulfill our individual and collective limitations. The rational and empirically rooted pessimism with which Royce regards our human limitation as such thus becomes the grounds for a "believing" optimism.[28] We foresee a situation in which all our partial experiences, thoughts and will-acts will be completed. We live in hope because of our initial assumption of that ultimate fulfilment. With such support it is practically possible to overcome the individualism towards which we are naturally inclined. Moreover, even an innate tendency towards selfishness can be utilized in promoting the universal good which is the goal of all individuals. For selfishness is

half realization of the truth expressed in unselfishness. Selfishness says: *I shall exist.* Unselfishness says: *The Other Life is as My Life.*[29]

Our selfishness itself can be made effective, since one must love and respect himself before he can act in a similar vein towards others.

Royce admits that there is a brand of selfishness or individualism to which idealists are particularly addicted. The main symptom is a total preoccupation with oneself through an attitude of constant self-examination. Generally speaking this attitude belongs to the second phase of individualism described above. In his search for "the better consciousness," the idealist is led to make and live by the judgment that *he* must at all costs be saved, no matter how much his saving hurts others. Eventually, such selfishness ends in a fixed idea that "all the world must serve me, and that I must serve my pet phantoms."[30]

When Royce looks around for a cure for the individualism or selfishness towards which we all (but especially idealists) are prone, he can find none other than the oft repeated emphasis on the Absolute as ultimate Truth. Involvement in other-directed enterprises such as art or politics are helpful but insufficient as efforts to overcome individualism by leading men to a higher

---

[27] RAP, 186.
[28] "Believing" is used here in the broad context referred to in Chapter IV, section A, *supra.*
[29] RAP, 161.
[30] Vol. 79, "Unfinished rewriting of an essay: a critique of transcendentalist or idealist selfishness," 21.

plane of life. Better success is obtained, he maintains, when one passes to the activity of truth-seeking, for truth is a more common possession than beauty or peace.[31] Truth is the Absolute which can order our individualistic bents towards the common Good which is the source and goal of the beauty and peace which we promote and share only relatively through art and politics.

Thus Royce's practical answer to individualism involves his positive appreciation for the pessimism which is to him a matter of experience. It means using our very awareness of the selfishness towards which we are inclined as a lever through which to lift ourselves and others away from ourselves and towards the Other. That no one can do this alone is obvious. Consequently, "all life for Self is worthelss."[32] Paradoxically, we can find happiness only when we cease to seek it for ourselves and seek it instead for all mankind.

C. The nature and significance of progress for the individual

Regarding the nature of progress for the individual Royce makes a distinction which is particularly pertinent by way of contrast with the later pragmatist John Dewey.[33] Not all growth, Royce asserts, is improvement: "One may grow while growing ever worse."[34] Evolution or growth is an "increase in the complexity, definiteness, individuality and organic connection of phenomena," while "progress is any series of changes that meets with the constantly increasing approval of somebody."[35] Ultimately, that somebody is the Roycean Absolute, whose will is incarnated in our world of change through human purposiveness. All progress is thus viewed as evolution, but not all evolution is judged progress. The latter occurs only when evolution fulfills a good purpose, i.e., when the increasing complexity is ultimately directed towards a final synthesis.

That all progress is dependent upon and verified through experience is an underlying notion in Royce's treatment of its meaning.[36] But his emphasis on the will is an added element in considering the progress of the human indi-

---

[31] Cf. RAP, 213.

[32] FE, 153.

[33] Dewey seems to see all growth or change as progress, admitting of no teleological principle which might explain the growth as directed towards some good end. E.g., in *Reconstruction in Philosophy* (Boston: Beacon Press, 1957), he remarks: "Growth itself is the only moral end." (177) And again: "Change is associated with progress rather than lapse and fall." (116) To the writer, such optimism appears justifiable only insofar as a teleology is presupposed.

[34] RAP, 29.

[35] RAP, 28.

[36] See Chapter I, section D, and Chapter III, section C *supra*.

vidual. No real progress is possible to man unless that progress is voluntary. Moreover, such voluntary progress is itself individuating: the fact that each one's progress is influenced by his volition tends to distinguish him more and more from other individuals.[37]

Under normal conditions, Royce claims, there are two principal tendencies that appear in all voluntary progress, viz., conservatism and optimism. By conservatism, he means "the tendency to change old conditions to meet new needs, in such a way as shall involve the least possible expenditure of energy."[38] Since Royce regards this tendency as a universal human desire he does not believe that absolute radicals really exist. For so-called radicals are actually trying to conserve the values and forms that they hold dear and essential; their aim is to alter the present situation by whatever means is most efficient to effect that conservation.[39]

The second tendency involved in all voluntary progress is defined by Royce as "the belief that things are in some respect growing better, and that human effort can make them grow better."[40] Our idealist admits that such an outlook is not uninfluenced by disposition. "Confidence in success is to a great extent a matter of temperament and earnestness."[31] Perhaps, he suggests, Americans are more dispositionally inclined to optimism than other peoples, partly because of their revolutionary origins. For "[a]ll upholders of revolution are believers in the success of human effort, are therefore optimists."[42] Less dramatically but nonetheless truly, the same attitude is evidenced in the competitive spirit of sports for any age group. As instance, consider the "Sand Lot." "No modern institution," writes Royce, "is more purely optimistic [than this]."[43] All forms of competition involve some degree of rebellious optimism.

Of the four forms of optimism described by Royce, only the first applies exclusively to the individual.[44] Moreover, as so limited, it is a rather naive or childish kind of optimism, destined to be rudely awakened to the facts of adult experience. The second and third types, patriotic and humanitarian optimism, both sound their note of hope on the basis of a commonness with other men, but these attitudes cannot cope adequately with the social frustrations that are unavoidable in life. The fourth kind is more realistic. It is a

---

[37] Cf. FE, 98.
[38] FE, 99.
[39] Cf. FE, 100.
[40] FE, 104, 5.
[41] FE, 105.
[42] FE, 106.
[43] Ibid.
[44] Cf. FE, 106-9.

modified optimism – so modified, Royce admits, that it is commonly called pessimism. Finding no solid reason for hope in this ordinary world of ordinary men, this type of optimism looks elsewhere (e.g., to the Absolute) to discover a basis for believing that things are really getting better. To Royce, one or other form of optimism must be present in every individual. No one can exist for any appreciable stretch of time as an absolute pessimist, for to live at all requires at least some modicum of hope.[45]

In considering different types of voluntary progress, Royce focuses his attention on individual activities only insofar as these throw light on social or universally orientated activities.[46] Always and everywhere, the meaning, worth and progress of the individual is in terms of the universal, the Absolute. Royce remains respectful of the individuals whose progress constitutes the Universal Will, even while claiming "a concert of individual actions produces a resultant greater than the numerical sum of the individual contributors or else different in kind from this sum."[47] Whether near or far from the Wholeness which is its goal, however, all voluntary progress is attended by the tendencies of conservatism and optimism.

The individual activity which Royce consistently esteems most highly is the activity of thought. In explaining his own understanding of the role of thought in voluntary progress, our idealist sounds much like Peirce and James.[48] "Thought," he claims, "is the process of consciously forming beliefs," and "beliefs are always the satisfaction of individual wants."[49] The empirical aspect of belief refers to the fact that the individual who believes has had, will have or might have a specific experience or experiences which he interprets through his act of believing. On the "subjective side,"[50] beliefs are always uniquely related to the believer himself: the content of belief fills up what is wanting to him as a knower.

But besides the empirical and subjective aspects of the thought process, Royce adds a third requisite for voluntary progress through the activity of thought, viz., "the ability to form an ideal of a perfect system of beliefs in those matters wherewith the thinker is immediately concerned."[51] Obviously, the ideal is a conception of the Absolute through which the believer is

---

[45] Cf. FE, 109.
[46] Cf. FE, 111.
[47] Ibid.
[48] Besides describing the thought process as one of "consciously forming beliefs" (Cf. Peirce), Royce explains the meaning of "true" in a passage that one might well mistake for James: "The adjective 'true' is applied to a belief by the one whose intellectual wants it satisfies, at the time when it satisfies them." (FE, 113)
[49] FE, 112.
[50] Ibid.
[51] FE, 114.

able to anticipate an ultimate synthesis of all beliefs. Having accepted this ideal, along with the empirical grounding for belief in general, and the possibility of its verification through the satisfaction of the subject, then the individual thinker or believer is capable not merely of the process of thought but of progress in thought through volition.

Since thought is a process, the beliefs formed through thought are subject to modification by means of that process. Consequently, Royce maintains that the voluntary thought-process may occur in three different ways: (1) through the modification of old beliefs in order to meet the demands of new experience, (2) through formation of new beliefs for the same reason, and (3) through the expression of new interests occasioned by one's experiences.[52] To Royce, all beliefs not only are, but ought to be flexible in terms of experience, the general criterion of their worth being the extent to which they promote the unity of truth and purpose.

As with individual progress in the activity of thought, so also with voluntary progress in industrial, political, and moral activities.[53] In each of these, Royce sees the presence of conservatism and optimism, and describes their progress as taking place through modifications based on experience. In each of these also the existence of the Absolute is necessary as the only guarantor of individual progress. According to Royce, if the Absolute were utterly separate from the individual as the realists believe, no one could ever make genuine progress.[54] While seeking union with the Absolute through different human activities is not the easiest engagement of our lives, it is nonetheless the most worthwhile one, for insofar as we lose our lives in the Spirit we take them up again renewed and enhanced with the power of Universal Love and Truth and Life.[55] All progress of the individual is procession towards this union.

While this chapter has been devoted primarily to Royce's conception of the individual there have also been many references to his notion of the Absolute and his theory of knowledge. The interrelatedness of the three topics is not only inevitable but necessary for an adequate understanding of any one of them. Moreover, it is only through the kind of overview that the interrelatedness makes possible that we can discern the general pragmatic trend of Royce's thought.

Within the more specific context of his treatment of the individual it does

[52] Cf. FE, 115-22.
[53] Cf. FE 123-28.
[54] Cf. RAP, 371.
[55] Cf. Vol. 55, "Papers written 1877-78," MS of *The Spirit of Modern Philosophy*, 23-4.

seem from the texts considered here and in the two preceding chapters that individuality is not overly esteemed in the thought of the early Royce. Except as an instrument to be employed in the service of the Absolute, the individual has no inherent meaning or worth. Even the voluntariness which our idealist so emphasizes derives its significance only in terms of its adherence to the Universal Will. On the whole, while Royce's brand of "instrumentalism" certainly differs from that of a John Dewey, and while appreciation for the individual as such is clearly not that of a William James – there is a pragmatism involved in the Roycean notion, a pragmatism quite consistent with his idealism, a pragmatism which judges the truth, value and reality of any and every individual according to its practical usefulness. The usefulness derives solely from the totally fulfilled future experience which is the Absolute. Apart from this reference, one certainly much emphasized by Royce, there can be no genuine individuality and no real progress.

PART TWO

THE MIDDLE PERIOD

(c. 1890-1906)

CHAPTER VI

THEORY OF KNOWLEDGE PRAGMATICALLY ALLIED
WITH DOCTRINE OF INTERPRETATION

In an article published in the March, 1904 issue of *The Philosophical Review*, Royce made the claim that all of us are pragmatists, though we might not like to admit it, in that our thinking is empirically rooted and practically directed:

Whatever may be the rationalistic bias or tradition of any of us we are all accustomed to lay stress upon practical considerations as having a fundamental, even if not the most fundamental, importance for philosophy; and so in a general, and, as I admit, in a very large and loose sense of the term, we are all alike more or less pragmatists.[1]

Moreover, while pragmatism, taken in this broad but true sense, is as old as the history of philosophy, there is nonetheless a pragmatism that is new in every age, even as the world it represents is in a certain sense new to each generation. Each moment of the present looks to a new future, i.e., one yet to be experienced. At the point of history in which Royce lived, an appreciation for that newness had been much deepened through the doctrine of evolution, and his pragmatist colleagues had conscientiously noted the effects of the deeper appreciation, insisting that man's process context necessitates his being practically orientated towards the future.[2]

For a time at least Royce himself had seriously struggled "not only to be what is now called a pragmatist, but also to escape falling into the clutches of any Absolute."[3] When he later fell prey to the "bondage of absolutism," he considered himself still to be a genuine pragmatist, though not in the same sense as before.[4] Like the other pragmatists he continued to hold that the object of belief is also the object of one's will to believe, that knowledge is

[1] "The Eternal and the Practical," 113-4. Hereafter we refer to this article as EP.
[2] Cf. EP, 115. Royce here mentions pertinent works of Dewey, James and Schiller.
[3] EP, 117.
[4] EP, 116.

action (though never mere action), and that the world of truth is not a finished world but one which is ever in the making.[5] Unlike the others, however, Royce maintained – no less pragmatically than they claimed otherwise – that one function of truth is to be "actually true."[6] In the course of explaining the pragmatic value of this theory of truth, our idealist first showed the inadequacy and impracticality of other conceptions. In our effort to trace the development of a Roycean pragmatism, we will therefore follow a similar procedure.

A. Other theories of being as interpretations

Since any theory of knowledge or truth is basically determined by one's view of reality or being, Royce examines three historical conceptions through which men have interpreted the being of the world. In the order in which he treats them in the first volume of *The World and the Individual*, the three theories are realism, mysticism, and critical rationalism.

According to the first and best known conception, the real is interpreted as that which is independent of the ideas or experiences that relate or may relate to it.[7] While preserving its external independence, reality is also the absolute determinant of the validity and worth of our ideas. Thus, the ideas depend upon reality, but not conversely. Moreover, as independence of the knower constitutes the very essence of real being, dependence characterizes the unreal. In the estimation of Royce, although the realist tries to distinguish between essence and existence, i.e., between what a thing is and that it is, he can never do more than point to a difference of "thatness" in regard to the real and the unreal. The essence of the unreal *may be* precisely that of the real, but it is impossible to know this, since the real must remain independent of the knowing process.

There have been many varieties of metaphysical realism in the history of philosophy. As examples, Royce cites the Eleatic One, the Platonic ideas, the Aristotelian individuals, the created entities of the scholastics, the divine substance of Spinoza, and Kant's things-in-themselves.[8] In each position in a different way, the real is the source of intelligibility and truth, even as it remains independent of the knower.

To Royce, the trouble with all types of realism is that they contain an inherent contradiction: the total independence of the object is incompatible with genuine knowledge of the object.

---

[5] EP, 117. Note that all of these factors imply an emphasis on future experience.
[6] *Ibid.*
[7] Cf. WI I, 61, 62.
[8] Cf. WI I, 63.

[N]o idea, as we know, can refer to any independent reality, since in order for such reference to be itself real, two irrevocably sundered beings would have to destroy the chasm whose presence is determined by their very essence.[9]

In short, the realm of being for a consistent realist is a realm neither of One nor of Many, but a realm of "absolutely Nothing."[10] Through its own definition of being (i.e., "a total Independence of any idea whose external object any given Being is"[11]) realism annihilates the very being it proposes to interpret. According to Royce, by laying stress upon our disquieting inadequacy to achieve oneness with other beings, realism marks a good beginning for metaphysics, but it can never provide an ultimate and complete metaphysical doctrine.

The second historical conception of being is mysticism. To Royce, the mystics are "the only thorough-going empiricists in the history of philosophy."[12] He calls them so legitimately because their notion of truth and of being is bound up with their concept of immediacy.

[T]hat is real which is absolutely and finally *Immediate*, so that when it is found, *i.e.*, felt, it altogether ends any effort at ideal definition, and in this sense *satisfies* ideas as well as constitutes the fact.[13]

In mysticism, then, real being is interpreted as essentially and wholly within immediate feeling. As independence is to the realist, so immediacy is to the mystic.

Royce admits that the mystical conception of being has been frequently misunderstood in the course of its history. Its critics tend to interpret it as an exaggerated realism which is little more than mere sentimentality.[14] But such criticism misses the main mystical insight, viz., that reality really is given to us through direct experience. Since thinking inevitably gets in the way of an absolute awareness of real being, the philosophical mystic seeks being within the very life of the knowing process. Only by plunging oneself into that life through mystical experience can one truly discern the nature of what is.

Although all mystics reject the contradictoriness inherent in realism they find different ways of explaining the "how" of mystical experience. Types of

---

[9] WI I, 135-6.
[10] WI I, 137. Most realists of course would not go so far as Royce suggests. Independent existence of the object of knowledge would be construed as perfectly consistent with knowledge of the object.
[11] WI I, 86.
[12] WI I, 81.
[13] WI I, 61.
[14] Cf. WI I, 79.

yoga performed by Buddhists in order to achieve their ideal of the Atman, or forms of Christian ascetical practice such as those of a Meister Eckhardt – are equally intended to lead one to an experience of reality that is wholly inaccessible through mere thought. Consequently, all genuine mysticisms dismiss knowledge as incapable of effecting the oneness with the other which is its aim; all of them emphasize experience as the means through which the union with the truth or reality might be achieved.[15]

To Royce, the inadequacy of the mystical interpretation of being lies in its negativeness. Knowledge is so thoroughly rejected that we are left with no positive content at all for our theory of reality. While pure experience *may* be possible, we cannot actually know what such experience entails, still less talk about it with any degree of coherence or clarity. This means that we are incapable of obtaining any real *conception* of being. In claiming immediacy as the only legitimate link with reality, mysticism thus involves us in another contradiction: the transcendence of absolute experience which the mystic proposes is incompatible with the required immediacy. Hence, writes Royce, we must acknowledge the inadequacy of mysticism as a philosophical interpretation of being, and look for another more satisfactory explanation.

The third conception is certainly more satisfactory to our idealist. For this view, the real is whatever is valid or true. Rather pragmatically, he interprets validity and truth as that "which Experience, in verifying our ideas, shows to be valid about these ideas."[16] Actually, Royce regards this position as the outcome of mysticism. For not only is the mystic right in asserting that the real cannot be wholly independent or inaccessible. He is equally correct in affirming the reality of the being that we seek, and in claiming that our consciousness of being depends upon the contrast through which we set all our finite experience over against the being of the other.[17] There is another important point to be made, however, which the mystic fails to consider, viz., that

it is not only the goal, but the whole series of stages on the way to this goal that is the Reality.[18]

According to the critical rationalist, therefore, being must be attributed both to the seeking and to the attainment of the other which is the truth.

---

[15] Note the implied difference between knowledge and contemplation. For the mystic, even the practice of contemplation is a type of *experience* through which one achieves union with the Other. The Other to which Royce here refers is perfectly fulfilled Being or Truth.
[16] WI I, 61. Note that Royce uses the terms "valid" and "true" correlatively: "For the third conception, that is real which is purely and simply Valid or True."
[17] Cf. WI I, 193.
[18] WI I, 193.

In interpreting being as the validity of our ideas, critical rationalism overcomes the contradictoriness of realism and mysticism while retaining the positive content of both positions.[19] The truth of being lies in the relationship between thought and thing, but this relationship is never a perfect adequation. Man knows the truth but does not, because he cannot, encompass it. To the extent that his conception of being is a true one, it is to that precise extent both valid and real.

As with mysticism and realism, Royce sees many different species of critical rationalism, among them such diverse positions as post-Kantian idealism and St. Thomas' explanation of the relation of the Ideas to God.[20] While we do not have space here for a detailed consideration of these, we would mention a factor that Royce regards as uniquely characteristic of their general view, viz., a conscious attempt to define the real as explicitly and only "the Universal."[21] Relative being and truth can only derive their realness from the being of that universal.

From what has already been said of Royce's early philosophy, one would expect that the third conception of being is most suited to his absolute idealism. The expectation would not be disappointed, for Royce accepts the whole of the theory of critical rationalism in regard to being. Nevertheless, he sees the possibility of extending this doctrine beyond its present contentions, thus developing what to Royce is not only a more adequate interpretation of being, but the only adequate one, viz., his own and the synthetic view.

B. *The synthetic view of Royce*

Royce could have presented the metaphysical base for his theory of knowledge without having examined other conceptions of being. That he chose to do otherwise suggests that while pointing out the defects of those theories he wished to preserve their positive elements in support of his own. In calling it "the Synthetic, or the constructively Idealistic conception of what it is to be," he implies that the workability of his interpretation supersedes that of the others.[22] The criterion by which its workability is judged superior is its application to actual and possible experience, and to individual as well as universal existents.

In explicating his own theory of being Royce begins with a discussion of

---

[19] Cf. WI I, 204.
[20] Both positions are developed as applications of critical rationalism in WI I, 228-38.
[21] Cf. WI I, 240.
[22] WI I, 61.

two time-honored concepts of truth. The first, given in terms of external meaning, defines truth as "that about which we judge." The second applies more to the internality of the knowing process as a search for truth, defining truth as "the Correspondence between our Ideas and their Objects."[23] Certainly, Royce concedes, there is an important relationship between the two definitions. For

[t]he ideas, when we judge, are also to possess external meanings. If we try to sunder the external meaning from the internal... we find then that weaving the ideas into new structures is a mere incident of the process whereby we regard them as *standing for the valid Reality*, as characterizing what their object is.[24]

The last two clauses in the above text are indicative of the course that Royce pursues in elaborating his interpretation of truth and being. To claim that "standing for the valid Reality" is the same as "characterizing what their object is" is definitely to adopt the stance of the idealist. In adopting it Royce regards the second notion of truth (correspondence) as presupposed by the first (objective reality) notion. The first is ultimately reducible to the second and expressible in terms of it. Or, to put the matter in another way, truth is finally a question of internal, not external meaning. The reduction is effected and Royce's theory explained by considering the role of purpose or intention in the thought process.

During all three periods of his philosophizing, Royce defines ideas in terms of purpose. General ideas, like beliefs, are habits of action formed from more specific ideas.[25] The latter are defined as particular plans of action which we arrive at through our acting in experience.[26] Any idea, whether general or specific, is a

state of mind, or complex of states, that, when present, is consciously viewed as the relatively completed embodiment and therefore already as the partial fulfilment of a purpose.[27]

The purpose embodied in the idea is what constitutes its "internal meaning." Royce asserts that the notion of external meaning in regard to our ideas arises through our awareness of a discrepancy existing between the internal meaning, as partial embodiment of purpose, and the totally fulfilled purpose or meaning. The latter is what constitutes "external meaning." In other words, the external meaning is the whole of the reality which is intended

[23] WI I, 270. (The italics in text were omitted.)
[24] WI I, 271.
[25] Cf. Vol. 75, "Andover Lectures," 54, and Vol. 63, Lecture III, 20.
[26] Cf. Vol. 74, "Columbia Lectures," 8, and Vol. 70, Lecture III, 14.
[27] WI I, 24-5.

through the internal meaning of ideas. This is why the problem of knowledge is inseparable from metaphysics. Whoever wishes to investigate the nature of being is necessarily concerned with the apparently external meaning of ideas.[28] Ultimately, our metaphysical question thus reduces to an epistemological one, viz.,

> How is it possible that an idea which is an idea essentially and primarily because of the inner purpose that it consciously fulfils by its presence, also possesses a meaning that in any sense appears to go beyond this internal purpose?[29]

Or, more succinctly, what is the relationship between the internal and external meaning of ideas?

In answering the question Royce shows that it is not mere agreement, but intended agreement that constitutes truth.[30] Since our notion of external purpose is founded upon an appeal to the truth, and since truth is the completed expression of the internal meaning or purpose of the idea, then one is related to the other (external to internal) as whole to part, each possessing the same being or reality. As actualized and fulfilled purpose, external meaning is only apparently external, for when it is truly comprehended it is not more and no less than the perfect embodiment of purpose. Hence, purpose is the only adequate criterion in regard to truth and being.

Through his doctrine of purpose Royce fills up what is wanting in the third conception of being. For what that theory fails to explain is the type of being represented through possible experiences. If truth is defined as validity, then when there is no way of validating or verifying through experience as in the instance of the possibles, the truth of their being is either indefinable or inaccessible. In either case, the definition is inadequate. Another kind of being which the critical rationalist fails to explain is that of the individual. "Validity," Royce claims, is a universal notion which as such cannot account for the truth of being in individuals as individual. In the absolute voluntarism of his synthetic view of being Royce finds a means of supplementing the inadequacies of the third conception. For the validating or truth- ascertaining process suggested by the critical rationalists can only be extended to "possibles" and to individual entities by positing some voluntary agent or absolute will as the ultimate source of purpose for everything that is: actual and possible, individual and universal. Other theories (including realism and mysticism), Royce maintains, are useful in explaining some types of being,

---

[28] Cf. WI I, 27.
[29] WI I, 32-3.
[30] Cf. WI I, 307.

but only his voluntaristic idealism is adequate to all types. As such it is justly judged more useful than the others.

Actually, the synthesis announced by Royce as the fourth conception of being is a rather eclectic interpretation of the other three views:

> What is, is authoritative over against finite ideas, as Realism asserted, is one with the true meaning of the idea, as Mysticism insisted, and is valid as Critical Rationalism demanded.[31]

In short, what is is the fulfilment of any and every purpose that ideas involve. Each individual, universal, possible, and actual entity derives its reality, i.e., its individuality, universality, possibility, and actuality from the perfectly fulfilled and fulfilling purpose of the Absolute.

Insofar as purpose is construed as practical orientation of consciousness, we find that purposefulness is not only the key to Royce's conceptions of being and theory of knowledge; it is also a key to our appreciation of a developing pragmatism in his thought. In elaborating upon the latter notion, however, we ought next to consider a factor which goes unmentioned in the writings of the early Royce, viz., the social character of the knowing process.

C. *The essentially social character of the knowing process*

In several important unpublished manuscripts preserved at the Harvard University archives, Royce discusses the essentially social character of the human knowing process.[32] An understanding of this dimension in the middle period of his philosophizing is central to an appreciation of the relationship between Royce's theory of knowledge at this time, and his mature doctrine of interpretation. That this development is pragmatic in its grounding and in its aim will be evident through a consideration of the social origin of our fundamental ideas, the social basis of reasoning, and the social criterion by which we judge the relative truth of our ideas.

1. *The social origin of our ideas*

As indicated earlier in Royce's works and earlier in this study, the term "belief" is used to designate the end of the knowing process.[33] To show the

---

[31] WI I, 358.

[32] E.g., there are three volumes in particular (68, 69, 70), in which the main theme is the relationship between social factors and the knowing process. The fact that this theme is scarcely present in the early writings makes it especially pertinent in tracing the development of Royce's thought.

[33] See Chapters III and IV, *supra*.

social origin of our ideas, Royce classifies the whole great field of human beliefs into two groups. In one group are our more or less probable opinions about facts. The data of history, our knowledge of the world, even our awareness of an individual calling or vocation – these are included in the first group of beliefs. All are assents to matters of fact or (in the case of mathematical facts) to what is implied in our own meanings. None are necessarily true; they might have been otherwise than we find them to be.

But there are a great many propositions, Royce maintains, which do not fit into this category. One example he notes is: "Whatever happens must have a cause." Another is: "Two straight lines cannot enclose a space."[34] Propositions such as these constitute the second great field of human beliefs, the field of our fundamental ideas. So starkly fundamental are they that men ordinarily do not question them at all. Only occasionally are people provoked to inquire about the nature of what is beyond observable facts. Nonetheless, in every age there is a peculiarity in human nature which is particularly sensitive to that philosophical provocation. Men have always looked for answers to fundamental questions and they always will, even though this will not generally be the preoccupation of their day to day living.

According to Royce the fundamental truths which form the second category of beliefs contrast with the first type in that they are necessarily true, and their meaning stretches beyond mere reports of facts or implications of ideas. The human mind arrives at its knowledge of them "not by mere analysis of what our ideas mean, but by an assurance that enables us in advance to predict the yet unseen truth."[35] That assurance is so great as to account for the necessity of truth "in advance of any experience and apart from any verification or report of particular facts."[36]

Frequently, such fundamental truths are the presuppositions for all our other ideas and beliefs. Take, for example, the different accounts of creation. Royce maintains that at least three ideas, all of them fundamental, are involved in all the accounts.

The first is, *That the world must have had an origin*, which antedates the coming of man. The second is, *That this origin must have depended upon some preëxistent real being*, to be called water or night, or chaos, or in the Christian view, God himself, who made the world out of nothing. The third is, *That the process of creation, must have involved the working of causes*, whose powers can be defined in more or less necessary terms, so that, when they work, the world and the living creatures must necessarily be produced.[37]

[34] Vol. 68, Lecture IV, "The Social Origin of Our Fundamental Ideas," 4.
[35] *Ibid.*
[36] *Ibid.*, 5.
[37] *Ibid.*, 7.

No matter who tells the creation story (e.g., North American Indians, Polynesians, African Negroes, Hindus or Hebrews[38]), all of the above ideas are presupposed. As presupposed so universally they cannot be construed as mere comments upon the meanings of a man's private ideas. Thus they can only be properly interpreted as necessary beliefs based on content that transcends individual human experience.

But what is the content from which our fundamental ideas are drawn? Or how, asks our idealist, do men acquire these truths? Since they are not drawn from individual experience, and since they are not the product of our own ideas (whether innate or acquired), Royce looks to the context in which man becomes aware of the fundamental ideas. That context he sees as an essentially social one. After an initial awakening to the world in general as an object of knowledge, man becomes conscious of the society in which he lives, the people in the midst of whom he thinks and acts. The society in turn elicits from man an awareness of his own social consciousness, and included in that consciousness are the fundamental ideas. Hence, "it is a fact that man first hears them [the fundamental ideas] from his fellows. . . .. It is a fact that man becomes rational in social surroundings, and in those alone."[39] Moreover, it is a fact that every man believes these truths, in one way or another, whether he adverts to them or not, for they are the starting point for all mental activity. According to Royce, therefore, it is always through interaction with his social environment that man comes to know the most basic truths of life and living, those principles which all his other knowledge presupposes. Man's intellect is "thus socially determined, not only in its spirit, but in its deepest assurances."[40]

2. *The social basis of reasoning*

Not only is society the starting point for our fundamental ideas; it is equally essential to the continuation of the knowing process through reasoning. Thinking, as a conscious social process, is a first step towards the type of communication which is demanded for the growth of our ideas. Our knowledge develops by sharing ideas with other people. As a matter of fact, Royce remarks, social communication can only take place on an idea or ideal level.

Not our experiences therefore, but the relations between our experiences are the common matters of social communication. But when we are aware of the relations

---

[38] *Ibid.*
[39] *Ibid.*, 12, 13.
[40] *Ibid.*, 12. Cf. Dewey's emphasis on social interaction in *Reconstruction in Philosophy*, especially Ch. IV and VIII.

between our experiences, we have what are called ideas.... It follows that if the relationships of our various experiences are the socially communicable side of our inner life, and if to be aware of these relationships is to have ideas, then the part of our inner life which, from a common sense point of view we do most directly communicate, is precisely the ideal side of this mental life.[41]

Admittedly, even the ideas are inadequate tools because total communication is impossible between separate individuals or groups. While some form of language is obviously necessary, ideas are yet more fundamental, for there can be no language without ideas. Consequently, in any effort to communicate, ideas are our most essential and useful tools.

Perhaps the best way to illustrate the social character of the reasoning process is through Royce's notion of the social contrast effect.[42] Our ideas of ourselves (the Ego) and of others (the Alter) are expanded and clarified by means of this contrast. The more we know about ourselves the more we know about others, the more we know about others the more we know about ourselves, in both cases through our increased awareness of differences between Ego and Alter. Neither idea is possible outside of a social context.

In explaining the role of social contrast in the human reasoning process Royce distinguishes between the form and content of consciousness. The *contents* consist of masses of sensations and feelings; they are never a sufficient source for definite knowledge. All the meanings which our consciousness comes to acquire are dependent upon the *form* which consciousness assumes in relation to the contents.[43] Thus meanings *quâ* meanings can never be reduced to mere contents of consciousness.

The form of consciousness depends in part on our social experience, or more specifically upon the contrasts or differences presented to us through our social situation. More specifically still, Royce notes that "the Form of our consciousness grows more definite in proportion to the definiteness of the *habits of action* which at any time we have acquired through former acts."[44] Accordingly, as the form becomes more definite, i.e., as the contrast between Ego and Alter becomes more evident, another contrast manifests itself, viz., that between the ideas and the presented facts of consciousness. this contrast grows as our habits grow: ideas as mental states directed beyond the presently presented facts. According to Royce, then, there are two instances of contrast involved in our reasoning process: one between form and content, another between ideas and presented facts.

---

[41] Vol. 68, Lecture II, "The Social Basis of the Intellectual Life," 14.
[42] Cf. Vol. 70, Lecture V, "Theory of the Origin of the Ideas of Ego and Alter," 1.
[43] Cf. *Ibid.*
[44] Vol. 70, Lecture V, 2. (Italics in text.)

In the specific case of Ego and Alter, these "come to our consciousness mainly as Ideas, whose relation to one another and to presented facts has a certain form."[45] At the outset the form is one common to all social situations as the contrast between alter-contents and ego-contents. The former, Royce claims, are states of mind due to other people's presence and deeds, while the latter are due to one's own deeds. The alter-contents are relatively "cold"; the ego-contents are "warm" because they involve both bodily acts and states of feeling.[46]

As man's social consciousness develops, the contrast between ideas and facts acquires greater significance. Since the ego contents are modified through one's conscious choices, "the ideas of which the alter is the source get more and more contrasted, as time goes on, with the ideas that the ego chooses, and proposes."[47] By deliberate decisions the field of ideas is enlarged, while factual content is left untouched. Thus the contrast between ideas and presented facts is extended in regard to both the Alter and the Ego as ideas of the same consciousness. "In consequence," writes Royce,

both the ego and the alter contents, always seen in the form of the social contrasts, and more and more interpreted in terms of ideas, rather than of presented facts, gradually get more and more sundered from and contrasted with one another, and with the presented facts of consciousness, until each set is viewed as a set of contents merely hinting of the existence of two sorts of Beings, the ideal Ego and the ideal Alter, neither ever a wholly present fact, and each in its way a mystery to the other.[48]

Eventually, our interpretation of these ideas gives rise to our interpreting the being of an absolute ideal, where the Ego and the Alter answer to the mystery of each other.

3. *The social criterion for truth*

Having come to an awareness of the Absolute through a social context, we might use the same social context as a means to guide our progress in the acquisition of knowledge. Gradually, our ideas are refined

by the process of mutual social criticism, until the lesson has been learned of the way in which one may contrast idea with idea, plan with plan, self with self, idea with visible truth, and all with the ideal that the self has formed of the universal Reason.[49]

---

[45] Vol. 70, "An advance resumé of Lecture V," 3.
[46] Cf. *Ibid.*
[47] *Ibid.*
[48] *Ibid.*
[49] Vol. 70, Lecture VII, "The Social Basis of Reasoning," 25.

Here again, we see the usefulness of social contrast, in facilitating constructive criticism of our ideas of others and of ourselves. All common knowledge, Royce claims, is subject to social verification in future experience. Our ideas of other persons and things pass their truth test only when we judge their content acceptable to all men, not merely to ourselves, and for all times, not merely for now. In regard to physical reality, for example,

> while for you personally, physical nature is always represented by what you regard as experiences that are permanently possible for you, you do still apply another criterion before you regard your experiences as standing for outer nature. This criterion is what I may call the social criterion.[50]

According to this criterion,

> [p]hysical reality is a permanent possibility of experience not for myself only, but for other men as well... and when we can repeatedly verify this fact by all sorts of social communications... then we draw the conclusion that beyond us all there must be some common possibilities of experience, and these we are accustomed to call the real nature of things.[51]

Thus "social communications" perform a necessary function in regard to the verification of our ideas.

To Royce, the Ego is also subject to the social criterion. Our self-consciousness is refined through the self-criticism which the social situation makes possible. Besides being an exercise of man's highest reflective powers, such self-criticism is also an extremely useful socially acquired art, one which sharpens the effectiveness of the Ego's judgments.[52]

The pragmatic value of the social criterion seems rather clear. Finding fault with the claim of (other) pragmatists that the truth of our judgments lies in their usefulness in answering individual needs, Royce offers a more workable criterion. What we really need, he says, is "that our judgment should be not only ours but true." Hence, our

> need for truth is the need that there should be other points of view, other actual judgments, responsive to the same situation, in other words, to the same object.... We conceive that all these judgments ought, despite their diversity of points of view, so to agree as to confirm one another, and so to unite in one system of truth as to characterize harmoniously the same object.[53]

The only way of course to guarantee the truths we need so much in each of our relative circumstances is through the notion of an eternal invariant

---

[50] Vol. 68, Lecture IV, "The Social Origin of Our Fundamental Ideas," 34-5.
[51] Ibid., 35, 36-8.
[52] Cf. Vol. 70, Lecture VII, 26.
[53] EP, 141.

Truth, a totally fulfilled future Experience, who is both source and judge of all our truths, an Absolute whose all-inclusiveness accomplishes the harmony we seek, while respecting our diversity and even our apparent contradictions. Supposedly "pure" pragmatism does not offer so practical a solution for this basic human need. The social situation certainly performs a pragmatic function in fulfilling individual and collective needs in regard to truth. But even this is not enough, for society itself needs a yet more fundamental and pragmatic grounding:

The need for the Eternal is consequently one of the deepest of all our practical needs. Herein lies at once the justification of pragmatism, and the logical impossibility of pure pragmatism... All that is practical borrows its truth from the Eternal.[54]

All that is practical regarding the social dimension in Royce's thought derives its practicality from the Absolute, the grounds for ultimate empirical verification.

In the first part of this chapter it was suggested that pragmatism, taken broadly as a philosophy which stresses practical considerations as fundamental, is open to whatever philosophical view is most practical in a given age. From the perspective of the pragmatist who lives in a process context, the future to which he addresses himself necessarily changes with the passage of time. His philosophizing is constantly being "renewed" through an effort to relate his thinking to that changing future.

Certainly, the theory of knowledge of Josiah Royce instances a new type of pragmatism – in that it involves an emphasis on absolute as well as temporal future experience. But Royce's divergencies from the positions of those philosophers whom we generally label "pragmatists" are actually based on what to him is a yet more practical interpretation of reality. Other theories, he maintains, do not work as well; other conceptions of truth and being do not, because they cannot, apply in all practical cases. His synthetic view can be properly described as a pragmatic interpretation, precisely because of its orientation towards future experience.

Probably the two aspects in Royce's theory of knowledge which best indicate a development towards his later (more pragmatic doctrine of interpretation are his emphasis on purpose and on the social character of human knowing. For the reality of "interpretation," as we shall subsequently see,[55] is wholly dependent upon our conscious practical purposes, and the community through which we know (by interpretation) derives its being and its

[54] EP, 142.
[55] See Chapter IX.

justification from the essentially social dimension and direction of all knowing. Together, these two concepts, which we found so predominant in the writings of the middle period, are our key to appreciating an increasingly pragmatic element in the thought of Royce.

CHAPTER VII

NOTION OF THE ABSOLUTE MORE PRAGMATICALLY ORIENTATED

Rather reluctantly, Royce concluded a philosophical conference given in 1903 with the admission that his own view of religion and of the Absolute had developed more pragmatically than he had intended.

In other words, I do not wish to take a pragmatic view of my own religious object; but my fate seems to be that I tend to do so. The religious object is to be exalted above my level, but on the other hand, it tends, as I discover, to be made in my image. Or again, God, instead of being absolute, becomes one of the people in the world, a being whom you propitiate, in so far as you have any definite relation to him at all; but in so far tends to cease to be divine. In brief *your religion becomes practical or not*.[1]

That Royce was correct in the general self-estimation that his thought tended in a pragmatic direction is the central thesis of this study. In applying this judgment to the religious object, our idealist hits the key point of his system, since that system (as he himself maintains) is essentially a philosophy of religion.

Obviously, however, Royce has a problem here: he does not wish to forfeit God's absoluteness even while he wants God to make a difference in the world. Insofar as he manages to retain both factors in his general conception of being, Royce is in a sense more pragmatic than those who would deny God's absoluteness. For the absoluteness of the Absolute is itself a useful and workable conception in that it grounds a present emphasis on future experience.

In examining the works of Royce in the middle period of his writing, three points stand out as indicating a more pragmatic orientation in his notion of the Absolute, viz.,

1) his explanation and definition of God in terms of Experience,

[1] Vol. 73, "Concluding Summary of the Philosophical Conference," (1903) 9. (My italics.)

2) his increased emphasis on the will in its relation to the Absolute, and
3) his description of the union between God and man.

Although all three points are hinted at in the earlier works, none of them receives as extensive consideration as in the middle writings, particularly in the two main works of the period, *The World and the Individual* and *The Conception of God*. In the early period, Royce seems more concerned to define and describe the Absolute in terms of Thought, and to retain the transcendent character of his Absolute. Here he proceeds from the notion of Absolute Thought to show the relatedness of that Thought to the life of man.[2]

A. An explanation and definition of God in terms of Experience

At the outset in his Conception of God address Royce defined the term being discussed.

> By the word "God" I shall mean, then, in advance of any proof of God's existence, a being who is conceived as possessing to the full all logically possible knowledge, insight, wisdom.[3]

"Omniscience" was undoubtedly the most appropriate attribute through which to define the Absolute and thus initiate his considerations on the conception of God. Besides the fact that this take-off point would lead most efficiently to the ideas he wanted to propound,[4] the audience to whom Royce was speaking had already spent time studying his *The Religious Aspect of Philosophy*, in which his notion of the Absolute centered more upon knowing than upon other divine attributes. Royce had no intention of merely repeating or defending the argument of that work.[5] Admitting that he had not reread it since correcting the galleys, he sought instead to indicate his present conception of God, a position not inconsistent with, but hopefully more developed than, that of his earlier work.

---

[2] Use of the sources and ordering of the three points treated in this chapter respects the sequence employed by Royce in developing his ideas in reference to the Absolute. The first section is based mainly on the famous *Conception of God* address given by Royce at the University of California in 1895; the second section, on Royce's *Supplementary Essay*, written after the critics' reactions to the address; the third, on the concluding chapter of the second volume of WI (1901), "The Union of God and Man."

[3] Josiah Royce et al., *The Conception of God* (New York: The Macmillan Company, 1909), 7. Hereafter this work is referred to as CG.

[4] An Omniscient Being who really exists necessarily possesses all the other divine attributes. Consequently, we might properly call this Being Omnipotence, Goodness, Perfection or Peace. But these other attributes do not serve Royce's purpose as well as Omniscience. Cf. CG, 8.

[5] His own comment on RAP is pertinent here: "I am not unwilling to confess that if I had to-night to pass an examination upon the text of my book, I might very possibly get an extremely poor mark." (CG, 6)

To Royce, any "really fruitful philosophical study of the conception of God is inseparable from an attempt to estimate what evidence there is for the existence of God."⁶ It is useless, he maintains, to define the term "God" unless one wishes to show that there is a reality corresponding to the definition. On the other hand, any proof that one can offer for the actual existence of God constitutes also the best exposition of what one means by the conception of God. The clarity and certainty of our concept of God's existence is in direct proportion to the clarity and certainty of our concept of his essence, and vice versa. Accordingly, the problem under consideration can be stated thus:

Does there demonstrably exist an Omniscient Being? or is the conception of an Omniscient Being, for all that we can say, a base ideal of the human mind?⁷

As Royce sees it, if we can demonstrate the existence of an Omniscient Being, we will have thereby communicated our conception of God.

Before attempting such a proof, however, Royce describes more specifically what he means by "Omniscient Being."

An Omniscient Being would be one who simply found presented to him, not by virtue of fragmentary and gradually completed processes of inquiry, but by virtue of an all-embracing, direct, and transparent insight into his own truth, – who found thus presented to him, I say, the complete, the fulfilled answer to every genuinely rational question.⁸

In other words, an Omniscient Being is one who has all the actual answers to all possible questions. To understand what this means, Royce suggests that we reflect on our human situation. We mortals question, he says, and our questioning always arises from our thinking of possible facts and experiences not now present to us. The thinking is itself a proof that there is a knowing involved in the very activity of questioning. For no one can question that of which he is absolutely ignorant. If one were to have no questions at all, he would be either a non-knower or an all-knower. As non-knower, he would have no answers; as omniscient he would have them all.

To be human is to live with a mixture of answers and questions, the former expressing what is actual, the latter suggesting what is possible. When ideas are verified through experience, the answers actualize the possibilities implied by questions. In other words, in the human knowing process, facts check theory; genuine knowledge can only occur when experience supports

⁶ CG, 6.
⁷ CG, 7.
⁸ CG, 8.

our ideas. Since the two factors never perfectly coincide in life, we continue to question. But in the omniscient Being, experience is perfectly fulfilled: all possible questions are answered. Not that the two elements (ideas and experienced facts) are indistinguishable. The Omniscient Being both knows and experiences, but these are not identical activities. His thought and his feeling are both perfectly fulfilled. Herein, then,

> lies the essence of his conceived Omniscience, – in him and for him these facts would not be, as they often are in us, merely felt, but they would be seen as fulfilling his ideas; as answering what, were he not omniscient, would be his mere questions.[9]

So much for Royce's starting point. In defining God in terms of Omniscience, he shows the necessary connection between the Absolute Thought and Absolute Experience. It is through the union of the two that "our Omniscient Being is technically to be named simply the Absolute; that is, the being sufficient unto himself."[10] The Self-sufficiency of the Absolute suggests one more point that Royce makes before endeavoring to promote the Absolute from hypothetical to existential status, viz., that because of the wholeness of thought and experience in the Absolute, both must be considered fully *organized*. The existence of the Absolute can only be established on the basis of his uniting a perfectly organized Experience with perfectly organized Thought.

In contrast with the procedure he had earlier employed, Royce here pursues his intent of proving the existence of the Absolute by concentrating his attention on the realm of experience. While admitting that experience is always necessary for human knowledge,[11] he nonetheless maintains that the verification process through which we arrive at truths is never accomplished apart from a contrast between two types of experience, actual and possible. The actual experience of man is inevitably lacking in organization, while possible experience is not. Thus the scientist hypothesizes concerning the organization of possible experience, and applies this theory to unorganized actual experience. Scientific verification occurs by contrasting the ideal with the real, indirect with direct experience. The work of science continues precisely because it never succeeds in putting perfect order into experience. Nor can it. As long as men remain human they will suffer a disparity between the ideal and the real, between actual and possible, between ideas and facts.

[9] CG, 11. Note the use of the hypothetical *would*.
[10] CG, 14.
[11] Cf. CG, 16.

Certainly the experience of life provides a sufficient number of instances to convince us that the disparity itself is undeniable.

Royce next addresses himself to the notion of "organized experience." Such a notion, he maintains, is necessarily associated with the meaning of "reality."

The terms "reality" and "organized experience" are correlative terms. The one can only be defined as the object, the content, of the other.[12]

Not that the two terms are identical. But if there is any reality at all it is experience-able, and what is experience-able is real. Moreover, by experiencing the real world man knows it through its organization, though fragmentarily. Thus, the fact of *organized* experience is essential to actual knowing. Without such experience there is no knowledge, and without knowledge there is no truth, "for truth *is*, so far as it is *known*."[13] Hence, if reality itself is not illusory, knowledge, truth and organized experience are not only possibilities but actualities.

Another factor about human experience which Royce regards as important in his effort to arrive at a proof of the existence of Absolute Experience is its social aspect. In the course of experience,

[e]very man verifies for himself. But what he verifies, – the truth that he believes himself to be making out when he verifies, – this he conceives as a truth either actually or possibly verifiable by his fellow or by some still more organized sort of experience.[14]

Other people's experience supplements our own, Royce claims, in two ways: first, in taking the experiences of others to be as live and real as ours, and secondly by suggesting that there may be a total experience which would unite the experiences of all mankind.[15]

Thus we are brought to the main consideration of Royce's address to the Philosophical Convention, viz., his demonstration of the actual existence of Absolute Experience, i.e., God. So far, according to Royce, we have seen that organized experience exists, and that the idea of Absolute Experience exists. The question which remains is: Is there any absolutely organized experience?

---

[12] CG, 36.
[13] CG, 41.
[14] CG, 33-4.
[15] Royce claims that such an idea could be provoked, for example, through a realization that the judgment of a consensus results in a more complete organization of our own fragmented experience. Cf. CG, 34.

Royce's answer involves a dialectic. First of all, we must acknowledge that men generally regard experience as suggesting truth.

Now, to regard our experience as suggesting truth is, as we have seen, to mean that our experience indicates what a higher or inclusive, *i.e.* a more organized, experience would find presented thus or thus to itself.[16]

Admittedly, suggestion alone is not sufficient grounds for claiming anything more than the will or aim or intent towards a fulness or unity of experience. "Perhaps," one might justifiably assert, "there is no absolute truth, no ideally united and unfragmented experience." Certainly, mere intention that there be an Absolute Experience does not make the Experience to exist.[17]

In response to such legitimate criticism, our idealist dialectician offers a counter-suggestion. Grant then, he proposes,

that there is no universal experience as a concrete fact, but only the hope of it, the definition of it, the will to win it, the groaning and travail of the whole of finite experience in the search for it, in the error of believing that it is.[18]

What such a proposal would have to entail, Royce maintains, is that its own assertion be absolutely true. Like it or not, we can only avoid total scepticism through the supposedly absolute truth of the unalterable finitude of experience. But by what authority, Royce asks, do we claim this ultimate truth? If we concede the finitude of experience we thereby render ourselves powerless to make any valid assertion in regard to what is beyond experience. Thus we can no more legitimately deny a unity beyond the fragmentariness than we might legitimately claim otherwise. We thus contradict our own position in the very act of asserting it.

Hence, – and here indeed, is the conclusion of the whole matter, – the very effort hypothetically to assert that the whole world of experience is a world of fragmentary and finite experience is an effort involving a contradiction.[19]

By contradicting the counter proposal we prove the truth of the original suggestion of experience, viz., that there is a unity of organized experience that ultimately answers all our questions. As a matter of fact, then, "[e]xperience must constitute, in its entirety, one self-determined and consequently absolute and organized whole."[20] Every intelligent interpretation of pre-

---

[16] CG, 39.
[17] Cf. CG, 38.
[18] CG, 39.
[19] CG, 41.
[20] Ibid.

sent human experience necessarily involves the assertion of the existence of an absolute future Experience as the only adequate explanation and completion of its meaning and reality.

B. *The relation of will to the Absolute*

Following upon Royce's Conception of God address at the University of California, three of his colleagues contributed their criticisms and comments to the discussion. While all four philosophers (besides Royce there were Prof. Joseph LeConte, Prof. George Howison and Prof. Sidney Mezes) projected an idealistic conception of a personal God, each had his own way of doing so. Among their diverse reactions, Prof. Howison's pluralistic view showed the sharpest contrast with Royce's monistic doctrine, while Prof. Mezes' remarks most nearly accorded with the Roycean position.[21] As a fruitful upshot of the critical exchange, Royce was provoked to write a Supplementary Essay, in which he elaborated upon the original argument, clarified some of its points, and replied to its criticisms. One important notion treated in this Essay is the relation of will to the Absolute, a topic which Royce had only rather sketchily considered in his earlier philosophizing.[22]

In the preceding section we saw that Royce's argument for God's existence in the Conception of God address not only begins with the notion of experience, but ends there too. By defining God as Absolute Experience he presents a nuance in comparison with his previous position, a nuance which is indicative of a more pragmatic orientation. In the Essay, Royce draws upon the implications of this definition in order to show that the Absolute is Will as well as Thought.

First, however, he examines the general conception of will, trying to distinguish its most essential features. Three are rather readily uncovered, viz., desire, choice and efficacious effort. Desire, writes Royce, is "a name for feelings that can arise in our minds with various degrees of vigour and clearness."[23] At times our desires can be unreasonable, capricious, and even contradictory, but this is not the case with choice. According to our idealist,

[c]hoice is a mental process that involves the presence of plans for the satisfaction of desires, a foreknowledge of relatively objective ends that constitute the conscious aims of these desires, a more or less reasonable estimate of the value of these

---

[21] An interesting and possibly relevant factor here is the relationship that two of the reactants had to Royce. Prof. Joseph LeConte had been Royce's teacher at Berkeley, while Prof. Sidney Mezes had been his pupil.
[22] Cf. Chapter IV, section C, *supra*.
[23] CG, 187.

aims, and then some process which involves the survival of some, the subordination, or perhaps the suppression, of other desires.[24]

So, desires precede choice as irrational feelings which motivate our conscious preferences.

The third feature of will is one not so commonly recognized as essential, since effectiveness is a factor relatively external to the will. Kant's "man of good will," for example, would remain such, even if his good intentions were forever thwarted. To Royce, however, some element of effectiveness must be present in every genuine will act, regardless of external circumstances. This is the "efficacious effort" that involves a kind of active readiness to utilize whatever means are available for actualizing a chosen possibility.[25]

All three aspects of the will are primarily manifest as facts of our own experience, and secondarily attributed to the experience of other persons. Nonetheless, asks Royce, does the mere fact that we find these three factors generally present in human willing provide sufficient grounds for predicating them of the Absolute? So far, we have shown only that an Absolute exists as the fulfilling unity of Thought and Experience. Now what, if anything, justifies our ascribing to God the activity of Will?

In reply Royce points to a characteristic of willing that has (in his estimation) been frequently overlooked, viz., *attention*. All our voluntary processes, he observes, involve this element. Even those will acts which are generally construed as "creative" are actually more attentive than inventive.

You can will nothing original, – no novel act, – nothing except what you have already and involuntarily learned to do.... In these cases, it is the situation that is novel, not the act really willed.... The essence of the will here is not inventiveness but attention.[26]

It is by attention, then, that we turn possibility into actuality through our will acts. Moreover, included in the notion of attention are the three elements already mentioned: desire, choice and efficacious effort. For choice is explicitly an attentive selection of one possibility over others; desire entails an attentive favoring of one type of conscious content over other, and in regard to efficacious effort – one always attends most closely to the deed he attempts to perform. Royce therefore concludes that the term *will* is best defined as "a process involving attention to one conscious content rather than to another."[27] From this consideration of the nature of will we might more

[24] CG, 188.
[25] Cf. *Ibid.*
[26] CG, 191-2.
[27] CG, 192. (Italics omitted.) Cf. James's chapter on "Attention" in his *Principles of Psychology*, Vol. I (New York: Henry Holt and Company, 1927; originally published in 1890), Ch. XIII.

94   THE MIDDLE PERIOD

efficiently examine whether the Absolute is also Will. If we find that Absolute Experience involves such a process as here described then we will know that a divine Will is being exercised.

In his original address, Royce had indicated that the Absolute is a unity of Thought and Experience. Upon closer scrutiny, however, he admits that it is not at all clear how the relation between the two can be a unity. On the one hand, if Thought defines the contents of an infinite series of possible experiences then that Thought must transcend Absolute Experience as an actual Being. On the other hand, one could validly argue

that a true thought, even about a bare possibility, is simply an expression, in thought's terms, of something which, just so far as it is true, must be somewhere presented to a concrete experience.[28]

There are thus two conflicting but supportable views as to the relation of idea and content in Absolute Experience. How, asks Royce, can one reconcile the two positions without losing the fundamental truth that each of them asserts?

In attempting the reconciliation, Royce reminds us of an experience that exemplifies a solution. It is our experience of the truth of hypothetical propositions. The truth of such judgments, he claims, is expressed by means of contrast. Consider, for example, the following statement: If you ask me no questions, I will tell you no lies.[29] Here the actual truth disclosed is that the person is more concerned to be discreet than to be truthful. Whether the possibility is realized or not, the proposition expresses the essence of the person's intent. Now consider a hypothetical contrary to fact judgment such as: If the Persians had won at Marathon, the face of Europe would be different today. The Persian victory to which the first part of the proposition refers is of course an abstract, unreal idea. But the concrete truth that the entire proposition indicates is that the Persian loss has really affected modern Europe.[30]

From an examination of the above and other propositions, Royce draws the following conclusion:

If, then, hypotheses contrary to fact can be present as expressions of concrete truth to an experience that faces truth, the presence of such hypotheses contrary to fact is not excluded from an Absolute Experience, even in so far as it is absolute.[31]

Furthermore, the presence of such hypotheses as elements of an Absolute

[28] CG, 195.
[29] CG, 197.
[30] Cf. CG, 197, 198.
[31] CG, 198.

Experience reconciles the two conflicting views of the relation of idea and experience in the Absolute. Thought must always transcend experience – even in Absolute Experience – in the sense that our ideas as such may extend to possible as well as actual beings, thus anticipating future experience. As hypotheses contrary to fact, our ideas can do this without being expressions of genuine and unfulfilled truth. In other words, the truth even of the "possibles" is connected with facts of experience by means of contrast. The real meaning of possibility is necessarily linked with the real meaning of what is actual, and through that linking the ultimate unity of Thought and Experience is maintained. "So, then," writes Royce,

an Absolute Experience could and would at once find its ideas adequately fulfilled in concrete fact, and also find this fulfilment as an individual collection of individuals exemplifying these ideas, while, as to other abstractly possible fulfilments of the same ideas, the Absolute Experience would find them as hypothetical or ideal entities, contrary to fact.[32]

Here, then, the antinomy is resolved: Thought and Experience are a unity in God. All our present thoughts and experiences are orientated towards their final future fulfilment in him.

Royce next focuses on what this unity means in terms of specific relationship between facts as individuals, and their corresponding ideas, which are universal types. In the course of explaining how the Absolute is both Thought and Experience we have inadvertently but necessarily hit upon a key point, viz., that of attention. While not using that precise word we have described its essential nature in terms of the contrast between possibility and actuality. For what is attention but

an ignoring of possible experiences for the sake of fulfilling, in sharply differentiated individual experiences, ideas that could not be fulfilled except through the ignoring of such possibilities.[33]

Attention is thus a sacrifice of ideal possibilities in order to realize ideas. "It is losing to win," or "losing bare abstractions to find life full of contrasting individuals, of sharply differentiated fact, of discrete realities."[34] Clearly, then, attention is an essential element of Absolute Experience.

Now recall, however, that attention is a factor that is always present in the life of will. If the Absolute is an attentive Being, he must also be a willing

---

[32] CG, 200. Note that use of subjunctive ("could" and "would") points to fulfilment in future experience.
[33] CG, 201.
[34] Ibid.

Being.³⁵ His divine Will, according to Royce, is simply "that aspect of the Absolute which is expressed in the concrete and differentiated individuality of the world."³⁶ So our Absolute becomes not only a dual but a triple unity. He is Absolute Thought, Absolute Experience, and Absolute Will.

A perennial problem involved in any doctrine of will – whether it is applied to God or man – is that of freedom. In describing the "divine freedom" Royce again directs our attention to "attention." The attentive aspect of the Absolute, he maintains,

> cannot be conceived as determined by any of the ideas, or by the thought-aspect of the Absolute in its wholeness, or as necessitated by thought, to attend thus or so. In this sense the attentive aspect of the Absolute Experience appears as itself possessed of absolute Freedom.³⁷

That God shall adequately fulfill all ideas is necessary from our point of view. But what individual fulfilment is given to these ideas, neither we nor the ideas themselves can predetermine. The fulfilment is accomplished at some time in the future by Absolute Experience "as absolutely free, and still as absolutely rational."³⁸ In the totality of his Being as Will is contained the fulness of freedom, a "transcendent Freedom" in which all individual "free" beings are but elements.³⁹

C. The union between God and man

The notion that all individual beings are but elements in the Absolute suggests the topic of this last section. In treating of the union between God and man Royce tries to make practical his doctrine of the Absolute. Whether he succeeds or not remains an open question.

By indicating that the Absolute is Thought, Will and Experience we thereby describe a divine Being who is at once universal, individual and personal. He is universal because he is the fulness of thought and experience, he is individual because he is really existent in the here and now,

---

[35] Royce has a pertinent remark regarding the relationship between "must" and "is" (pertinent especially because the freedom of the divine will is next discussed). "The *must*," he says, "is our comment. The *is* expresses the ultimate fact." (CG, 206) In other words, the fact has greater force and importance than necessity. We use the latter merely to arrive at an awareness of the former; once we get there the *is* judgment is the essential one. That the Absolute *is* Will thus replaces the judgment that the Absolute *must be* Will.

[36] CG, 202. (Italics omitted.)

[37] CG, 202.

[38] *Ibid.*

[39] Cf. CG, 203, and note that "free" ≠ "transcendent Freedom."

he is personal because through the divine Will he acts with responsibly perfective import. The last point now deserves elaboration.

Personality, according to Royce, is an essentially ethical category.

A Person is a conscious being, whose life, temporally viewed, seeks its completion through deeds, while this same life, eternally viewed, consciously attains its perfection by means of the present knowledge of the whole of its temporal strivings.[40]

Temporally viewed, God is a Person because his life of Absolute Consciousness involves the entire temporal succession of conscious efforts towards perfection or fulfilment. Eternally viewed, however, "God's life is the infinite whole that includes this endless temporal process, and that consciously surveys it as one life."[41] Our temporal view of the divine Person is necessarily associated with a conception of his Individuality. He is the Individual of Individuals whose transcendent freedom acts in time, and which we discern as acting in each successive moment.[42] He is thus the basis upon which we make our present judgments by anticipating the effects of those judgments in temporal future experience. On the other hand he is the Whole who eternally unites individual existents and ultimately fulfills them. God as Person is thus correctly viewed as Individual and Whole, as temporal and eternal. According to Royce, personality is a category broad enough to include all these aspects of the divine nature.

This all-inclusiveness of the Absolute Person is necessarily illustrative of the pantheism that Royce disclaims. Though he tries verbally to justify a distinctness among the individual selves, the only basis for such distinction is quantitative, not qualitative: their individuality is constituted by their partialness, as elements of the Absolute Individual. Each individual self may be conceived "as a Part equal to the Whole, and finally united, as such equal, to the Whole wherein it dwells."[43] Moreover, only insofar as all the various selves are fulfilled in the Absolute are they individual at all. In the present life, our individuality is curtailed through its transiency. Hence, not until the "eternal world" can we be truly "aware of what our individuality is."[44]

Such a view of individuality calls for a closer consideration by our idealist of the problem of death. According to his general position, death is hardly explicable simply as the cessation of existence. For how can an individual die

---

[40] Josiah Royce, *The World and the Individual*, Second Series (New York: Dover Publications, Inc., 1959; an unaltered republication of the First Edition published by the Macmillan Company, 1901), 418. Hereafter, WI II.
[41] WI II, 419.
[42] Cf. WI II, 447.
[43] WI II, 452.
[44] WI II, 435.

at all if his individuality is only completely achieved in the eternal world? It would seem that either one never truly achieves individuality or else death is an illusion. On the other hand, the fact of death is a commonplace of experience, one closely associated with the temporality of man's existence. Consequently, while we know that "the lives of human individuals meet with a termination in physical death,... [h]ow, from our idealistic point of view, is such death possible at all as a real event?"[45]

The question cannot be adequately answered by pointing out that the "eternal perfection of the divine Will can only be expressed in a realm of temporal deeds, each one of which, as temporal, is transient, and, as an individual deed, is irrevocable."[46] For we are not asking about death as the mere cessation of temporal existence, but as a reality which "seems to defeat all the higher types of individual striving known to us."[47] Actually we are questioning the meaning of the experienced transiency of individual human existence. Our problem is rooted in man's experience as a "series of events wherein something individual is attempted, but is, within our ken, never finished at all."[48] Man's awareness that his temporal future experience is inevitably limited provokes him not only to consider the possibility of an after-life, but also, and perhaps more poignantly, to question the meaning of life itself.

To interpret the meaning of death in a way consistent with idealism requires for Royce a return to the fourth conception of being, viz., that "to be means to fulfil a purpose."[49] If death is real at all, he says, "it is real only insofar as it fulfils a purpose."[50] But the only purpose that death can fulfil is the purpose of another than him who dies. The very possibility of death, therefore, "depends upon the transcending of death through a life that is richer and more conscious than is the life which death cuts short."[51] Ultimately, the only consciousness which is not itself subject to death proves the existence of the Consciousness whose divine purpose furnishes the only positive meaning for its reality. If death is a fact at all, it can only be justified as such through the consciousness of the Absolute.

Apparently, the purposes of finite individuals are defeated through death. Actually, however, the event of death which is the cessation of finite life becomes assimilated into the Absolute Purpose who fulfils all finite individuality

[45] WI II, 438.
[46] WI II, 439.
[47] WI II, 440.
[48] Ibid.
[49] Ibid.
[50] Ibid.
[51] WI II, 441.

and purpose. In him, one's "whole individuality is continuous in true meaning with the individuality that dies."[52] The "deathless individuality" in which finite selves thus partake is another way of expressing Royce's doctrine of immortality. The continuity through which he describes the ultimate fulfilment of finite purposes is explicable only in terms of human immortality. As the assimilation of finite beings into the life of God, immortality thus becomes a necessary element of his absolutistic doctrine, giving meaning to present human existence.

Towards the end of his chapter on "The Union of God and Man," Royce concludes that there are three ways in which our union with God implies an immortal and individual life for man. The first is that "in God, we are real individuals, and really conscious Selves,"[53] a fact which finite consciousness and experience can never adequately explain. Secondly, "the death of an individual is a possible fact, in an idealistic world, only in case such death occurs as an incident in the life of a larger individual,"[54] viz., God. Thirdly, Royce asserts that

no ethical Self, in its union with God, can ever view its task as accomplished, or its work as done, or its individuality as ceasing to seek, in God, a temporal future.[55]

Only in eternity can we finite beings claim that all is done. In time there is no end to the individual's ethical task.

Admittedly, some of these notions in Royce suggest a pantheism. There are several ways, however, in which they also indicate a pragmatism. For the Absolute gives practical meaning to our present and subsequent situations. In regard to the present, he is the basis for a self-respect and other-respect which is wholly in order because of our participation in divine life. Further, he is the basis for our hope – a hope that makes a difference in the here and now – a hope that ultimately our inevitably frustrated purposes will be fulfilled in future experience. Hence in treating of the union between God and man Royce does seem to succeed in showing that there are practical consequences that follow from his doctrine of the Absolute.

At the beginning of this chapter it was suggested that at least three points are illustrative of the development of a more pragmatic orientation in Royce's notion of the Absolute. In regard to the first and second points, the texts clearly indicate increased emphasis on experience and will in Royce's proof for the existence of God and in his description of the life of the Ab-

---

[52] WI II, 442.
[53] WI II, 445.
[54] *Ibid.*
[55] *Ibid.*

solute. Both emphases indicate the practical and empirical thrust of Roycean philosophy. Both points contribute also to the third pragmatic factor which we have considered here, viz., the relevance of the Absolute to the life of man. In the development of his thought Royce seems more and more interested in applying his idealistic doctrine to the concrete human situation. That the being of the Absolute makes a practical difference in a practical world is a conviction to which his writings in the middle period give abundant testimony.

CHAPTER VIII

CONCEPTION OF THE INDIVIDUAL PRAGMATICALLY LEADS TO CONSIDERATION OF COMMUNITY

In the sixth of his lectures for the Lowell Institute in 1906-7, William James described truth, according to his pragmatic theory, as the "agreeable leading" of our ideas towards their verification in future experience.[1] That this description applies to the development of Royce's concept of the individual is a claim that the present chapter hopes to justify. Through his own consideration of the meaning and role of the individual in his absolutistic system, Royce was led to place increasing emphasis on the notion of community. Several themes which illustrate this "agreeable leading" of pragmatism as a way of philosophizing form the subject matter for the sections which follow. Collectively, these ideas not only motivate but necessitate Royce's later more extensive treatment of community.

A. *Royce's conception of the self*

The differing historical conceptions of being which Royce discusses in the first volume of *The World and the Individual* give rise to three general views of the self as this term is applied to the individual man. Although each of these is open to diverse interpretations, all three have certain advantages and disadvantages which are utilized by Royce to explicate his own conception of the individual.

First, then, is "the more directly empirical way of conceiving the Self." By this, according to Royce,

you mean a certain totality of facts, viewed as more or less immediately given, and as distinguished from the rest of the world of Being.[2]

These facts may be but need not be predominantly corporeal. States of consciousness, feelings, thoughts, desires, memories, emotions, and moods be-

[1] Prag, 134.
[2] WI II, 257.

long as equally to this empirical, phenomenal self as do its physical appearance and deeds. With such a broad and multifaceted empirical base, the question that naturally arises is: how might the uniqueness of the Ego be explained and/or maintained? In our idealist's view, the only basis for deciphering some continuity or self-identity amid this multiplicity of empirical facts is social contrast. In origin, then, "the empirical Ego is secondary to our social experience."[3] One becomes aware of his own uniqueness, his individuality, through the discernment of differences and similarities between himself and his fellows. Outside of such a social context, there could be no empirical Ego.

The second general conception of self is the view that regards "the Self as in some metaphysical sense a real being, without defining the true Being of this Self in strictly idealistic terms."[4] Here, insofar as the self is construed as a distinct and independent entity, its individuality is essentially separable, not only from the body, but from other selves as well. To Royce, such a doctrine of the self as a "Soul-Substance" is useful in explaining the perdurance of the human individual through a multiplicity of changing experiences, but the doctrine stands or falls with the realistic theory of being from which it arises. Since Royce has already disposed of that theory, the metaphysical concept of the self is likewise unsatisfactory. "Whatever the Self is, it is not a Thing," i.e., an independent substance.[5]

A third conception of the Ego remains. This is a "strictly idealistic" notion, originating from man's experience of the ethical dimension of his life.[6] "A man has," Royce writes, "...two Selves, – the inner and the outer, the nobler and the baser."[7] Even common sense is able to distinguish between these two aspects of the same individual. Accordingly, in the experience of a gap between his higher and lower tendencies, between the real and the ideal, a man discovers who he is – "not a Thing, but a Meaning embodied in a conscious life."[8] His individuality is constituted through a reference to a higher purpose that transcends his present situation. Consequently,

---

[3] WI II, 264.

[4] WI II, 266.

[5] WI II, 268. Cf. James's critique of the notion of self as a metaphysical entity in *Principles of Psychology*, Vol. I, Ch. XII.

[6] Cf. WI II, 268.

[7] WI II, 249.

[8] WI II, 269. Cf. James's notion of self as stream or flow of consciousness in *Principles of Psychology*, Vol. I, Ch. XI. The dialectic which Royce ascribes to self-consciousness suggests a process context similar to that of James.

even what is most individual about the Self never appears except in the closest connection with what transcends both the meaning and the life of the finite individual.[9]

No self is truly individual except insofar as it relates to a purpose which projects beyond its finitude.

Royce adopts this last conception of the self, translating it into terms that readily accord with his absolutistic voluntaristic epistemology. Through the successive instants of existence, he maintains, we catch fleeting glimpses of ourselves as individuals, expressing our uniqueness in deeds and ideals. At the same time we obtain fragmentary flashes of insight into "the way in which this Self is linked to the lives of its fellows, or is dependent for its expression upon its relations to Nature, or is subject to the general moral order of the universe."[10] All our idealistic accounts of the self are thus the record of what we have understood by relating internal and external purposes. As Royce puts it,

[a]ny instant of finite consciousness partially embodies a purpose, and so possesses its own Internal Meaning. Any such instant of finite consciousness also seeks, however, for other expression, for other objects, than are now present to just that instant, and so possesses what we have called its External Meaning.[11]

Ultimately, if the whole meaning and intent of any finite instant of life or any finite self is fully developed and perfectly embodied, the entire meaning of that self "becomes identical with the Universe, with the Absolute, with the life of God."[12] Again then, as we have already seen in Chapter VII, individuality is summarily absorbed into Royce's doctrine of the Absolute.

While insisting upon the uniqueness of each individual self as a real existent human being, Royce nonetheless concedes his inability to explain the nature of man's individuality. Reason and experience can assist our understanding of universal concepts, but not of individuals as individual.

For whatever is a truly individual character of any existent thing is a character that simply could not be shared by another thing; and whatever makes you an existent individual being forbids anybody else, whether actual or possible, to be possessed of precisely your individual characteristics.[13]

Accordingly, one can explain the term "man," but not "this man."

[9] WI II, 269.
[10] WI II, 270.
[11] *Ibid.*
[12] WI II, 271.
[13] Josiah Royce, *The Conception of Immortality* (New York: Houghton, Mifflin and Company, 1900), 16. Hereafter, CI.

you can define; but the true essence of any man, say, for instance, of Abraham
Lincoln, remains the endlessly elusive and mysterious object of the biographer's
interest, of the historian's comments, of popular legend, and of patriotic devotion.
There is no adequate definition of Abraham Lincoln just in so far as he was the
unique individual.[14]

Thus the precise being of any individual remains a "mystery." Our only approach to an understanding of the mystery of a man's individual nature lies in conceiving him to be "so related to the world and to the very life of God, that in order to be an individual at all a man has to be very much nearer to the Eternal than in our present life we are accustomed to observe."[15] To the degree that one unites himself with the being of the Absolute the more truly individual he becomes.

B. Love as the principle of individuation

Although Royce acknowledges the impossibility of adequately explaining the "nature of the individual," this does not impede his considering the principle by which individuation occurs, i.e., the principle by which one recognizes the individual as such. Since the conception of self in his idealism originates in an ethical context, he naturally looks to this context for an explanation of individuation. As God individuates beings through the exercise of the divine Will, the same is true of man.

Man individuates the object of his knowledge because he is an ethical being. God
individuates the objects of his own world, and knows them as individuals, for no
other reason.[16]

Hence, the principle of individuation is "identical with the principle that has sometimes been called Will, and sometimes Love."[17] While individuality remains theoretically indefinable, individuation is practically, i.e., voluntaristically or ethically, explicable.

To illustrate his notion of love as principle of individuation Royce describes the development of the human ability to individuate among a multiplicity of like objects. As Aristotle first noted, all knowledge is initially of what is vaguely universal. Only gradually does one come to distinguish the "one" through the "many." "If you do not believe this," says Royce,

watch any young child calling flies "dogs," or independently recognizing pine cones

[14] *Ibid.*
[15] CI, 5.
[16] CG, 259.
[17] *Ibid.*

as potatoes, or thoughtfully saying "piece of moon all torn" when he happens to observe a bright star, – and you will know what I mean by asserting that not only the first unconscious general ideas, but also the first explicitly conscious ideas, are of the universal, as such.[18]

If he continues in this way, i.e., on a purely theoretical level, the child might never reach an awareness of what true individuality means. The process through which he vaguely recognizes universals could proceed indefinitely. But suppose the same child is given a tiny lead soldier as a toy. Suppose that after he grows to love the toy, he accidentally breaks it. What would happen if one were to offer him another lead soldier, one similar to the one just broken? Would the child, who intellectually is so naturally fond of universal types, be very likely to accept the new soldier as a compensation for the broken one? No, says Royce. In fact, "[h]e is very likely to mourn the more vociferously in view of your offer."[19] Certainly the child does not intellecually recognize the first toy soldier as observably unique in type or definably different from all others. Rather, it is that his love for his toy is an "exclusive passion,"[20] i.e., a feeling that involves the recognition that something is existentially, not theoretically, unique. At the moment when the child rejects the second soldier,

at this very moment he *consciously individuates the toy*. And he does this because he loves the toy with an exclusive love that *permits no other*.[21]

It is not the object as presented, nor the object as thought, but the object as loved which is uniquely, unrepeatably individual. Love, therefore, is the principle of individuation.

What happens in the case of the child, Royce maintains, happens over and over again in life. Whenever a person acknowledges uniqueness or individuality of an object, he does this not through any intellectual effort but through his will, i.e., by making a choice of one among many. The individual becomes known as such by being selected as an object of exclusive interest, whether by himself or others. I can know myself as individual, for example, insofar as I see myself as "essentially an actor, one who means to do so and so,"[22] one whose will-acts are inseparable from his uniqueness, whose life is

---

[18] CG, 260. Admittedly, the examples Royce here provides seem to illustrate the child's confusion of concepts rather than his knowing the universal first. Nonetheless, when one so "confuses" one object for another, it may be because he recognizes a yet broader universal which encompasses both objects. E.g., pine cones and potatoes are both small round brown objects that grow.
[19] CG, 261.
[20] Ibid.
[21] Ibid.
[22] Vol. 63, "Lectures to Teachers," 1893, Lecture III, 45.

best described through his intended "plans of action."²³ I thus become an object of my own exclusive interest in the course of my knowing myself as uniquely me.

Or, in regard to others, in preferring one to another I recognize real but indescribable individuality. Ask a lover, for instance, why his beloved is unique, and he can only mutter inadequate generalities, nothing that explicitates the nature of the uniqueness on which he insists.²⁴ His choice of the beloved among all others marks her as an object of exclusive interest.

[F]or our Will, however sense deceives and however ill thought defines, there *shall be* none precisely like the beloved. And just herein, namely, in this voluntary choice, in this active postulate, lies our essential consciousness of the true nature of individuality.²⁵

In regard to God, the divine Will is that which explains his awareness of each individual as object of his exclusive interest. Only to him can the individual be completely known as such; only in him can the existence of individuals as such be adequately explicated. While

human love is a good name for what first individuates for us our universe of known objects. . . [w]e have good reason for saying that it is the Divine Love which individuates the real world wherein the Divine Omniscience is fulfilled.²⁶

Accordingly, God's exclusive love is the universal principle of individuation.

Not all love, however, is individuating – whether it be divine or human. According to Royce there is much love of unindividuated types. What makes it individuating is the exclusive element that is present only in the ethically organizing interests of life.

Ethical love, organizing interest, is precisely the sort of interest that cannot consciously serve two masters, and that accordingly individuates, first its master, and then countless other individuals with respect to that master, – viz., individual means to the one end, individual objects of the one science, individual acts of the one life, and all the other individuals that in the end fill our known world of experience.²⁷

By an individuating or exclusive interest in living one life for one purpose a man becomes a moral individual, a unique self, and not a mere collection of empirical social contrast effects. His exclusive love for God, whom nobody

---

[23] *Ibid.*, 48.
[24] Cf. CI, 32-34.
[25] CI, 38.
[26] CG, 259.
[27] CG, 264-5.

CONCEPTION OF THE INDIVIDUAL PRAGMATICALLY 107

else can serve in just the way open to him, tends to individuate his idea of his own moral self. Ultimately, the only End sufficient to all of life's ethical demands, the only Master worthy of our ethical love in any and all circumstances is the Absolute. In him alone our ethically organized interests find final fulfilment.

C. Freedom and responsibility of the self

As man advances towards the ethical fulfilment which is the achievement of his selfhood he likewise grows in freedom and responsibility. According to Royce, the progress is effected in three overlapping stages.[28] At the outset the child is equipped with a basic impulse or tendency to strive toward ideal goals, vague and unformulated though these often are. As he gets older, through social processes of imitation and contrast, his ideals receive some measure of content and conscious formulation. Eventually, the mature individual emerges, as one faced with the problem of choosing among and reconciling a plurality of conflicting goals or ideals. Thus confronted the self is simultaneously aware of his freedom and responsibility. Through his acts of choice he acknowledges his willingness or unwillingness to meet the responsibility that he conceives as his. Through these free decisions he carves out of life the unique relationship to goals that constitutes his individuality.

Man's sense of responsibility is his awareness of his own ideal self – the self that he would be, not what he is. Consequently, each unique life plan affords the individual a conception of a potential existence which contrasts with and serves as a standard for criticizing his empirically observable "self" as it exists in the here and now. Moreover, a man's "ideal gives him all the more unity and permanence by virtue of its very remoteness."[29] In its light the individual can discern a yet sharper contrast between what he is and what he could have been.

You never know a man's self-consciousness, until you learn something of this graveyard of perished ideal selves, which his experience has filled for him, and which his memory has adorned with often very fantastic inscriptions.[30]

The ideal is thus the unifier in man's conception of his self as one whose individuality is constituted not only by present decisions but by past and future as well.

In Royce's idealism the notions of freedom and responsibility are clearly

---

[28] Cf. Fuss, 85.
[29] Vol. 70, "Some Aspects of Social Psychology," Lecture VI, 15.
[30] CG, 284.

inseparable from the ethical and teleological categories in which he defines the term "person."

> The term "person"... can mean only the moral individual, *i.e.* the individual viewed as meaning or aiming towards an ideal... for only the moral individual, as a life lived in relation to a plan, a finite totality of experience viewed as meaning for itself, a struggle towards conformity to an ideal, has, in the finite world, at once an all-pervading unity, despite the unessential accidents of disease and of sense, and a single clear contrast, in its wholeness, to the rest of the universe of experience.[31]

Personality is thus acquired, as the unique expression of a self, through the progressive merging of one's socially inculcated moral ideal with his free decisions relative to that ideal. A person is always a morally orientated individual.[32] He is not necessarily one who has speculated much about a moral way of acting, but he is one who really acts out of a moral consciousness. "It is not necessary," Royce writes,

> to be a philosopher in order to be a person, and often enough, as human nature goes, abstract ideas may be permitted so much to stand in the way of concrete devotion, that a given individual may appear all the more doubtfully to be a person by virtue of the fact that he has let himself become a philosopher.[33]

One cannot become a person merely by defining his moral ideal; one becomes a person through his efforts to live practically that ideal, by becoming a "self-conscious moral agent,"[34] i.e., one who acts from a sense of moral responsibility.

As Peter Fuss observes in *The Moral Philosophy of Josiah Royce*, our idealist generally handles the themes of freedom and responsibility from two more or less distinct points of view.[35] The first is the perspective of the absolutist metaphysician who attempts to preserve the freedom and responsibility of the finite individual in spite of his "inclusion" as part or aspect in an Absolute Consciousness or Will. Briefly stated, Royce's argument is that the very fact of the self's inclusion in an Absolute Will must be understood to mean that his own unique will is included in the divine Will as one of *its* purposes. Thus, he is free in the sense that he is a unique embodiment of the Will of the Absolute.[36]

---

[31] CG, 267.
[32] Or immorally orientated for that matter – for bad choices, says Royce, are also qualitatively moral. Cf. CG, 292.
[33] CG, 316.
[34] Ibid.
[35] Cf. 86 ff. and n. 28 *supra*.
[36] Cf. WI II, 330 ff.

The second perspective is that of the moral psychologist. From this vantage point Royce feels that he must somehow account for an element of personal initiative and self-determination on the part of the human individual, despite his conditioning by social environment. Here the philosopher employs a psychological concept prevalent in his day (and one which we have already discussed in the context of his epistemology), viz., attention. In his *Outlines of Psychology* Royce gives a full exposition of the psychological implications of this doctrine.[37] Involved in attentive selection, he claims, is a residue of "self-activity" which cannot be adequately accounted for in terms of habits formed through environmental conditioning. The residue is described as a "restless persistence," noticeable in the predisposition of children to endless experiment, and in the tendency of adults to persevere in seeking solutions to fundamental problems.[38] Royce believes that this element in the attentive process accounts for the spontaneity that is sometimes present in our will acts. He asserts that

the restless over-activity of the organism in carrying out its instinctive processes, or in seeking opportunity for the establishment of new functions, is the principal condition of every significant form of mental initiative.[39]

"Such persistence," he continues, "is the one initiative that the organism can offer to the world."[40] Its reality is only explicable in terms of the freedom of the individual.

In elaborating upon the relation between freedom and spontaneity or originality Royce distinguishes between acts of will that are *original* and those which are *originative*. He argues that we cannot consciously and directly will any new act, but only those acts which we have already learned how to perform. One can only choose among *known* alternatives. Choice is therefore an *unoriginal* power, but it is *originative* in the sense that the person who deliberately chooses one among the known possibilities may actually be beginning a new way of life for himself.[41]

Royce concedes that neither freedom nor responsibility can be taken as absolute in regard to finite individuals. Because of the limitations that are

---

[37] Cf. (New York: The Macmillan Company, 1916; first published by Macmillan, 1903) 306-31. Hereafter, OP.
[38] Cf. Fuss, 88-91.
[39] OP, 318. (Italics omitted.)
[40] OP, 325. (Italics omitted.)
[41] Cf. OP, 371. Also, cf. Fuss (91) for a critique of Royce's psychological account of freedom. A critique of his metaphysical view, as Fuss rightly observes, would require a point by point analysis of Royce's entire metaphysical system, something which other authors have already dealt with comprehensively (e.g., Oppenheim's dissertation cited in Ch. II, n.40, and Gabriel Marcel in *La métaphysique de Royce*).

part and parcel of human nature, both are relativized – but nonetheless real. The realm of future experience to which our freedom and responsibility are directed is restricted by time and space, by one's awareness, and by personal capability. Even within this restricted sphere, however, a man is free consciously to cultivate his powers of response, or deliberately to narrow his attentive concerns. In choosing the latter course, one betrays his responsibility, i.e., one sins.

To sin is *consciously to choose to forget*, through a narrowing of the field of attention, an Ought that one already recognizes.[42]

One cannot sin unless he is free to say No to moral responsibility. As Kant had noted long before, freedom is a *sine quâ non* for human ethical living – be it good or bad.

While Royce insists that the individual as such is truly free,[43] his justification for that freedom, as admittedly relative, is largely colored by his absolutism. One acts freely in regard to the immediate future only because there is a finally fulfilling future where perfect freedom may be had.

I shall, then, also strenuously insist that the individual, as I define him, is free, – free with the identical freedom of God, whereof his freedom is a portion. For there is (1) in his consciousness an element which is determined by absolutely nothing in the whole of God's life outside of this individual himself. Furthermore (2), this element, namely, his attentively selected ideal, is determined neither by the contents of the individual's experience nor by the mere necessity of the laws of the individual's thought.[44]

God, of course, is absolutely free. The individual, as a unique aspect of his free divine life, shares in that freedom in a relative way. Besides this, however, the same individual exhibits his freedom in the choice of his life plan or ideal, and in the unique purposiveness of all the lesser decisions which his life entails. He is free not merely by the effective proclamation of the free God who gives him being, but free in each of the choices in which he fashions that being according to his will.

D. *Community as fulfilling the individual*

So absolute an idealist as Royce could never be satisfied with the relative situation of human individuals as such. Given the optimistic trend of his general philosophizing he would be apt to find ways through which the limi-

[42] WI II, 359. (Italics omitted.)
[43] Cf. CG, 304: "A true individual, as such, is therefore itself a free fact."
[44] CG, 294.

tations of the various finite selves might be diminished so that their own worth and that of the world which they comprise might be enhanced. To this end Royce seems to have emulated Peirce in gradually developing a greater emphasis upon the notion of community.

It was through reflection on the meaning of freedom and responsibility that our idealist first developed this awareness. In a lecture delivered at Cambridge in 1898 Royce noted that any effort to define and solve social problems presupposes some understanding of who the self and others are.[45] First we believe that other men exist as other consciousnesses, then we look to them to tell us about ourselves. By contrast with others, i.e., by contrast with the ideals we learn from them, we discover both a social and an antisocial self.[36] The genuine existing self is one thrust purposefully towards his own fulfilment in a social empirical context, thrust towards that ideal out of presently anti-social elements contained within himself.

To Royce, "the human subject is essentially a suggestible, a socially plastic, an imitative being."[47] Our most ordinary habits certainly indicate the presence of social suggestion. But even in our specific and supposedly "individual" likes and dislikes, we show its influence. Consider the following, for example.

[I]f there were one man in the world who liked olives, and if he persisted in liking them despite vigorous and universal social suggestions to the contrary, he would probably prove to be a person whom it were dangerous to leave at large.[48]

So universal is the effect of social suggestion that one who acted contrarily would justifiably be considered "odd."

Nonetheless, men differ in types and degrees of social plasticity, and it is because of this that they interact differently with each other.

Many of us, and by no means the least intelligent or the least individual amongst us, are in one sense, in our conversational trains of thought, wax to be moulded, up to a certain point, by the current conversational impressions that we get from our whole social environment. There are people who force some of us to think and to say all our possible foolish or stupid things. . . [I]n the presence of these quenchers of our personality we are baffled, hesitant, slow, thoughtless, vaguely flippant, wearily dull. . . Other people there are who as it were unlock the doors of all our treasure houses. . . In their presence our thought flows like a river, not perhaps to their delight, but to our own.[49]

[45] Cf. Vol. 70, "Cambridge Conferences," First Lecture, Feb. 6, 1898, 3.
[46] Cf. Vol. 68, "The Social Basis of the Intellectual Life," Lecture II, 8 and Vol. 66, "On Certain Psychological Aspects of Moral Training," Lecture XII, Galley 4. Also see Vol. 62, "The Twofold Nature of Knowledge," 41-2: "I am one who look [sic] for myself in something other than what I now am."
[47] Vol. 62, "The Twofold Nature of Knowledge," 44.
[48] Vol. 64, "Lectures to Teachers," Lecture IV, 46.
[49] Vol. 63, Lecture III, 20-21.

It is inherent then in man's nature as a social being that he tend towards union with others, particularly those who are open to his thrust towards fellowship. By establishing ties with other selves a man's own individuality is enriched, and the unity of all mankind is thus increased.

Man's dependence on others and upon the world for his own self-realization is itself a sign pointing towards "the Absolute Individual who is the sole completely *integrated* Self."[50] In him alone can perfect unity be reached. It is attained in a relative but real sense in the here and now not only through individual directedness towards God but also through the directedness towards others which is community.

For it [the self] is not related to these other selves *merely* through the common relation to God; on the contrary, it is just as truly related to God *by means of* its relation to them. Its life with them is an eternally fulfilled social life, and the completion of this eternal order also means the self-conscious expression of God, the Individual of Individuals, who dwells in all, as they in him.[51]

Moreover, the dependence of which Royce speaks is not only a one-way relationship. Finite selves are mutually dependent upon one another and upon nature, and both are dependent upon God. In addition, however, the Absolute also relates to the world and to individuals in order to manifest himself phenomenally through them. Through "interpenetration" of the various finite selves by "processes of intercommunication"[52] he must express the unity which constitutes his very being. There is a sense then in which God needs man even as man needs God, the one to express himself, the other to find fulfilment. Both God and man need various selves united in such a way as to form community.

In the process through which the finite individuals approach an ultimate unity in the Absolute, the principle of their progressive integration is the development of what Royce calls "the social mind." This mind depends upon the individual minds who comprise it, who insure its growth through their collective experiences and actions, and its continuity through their collective memory and interaction.

The growth of the social mind depends, like the growth of the individual mind, upon the fact that all these experiences tend to express themselves in action, upon the fact that the experiences leave records of themselves in the individual or social memeory, and upon the fact that the consequences of former social activity tend to effect [sic] the later activities that express the same continuous social mind.[53]

[50] WI II, 447.
[51] *Ibid.*
[52] WI II, 448.

In learning about himself, the world and the Absolute from the social situation in which he lives, the individual is drawing upon the ever developing content of the social mind.

Not all communal contexts, however, actually facilitate the enrichment of the individual, as such. Certain situations might enhance some selves, others might exert no good effect at all.

Only certain social situations, only certain socially acquired habits tend to encourage the thinking process, to tend to develop the individual reason, or tend to cultivate that ideality whereby the individual self-consciousness gets the degree of self-directing independence which in the end it ought to attain.[54]

Nevertheless, whatever qualitative growth does occur in regard to any finite self is only possible because of his presence among other selves who teach him who he is and who he ought to be.[55] Through interaction with his fellows a man becomes more whole. Through a sharing of ideas, the meanings of each of the sharers become deeper and more integral so that the entire community of sharers are brought closer to a final unity of meaning.

If, for instance, I now have a genuine idea of your minds while I speak to you, or if you have any idea really referring to my own mind, then our minds are actually and metaphysically linked by the ties of mutual meaning. In other words, we are then not wholly sundered beings. We are somehow more whole of meaning.[56]

Thus the fragmentation of our separate human natures, which our idealist so frequently bemoans, is diminished through the process which constitutes community.

To Royce the differences between individuals is the basis upon which most of our social relationships are established. As a matter of fact, man's love for another is most likely to be elicited and sustained through a contrast between him and that other. The contrast not only sets up the possibility for a complementarity that is mutually enriching; it also communicates the element of mystery that is involved in all interpersonal relationships. In a sense it is because one can never wholly understand the other, that he contrasts with ourselves and remains unique. Thus

I love my neighbor most in social life when he genuinely, but not too violently,

---

[53] Vol. 91, "The Growth of the Social Mind," 1900?, 26.
[54] Vol. 70, "The Social Basis of Reason," 1897-8, Lecture VII, 5.
[55] Cf. Vol. 70, "Theory of the Origin of the Ideas of Ego and Alter," 1898?, Lecture V, 2: "It is on the whole my fellows who teach me what I ought to be, in so far as concerns all my early conceptions of my worth and position. My very self-assertion involves all sorts of social dependence."
[56] CI, 54.

contrasts in attitude, idea, and expression, with me, so that he baffles me a little, but entices me to pursue further the relation, and to get his ideas, since he has not merely reflected mine. This sort of cheerful baffling of one another by the absence of perfect agreement and analogy in conduct and expression, forms the basis for some of the most fascinating friendships that exist between people of contrasting character...[57]

Not that the baffling of which Royce speaks is an end in itself. But it is an indication that the person of the other with whom we establish social ties is respected for his unknowable uniqueness. He who is cheerfully baffled is thereby open to continued disclosures on the part of his neighbor. Communication provoked precisely by this "baffledness" is deemed important and pursued as the means by which one questions, responds, and grows through social intercourse.[58]

One of the offices of philosophy, Royce maintains, is to cultivate the sense of fellowship among men. The most vital interest of idealism is thus to explain the unity of the world, the Oneness towards which all finite beings tend and which they further through their oneness with each other.[59] Since "[w]e are related to God through our consciousness of our fellows," it is not until the individual

views himself as a member of a universal society, whose temporal estrangements are merely incidental to their final unity of meaning, that man rationally appreciates the actual sense of the conscious ideas that express his longing for oneness with an absolute life.[60]

In developing that appreciation philosophy performs a practical and effective function in regard to the individual as well as to the world at large. Moreover, the actuality of community among men provides the idealistic social criterion by which individuals preserve an awareness of ideals that motivate their own enrichment. Society teaches, remembers and reminds the finite self of goals he might forget or not yet know.[61]

Community, to Royce, even at this stage of his writings, is no mere aggregate union of separate individuals, the sum of many distinct parts. Rather community is an organic life, a personal being, a living reality which is more than all its members.[62] From the fulness of its personal life, the community

[57] Vol. 69, Lecture II, 20.
[58] Cf. Vol. 68, "The Social Factors of the Human Intellect," Lecture II, 16.
[59] Cf. WI I, 418, 417.
[60] WI, 418.
[61] Cf. Vol. 71, "On certain limitations of the thoughtful public in America," 7, 39 and Vol. 68, Lecture IV, 38.
[62] Regarding personality of community see Vol. 91, "Spirit of the Community," 1900?, 23. Concerning community as organic life see Vol. 65, Lecture VII, 54.

can and does contribute to the completion and ultimate perfection of those finite individuals who compose it. Royce's growing emphasis on community stems from his hope for a future of fulfilling experience.

Although Royce's specific references to "community" in the works of his middle period are somewhat sparse, the ideas developed during this time show a progression in his thought (i.e., an "agreeable leading" of his ideas) from an emphasis on the individual as individual (whether finite or infinite) to the grouping of individuals into a human society. By stressing love as the principle of individuation Royce paves the way for later considerations of love and loyalty as the unifying principle of community. In freedom and responsibility the individual establishes his own uniqueness, while effectively respecting the uniqueness of others. Through all three factors – love, freedom and responsibility – our notion of the individual is rather pragmatically pointed towards a closer study of community as a future-orientated way of lived philosophizing.

PART THREE

THE MATURE ROYCE

(c. 1906-16)

CHAPTER IX

KNOWLEDGE BY INTERPRETATION, A MEDIATING PRINCIPLE

Recent efforts in the direction of a Royce revival attribute great significance to his two volumed work *The Problem of Christianity*.[1] That the attribution is well deserved will be evident in this third part of our study. For the two themes that are central to Royce's mature philosophizing dominate his thought in that work, viz., interpretation and community. These form the subject matter for the present chapter and for Chapter XI, respectively. The basis for both themes and the element of continuity between Royce's later and early thinking is his notion of the Absolute and man's relation to that Absolute; accordingly, these topics are treated in Chapter X. Using texts primarily from *The Problem of Christianity* but also from pertinent later manuscripts and other published works of the period we expect to see that in regard to interpretation, God, and Community, the mature writings of Royce definitely show a more pragmatic strain than did his early works.

Concerning the Roycean theory of interpretation, then, its author first elaborates this after showing the inadequacy of other conceptions of cognition. A similar procedure is followed here.

A. Perception, conception, and interpretation

Much of the history of philosophy, Royce claims, has been occupied with a dualistic view of the classification of human knowledge. Generally, even positions as diverse as rationalism and empiricism agree that there are two processes involved in cognition, viz., perception and conception.[2] As parti-

---

[1] While *The Problem of Christianity* was out of print for over 50 years, *The World and the Individual* was generally considered the main philosophical work of Royce. Today, PC is justly given more attention as the fruit of Royce's mature philosophical development. In 1968 alone two editions of PC were published: one (used in these Notes) a single volume hardback introduced by John E. Smith, the other a two-volumed paperback foreworded by Jesse A. Mann. (See bibliography for specifics.)

[2] Cf. PC, 278, where Royce names Kant, James, Bergson and Russell as exemplars of dualistic theories of cognition.

cular examples Royce selects the theories of Henri Bergson and William James, which he uses as foils to support his own position. Both directly and indirectly, in describing and criticizing the ideas of these two thinkers, our idealist explicates his later view of knowledge.

1. *A critique of Bergson*

Through Bergson Royce examines the general worth of a dyadic theory of cognition. "Bergson's philosophy," he maintains,

> consists of two parts: a pragmatism which he [Bergson] regards as always incomplete and unsatisfactory, and a mysticism which, as he now more fully expresses himself, he tends to make more prominent.[3]

The "pragmatism" of Bergson lies in his explanation of the role of concept in human thinking and acting: the concept is an intellectual immobilization of reality for the purpose of handling that (actually mobile) reality. While concepts are extremely useful and necessary, their inevitable fixity prevents our grasping reality itself, which is essentially change or duration.[4] Nonetheless, the intellect is quite relentless in its tendency to identify the static concept with the changing thing. Bergson proposes that we check this fallible bent of human nature through the corrective of an intuition, with which one can actually "think" the reality which is duration.

The notion of intuition leads us into the realm of "mysticism" which Royce attributes to Bergson. As a "mystical" experience, intuition also involves perception, through which we are brought into contact with the real.[5] Where conception proves inadequate, perception is capable of taking over and filling the gap. Bergson's pragmatism thus *needs* the complement of his mysticism. To clarify this relationship Royce invites us to consider what would happen if we were *merely* "pragmatic." We would soon notice, he says, that all the "ideal leadings of the intellect" constitute at best an endlessly varied using of tools. Eventually,

> with Bergson and with the mystics, we would come to regard all this life of the varied ideas, this mechanical using of mere tools, this mere pragmatism, as an essentially poorer sort of life from which nature has long since delivered the nobler of the insects, from which the artists can and do escape, and from which it is the loftiest ideal of philosophy to liberate those who are indeed to know reality.[6]

In other words, Bergson's idea is that the truth of reality is attainable *only*

---

[3] PC, 355.
[4] Cf. PC, 292: "Reality, so Bergson tells us, . . . is essentially change, flow, movement."
[5] PC, 334.
[6] PC, 336-7.

through perception, and this perception is possible only through pure intuition.

Hence, perception and conception are really the only two types of cognition available to man. Through perception one knows the real; this is the mystical aspect of Bergson's philosophy. Through concepts one knows how to manipulate the real; this is clearly pragmatic. Such at least is Royce's understanding of Bergson's doctrine.

In criticizing the evolutionist's theory, Royce claims that Bergson neglects a third kind of cognition, one which involves a comparison of our perceptions and conceptions through a process of "interpretation."[7] Such a theory, Royce maintains, fills the gap left in the dualistic approach. To illustrate, he points out that Bergson's own notion of reality as duration, accessible only by intuition, is itself an interpretation of reality.[8] Even the artists whom Bergson is so fond of using as examples, whom he recommends for their intuitive approach, are interpreters of reality.[9] Their very intuition is an interpretation of the meaning of reality to them. For Royce, interpretation rather than intuition touches the heart of reality.[10] In the following passage, he indicates his own pragmatic preference, reflecting at the same time an almost wistful regard for Bergson's mysticism.

Only the more uncompromising of the mystics still seek for knowledge in a silent land of absolute intuition, where the intellect finally lays down its conceptual tools, and rests from its pragmatic labors... Those of us who are not such uncompromising mystics, view accessible human knowledge neither as pure perception nor as pure conception, but always as depending upon the marriage of the two processes.[11]

Although Royce may not himself be an "uncompromising mystic," he clearly refuses to compromise his thought with that of Bergson.

2. *A critique of James*

Royce is just as resolute, if not more so, in disagreeing with James's theory of cognition. Jamesian pragmatism, he maintains, points to the inadequacy of a dualism such as Bergson espouses, and attempts to bridge the gap by suggesting a "sort of synthesis of perception and conception" in the knowing

---

[7] Cf. PC, 277, 281.
[8] PC, 334.
[9] PC, 295.
[10] *Ibid.*
[11] PC, 279.

process.¹² It does this by focusing both forms of knowledge upon the experience of practical life. Through that focus,

> whatever really meets our need or at least for the time contents us, has to be known to us in the form of perceptual knowledge. The use of the other kind of knowledge, the value of conceptual knowledge,... is instrumental. The use of our concepts lies not in this, but in the immediate experience to which they may lead us.¹³

Or, to use a metaphor employed by all three thinkers, a concept gives knowledge only insofar as it is convertible into the cash of experience. Concepts and percepts are always practically combined in human knowing and living.¹⁴ The truth of their combination in concrete situations lies in the concepts leading us to certain desired percepts. Our fund of knowledge is increased as new facts blend satisfactorily with previous theories. Truth happens to our ideas as they show their usefulness in practical effects.

In contrasting his own view with James's theory, Royce presents his criticism rather bluntly:

> My general objection to your [James's] view is that it is not the whole truth about truth. It leaves out essential aspects.... My definition of truth: – A statement is true if the whole of the experience (and reality) to which that statement belongs fulfils the purpose which that statement expresses. This definition includes your workings and much more too.... A true statement of course "works." So may a lie.¹⁵

Actually, Royce accepts the partial truth of James's pragmatism, claiming that it just does not go far enough. The theory of knowledge thus defined still depends upon recognizing the dual contrast between concept and percept. To maintain that true ideas are agreeable leadings, which in turn are combinations of concepts and percepts, is to keep the two means of cognition quite separate and merely to assert that truth is verified in experience. Royce readily agrees, therefore,

> [t]hat synthesis of perception and conception which the pragmatists emphasize indeed exists; but the fact that we are indeed led from our concepts towards our percepts by various more or less practical tendencies does not itself constitute a genuinely third type of knowledge.¹⁶

Hence James's theory of knowledge marks no real advance on that of other dualists.

Inadvertently, however, James furnishes Royce with an example for his

---

¹² Vol. 84, Undated Material 1915? "The Triadic Theory of Knowledge," 29.
¹³ *Ibid.*, 17.
¹⁴ Cf. Ibid., 18.
¹⁵ Perry, *The Thought*..., Vol. II, 735-6.
¹⁶ Vol. 84, "The Triadic Theory of Knowledge," 27.

theory of interpretation.[17] In one of his earlier essays James had illustrated his position by telling of a man lost in the woods faced with a choice between two paths that might lead him homeward. According to James, whichever path "works" to get the man home is of course the correct path for him to take. But, Royce asks, *how* does the man know on arrival that the path he traversed was the right one? Not merely by his (satisfied) perception of home, not by his remembered concept of home, not by his concept of the path he actually took, and not by any *combination* of conceptions or perceptions. The man, Royce asserts, can only know that he is home through a third cognitive process, viz., interpretation. At the journey's end the wayfarer compares his concept of the home he perceives with his concept of the path just travelled. From the comparison (not combination) of the two concepts, he interprets the truth of their relationship, and judges truly: That path was homeward bound. Such a statement is true because it expresses the whole of the experience which fulfilled the intent of the traveller.

Through the mention of "intent" or purpose we are reminded of a more specific contrast between Roycean interpretation and James's theory of truth. One of the inadequacies Royce laments in Jamesian pragmatism is its vagueness. While James claims "[a]n idea is true if it agrees with its expected workings,"[18] he remains unclear in regard to the meaning of those "expected workings." What he thereby implies, however, as in the case of the traveller lost in the woods, is an intention or purpose on the part of the knower, i.e., a will to interpret. Through his will to interpret a man intends his thought to agree with future experience; he determines what shall constitute the agreement that is the truth of his ideas. Without such determination, i.e., without a will to interpret, the mere notion of agreement or even "agreeable leading" is hopelessly obscure as a theory of truth or knowledge. As Royce would put it, some kind of voluntarism is essential to any adequate epistemology.

Moreover, by one's will acts one determines truth absolutely, not relatively. In the acts of intended agreement in which truth happens to ideas, irrevocable decisions of the will mark the truth it judges as unalterable, as absolute.[19] According to Royce, Jamesian pragmatism presupposes this ultimate quality in attributing absolute status to its claim that truth is relative.[20]

---

[17] Cf. *Ibid.*, 20.

[18] Vol. 83, Philadelphia Lectures, Lecture II (second copy), "Theoretical and Practical Truth" (1910 or later), 12.

[19] Cf. *Ibid.*

[20] Cf. Josiah Royce, *The Philosophy of Loyalty* (New York: The Macmillan Company, 1924; first published by Macmillan, 1908), 373: "[M]y friends, the recent pragmatists,

Although James would scarcely delight in Royce's interpretation of his pragmatism, he would have to concede that his idealist friend usefully employs that theory of truth to support the absolutism which Royce construes as yet more workable and practical.

Certainly both views of human knowing – James's and Bergson's – when coupled with their Roycean critique, contribute to our own understanding of interpretation as a third process of cognition. Now our own will to interpret Royce must examine more carefully what he means by that doctrine.

B. The Community of Interpretation

In the second volume of *The Problem of Christianity* Royce describes how interpretation differs from other cognitive theories:

> Interpretation, viewed as a mental process, or as a type of knowledge, differs from other mental processes and types of knowledge in the objects to which it is properly applied, in the relations in which it stands to these objects, and in the ends which it serves.[21]

Unlike perception, whose objects are particular sensible existents, and unlike conception, whose objects are abstract universals, interpretation addresses itself to objects accessible through neither of these means. Individual consciousness – whether our own, our neighbor's, even that of the Absolute – can never be known through mere perception and/or conception. Nor can the reality of community be known or achieved except through the process of interpretation. "Were there, then, no interpretations in the world, there would be neither selves nor communities."[22] Bergsonian intuition and Jamesian pragmatism are equally at a loss to explain the existence of or our awareness of either of these objects of knowledge.

But there are other instances for which Royce feels that only his theory of interpretation can render adequate account. Consider the following, for example, as both a literal and symbolic application of the Roycean view:

> A traveller crosses the boundary of a foreign country. To the boundary he comes provided, let us say, with the gold and with the bank-notes of his own country, but without any letter of credit. This side of the boundary his bank-notes are good because of their credit-value. His gold is good because, being the coinage of the realm, it possesses cash-value and is legal tender. But beyond the boundary, in the land to which he goes, the coin which he carries is no longer legal tender, and

---

reassert my theory of truth even in their every attempt to deny it." Hereafter references to this work are abbreviated to PL.
[21] PC, 275.
[22] PC, 274.

possibly will not pass at all in ordinary transactions. His bank-notes may be, for the moment, valueless, not because the promise stamped upon their face is irredeemable, but because the gold coin itself into which they could be converted upon presentation at the bank in question, would not be legal tender beyond the the boundary.[23]

At this point, then, a new process is indispensable if the traveller is to be able to conduct monetary transactions after crossing the border. It is a process which consists neither in the presentation of cash-values (cf. perceptions), nor in offering or accepting credit-values (cf. conceptions). Rather, it is a process of interpreting or translating cash-values recognized as such in one country into that which is similarly recognized in another, so that one might proceed to act upon the basis of the interpretation. Such interpreting involves an anticipation of that future experience in which one's present judgment may be empirically verified.

Money-changing thus provides an excellent example of what men often do in their efforts to communicate with one another. For while individuals can acquire knowledge of certain objects through perceptions, conceptions, or combinations of both, they cannot communicate and thereby learn *through one another* except through this third means of cognition. The relationship between the process and its objects is such that interpretation both requires and establishes a community of knowers through the media of signs. When the traveller reached the boundary some interpreting agent read the set of signs presented to him and translated that set into another.[24] As mediator, he acted as a unifying principle in establishing what Royce calls the community of interpretation. Hence, the third way of knowing is a necessarily social affair, in which the interpreter clearly plays the most essential part. The accuracy of his "translations" is always subject to the test of other minds in future experience.

The aim of interpretation is also social. In some form or other, its result is always more than an individual's growth in knowledge. Through its connective links between individuals and groups of individuals, interpretation produces a mutuality of understanding that was previously non-existent. The community it thereby creates is no mere collectivity, but a unity of social consciousness, a whole which is greater than the sum of its parts. According to Royce, to the extent that any human knowing activity involves this social and socializing element it is always an interpretive process. It is for this reason that interpretation is the key to Royce's mature notion of community.

Acknowledging his debt to Peirce and regretting that he had not earlier

[23] PC, 282.
[24] Cf. PC, 31-32.

realized the importance of "the Peircean 'interpretation' " Royce explicitates his theory as triadic.[25] Accordingly, the three members of the triad are the interpreter, the mind to which he addresses his interpretation, and the mind which he undertakes to interpret. The process can only occur through an exchange of signs, i.e., communication. To put it graphically,

```
Individual A:              Interpreter:              Individual B:
                            principle
   Sign A ──→ Sign A ←─────────────→ Sign B ←── Sign B
                            of unity
```

Community of Interpretation

An essential factor in the process is some principle of unity through which the translation or communication of signs is made possible. Then, using signs as media, the members of the triad may reciprocally interchange the roles of interpreter, interpretant, and interpreted through the ongoing process of interpretation. Since every "interpretation of a sign is, in its turn, the expression of the interpreter's mind, it constitutes a new sign, which again calls for interpretation: and so on without end."[26] The term sign is used by Royce as it was by Peirce in a very general sense. It may take the form of words, gesture or physical fact – in brief, whatever is subject to interpretation by a mind or minds for the sake of another (or other) mind(s). "A sign, then, is an object whose being consists in the fact that the sign calls for an interpretation."[27] The sign serves its interpretive purpose by associating an already-received meaning with the future fulfilment towards which it points.

In contrast with Bergsonian intuitionism and Jamesian pragmatism, Royce sees Peirce's triadic approach as constituting the missing link in their cognitive theories.

Peirce insists that the signs, viewed simply from a logical point of view, constitute a new and fundamentally important category. He sees this category as a "third," side by side with the classic categories of the "universals" which form the "first" category, and the "individuals," which, in Peirce's logic, form the "second" category.[28]

Peirce's notion of comparison or interpretation of signs thus presents the

---

[25] Unpublished letter to Reginald Chauncey Robbins, November 8, 1914, preserved at the Harvard Houghton Library.
[26] PC, 345.
[27] Ibid.
[28] Ibid.

logical basis for Royce's theory of knowledge.[29] To be consistent with his idealism, however, Royce had to apply Peirce's theory to the order of being as well as thought.[30] Accordingly, his metaphysical thesis asserts that the entire universe consists of signs and their interpretations. As Royce puts it,

[s]ince any idea, and especially any antithesis or contrast of ideas is, according to our metaphysical thesis, a sign which in the world, finds its real interpretation, our metaphysical theory may be called a "doctrine of signs."[31]

For the idealist, a world of interpretation is an essential correlate of interpretation as a theory of knowledge.

In elaborating upon the world of interpretation which emerges from this application of his doctrine, Royce explains that the differences among our true ideas, all of which derive from our experience of the world, are only explicable if we look upon the one world as subject of our diverse interpretations. The notion of interpretation is as pragmatic a theory in Royce as it is in Peirce in that it provides for relative differences in the truths that men acquire through their reference to future experience. According to Royce, therefore,

[t]he world as interpreted by me is a fact different from the world as interpreted by you: and these different interpretations have all of them their basis in the truth of things.[32]

Thus, the one world of interpretation is the basis for whatever truths the community of interpreters truly interpret – whether as individuals, as a group or groups. In Royce's own estimation, his doctrine is open to the greatest diversity and unity, precisely because he manages to combine Peircean pragmatic interpretation with his absolute idealism, retaining all the essential elements of both. "Here," he claims,

...is a theory that allows for endless variety of individual "interpretation," and for endless change, growth and fluency, while "absoluteness" is nevertheless a "chronosynoptic" and universal, above all and in all the flow and the tragedy of this world whose unity means that it "contains its own interpreter."[33]

---

[29] Royce uses both terms in explaining the same theory of Peirce. E.g., cf. PC, 344: "The method of interpretation is always the comparative method. To compare and to interpret are two names for the fundamental cognitive process." Cf. also Peirce's section on pragmatism as interpretation in CP V, #470-93.

[30] That Peirce regards his own theory of knowing as a realism is clear in his writings. See, e.g., CP V, #423: "[W]hat distinguishes it [Peirce's theory] from other species is... its strenuous insistence upon the truth of scholastic realism."

[31] PC, 346.

[32] PL, 78. Cf. Peirce's discussion of Truth as ideal and absolute: e.g., in CP V, # 416 and #494.

[33] Unpublished letter to Robbins, Nov. 8, 1914, Houghton.

Interpretation, then (according to his interpretation of it), is more than a theory of knowledge and more than a theory of nature. It is the entire philosophy of Royce, his "absolute pragmatism."

In the second chapter of the Introduction three factors in Peirce's philosophy were mentioned as affecting the development of a Roycean pragmatism, viz., the doctrine of signs, the theory of interpretation, and Peirce's insistence upon the communal nature of man's quest for truth. We have seen now that all three notions are involved in Royce's mature conception of knowledge. As already noted, the pragmatism of Peirce was certainly not the same as that of James, and as Royce himself observed, "James's Charles Peirce and mine were never, so to speak, the same man."[34] All three men interpreted each other in whatever way worked most practically in the context of their own philosophizing. In regard to their theories of knowing, however, it is apparent that Roycean pragmatism is closer to the view of Peirce than to that of James. The texts of this chapter clearly support that claim.

Moreover, as interpretation is a third principle, a mediating method in the philosophy of Peirce, it performs a similar pragmatic function in the thought of Royce. Not only does the Roycean triadic theory of interpretation close the gap left by other explanations of cognition; it also "fills up what is wanting" to individuals who compose the triad, mediating through a reference to future experience the value of the whole to each of its parts. Without such mediation, the limitation of man's nature, which Royce so often bemoans, can never be improved upon. Hence the importance of interpretation as a mediating principle. Without the reality of community that the mediation effects, no man and no group of men can achieve any individual or collective ideal. The interpretive process is thus a necessity to all human progress, whether intellectual or moral. "Whatever else men need," writes Royce, "they need their communities of interpretation."[35]

C. *The role of the mediator*

It has already been remarked that the interpreter plays the most essential part in the community of interpretation. In the act of interpreting he is the one who is responsible for the growth in knowledge which the comparison of ideas effects. Every comparison involves the awareness of similarities as well as differences between the objects being compared. Only when this

---

[34] Vol. 84, "Illustrations of the Philosophy of Loyalty" (1915?), 10. Cf. Chapter II *supra*.
[35] PC, 318.

awareness is complete does the process constitute genuine interpretation. But the comparison will always be incomplete and therefore not an interpretation if the ideas which are being compared are merely understood as separate conceptions, and not brought together into a new synthesis though the interpreter's mediation. It is for this reason that the interpreter must be a third and distinct member of the triad, one whose being involves more than the mere capacity to comprehend and translate signs, one who is capable through that transmission of establishing a larger and real unity of ideas, i.e., community.

One good example of the mediating role of the interpreter appears in an unpublished paper which Royce read to colleagues representing various departments of research in the natural sciences in 1914.[36] Therein Royce distinguishes between two general approaches of science and philosophy, viz., materialism and vitalism. The differences between the two is such that any kind of unifying comparison would seem unlikely if not impossible. Vitalism is associated with the historical knowledge of objects, i.e., single events occurring to individual existents (e.g., a free will act, or an observed eclipse). Materialism involves objects of mechanical knowledge, i.e., unchanging natural laws which govern individual variation.[37] Despite the difference between them, both doctrines are obviously important and useful to man. Moreover, there is a patent similarity here between their relationship and the perception/conception dualism. Neither the historical nor the mechanical method, nor both together can provide an adequate account of a type of object with which modern science deals most frequently, viz., "statistically defined assemblances."[38] The method through which we obtain our knowledge of such objects is statistics. According to Royce, then, the statistical type of knowledge involves neither single events nor invariant laws, but

the relatively uniform behavior of some average constitution, belonging to an aggregate of things and events, and the probability that this average behavior will remain, within limits, approximately, although always imperfectly uniform.[39]

In man's quest for useful knowledge, statistics thus becomes an interpreter or mediator. By comparing ideas, it reads the signs, then translates them

---

[36] Josiah Royce, "The Mechanical, the Historical and the Statistical," Unpublished paper read at Harvard Club of Boston, March 1, 1914, preserved at Harvard Houghton Library. Hereafter, MHS.
[37] Cf. HMS, 12.
[38] MHS, 10.
[39] MHS, 12.

into the field of experimental action. It does this by working with probability or averages, i.e., the mediating viewpoint of statistics. The statistical groupings it thereby forms and utilizes are what Royce would call the scientific community of interpretation.[40]

Some would probably contend that the statistical mediator is a rather dead or dry interpreter. Royce asserts quite strongly, however, that it is a process that touches the reality of human life, possibly even more than either vitalism or materialism through their historical and mechanical methods. "Mechanism," Royce maintains,

is rigid, but probably never exactly realized in nature. But life, although it has its history, has also its statistics. And averages cease to be dry when they are averages that express the unities and the mutual assimilations in which the common ideals and interests, the common hopes and destinies of the men of the social orders, of the deeds, – yes, and perhaps of the stars and of all the spiritual world are bound up and are expressed.[41]

Whether we apply his doctrine in science through statistics, or to any other area of human knowledge, Royce insists that his mediating method is a practical one. The precise point of comparison or interpretation is to teach "us how to deal with the living, with the significant, and with the genuinely real."[42] In so justifying his theory, Royce is clearly pragmatic, always emphasizing its usefulness in terms of an orientation towards future experience.

The mediating role of the interpreter is also evident in Royce's description of situations of "estrangement" involving "dangerous pairs" of individuals or groups.[43] Such instances occur whenever the separate interests or needs of the parties of a dyadic relationship are so distinct as to clash or oppose each other. Admittedly, in some real life situations where mediation is impossible, the differing members must learn to live with the consequent tension. In other cases, however, an interpreter can actually effect consolidation and establish harmony. Hence Royce claims:

One remedy for such estrangement... is the appearance of the fitting third person, real or ideal, who may act as Interpreter, as the Spirit of a new triadic Community of Interpretation. So, for instance, in the natural community of the family, the child, as natural member of the family, may act as a mediator in holding together the family union. So, in the commercial community, the banker or broker has, in the modern world, acted as mediator to unite by ties of far reaching significance,

---

[40] Cf. Peirce's notion of truth as the object of a scientific community of minds, and Chapter II *supra*.
[41] MHS, 33.
[42] PC, 308.
[43] Cf. Vol. 95, "Comments upon the Problem of the Mid-Year Examinations," 11, 12.

the members of the Dangerous Pair, which, in the ancient world, had to consist solely of borrower and lender.[44]

In short, Royce ascribes great importance to interpretation as a general formula through which "the estrangements of pairs may, in many cases, be healed through the presence, through the inventiveness, through the interpretations of some mediating third person or group."[45]

By means of the Roycean process, men are interpreters not only in regard to others but also in regard to themselves. In either case interpretation establishes a greater unity than had previously existed. Moreover, the separate members of the triad need not be distinct conscious selves. In order for a man to achieve the unity within himself that is the harmony of self-possession, his ideas of himself require an integrating self-interpretation. As regards other selves, it is clear that one can only indirectly, i.e., through mediation, arrive at an awareness of consciousnesses other than one's own. By introducing a third idea into the process of cognition, the interpreter employs a kind of "creative insight."[46] This is the element that effects the greater unity. In that the mediating idea is necessarily broader than the ideas that it compares, it illumines while synthesizing the other members of the triad.

It has already been mentioned that it is the will to interpret which forms the community of interpretation. This will is the directedness of the interpreter towards a final ideal unity. "Community" is thus both the goal and the means in Royce's theory of interpretation.[47] In either case the interpreter remains the most essential member of the triadic process, while fulfilling his mediating role. To function effectively in this capacity, certain ideal and seemingly contrasting qualities are demanded. Hence Royce observes that the interpreter, as

one who is, in ideal, this chief, is so because he is first of all servant... And his own ideas can "work" only if his self-surrender, and his conformity to ideas which are not his own, is actually a successful conformity; and only if his approach to a goal which, as member of a human community of interpretation, he can never reach, is a real approach.[48]

The role of the mediator is clearly not self-serving but other-serving. Since such selfless service can only be effected through love, the quality of one's

---

[44] *Ibid.*
[45] *Ibid.*
[46] PC, 307.
[47] The notion of community as end and means in Royce's philosophy is treated in greater detail in Chapter XI below. Also see my article in *Transactions of the Charles Peirce Society*, "Community in Royce: An Interpretation," Fall, 1969 (V, 4), 224-242.
[48] PC, 317.

love becomes a guage of his mediating and interpretive effectiveness. "God the Interpreter" who is limitless Love is thus the only absolute and perfect mediator.[49] Nonetheless, while no human interpreter is adequate to the ultimate communal ideal, every man, insofar as he himself realizes the spirit of the community(ies) to which he belongs, increases his own capacity for mediation.[50]

It was William James who described pragmatism as a method of settling disputes. It was Charles Peirce, the founder of pragmatism, who described interpretation as a theory of knowledge, and the quest for truth as a communal affair. All of these factors that were extremely significant to two leading American pragmatists were just as significant to the idealist Josiah Royce.

In the doctrine of interpretation which Royce came to only in his later philosophizing, a decidedly pragmatic orientation is in evidence. Interpretation serves the mediating function which James claims is proper to pragmatism; interpretation supports Peirce's assertion that pragmatism is a method through which the truth is sought by a community of minds, whose judgments arise from a reference to future consequences. In texts such as those of this chapter, a pragmatic element in the later cognitive theory of Royce is clearly in evidence. A comparison of these texts with those of Chapters III and VI validates the (admittedly interpretive) conclusion that the pragmatic factor of Royce's thought, i.e., its emphasis on future experience, became increasingly present as his philosophy developed.

---

[49] PC, 319.
[50] Cf. PC, 317.

CHAPTER X

GOD AS PRAGMATIC POSTULATE

Through some of the ideas expressed in *The Varieties of Religious Experience*, in the last of the Lowell Institute lectures, and in his essay "The Will to Believe," William James left himself open to Royce's translation of his views into absolute pragmatism. In all three places James's pragmatic characterization of truth as that which works, as that which leads to verification in experience, is utilized in support of the value of religious experience and belief.[1] For James himself, of course, the "absolute" remains a finite god. There is no need to postulate a highest being, since

all that the facts require is that the power should be both other and larger than our conscious selves. Anything larger will do if only it be large enough to trust for the next step.[2]

Insofar as the existence of God makes a practical difference in the concrete situation, Jamesian pragmatism endorses his existence with all the relative weight at its disposal.

Inevitably included in its endorsement, however, is Royce's Absolute, for this is an "anything larger" that makes more of a difference in the here and now than anything "less large" can make. The point of Royce in regard to James in their lifelong "battle of the Absolute" is that a merely finite god cannot be "large enough to trust for the next step." Nothing short of an absolute deserves such trust. Thus, dissatisfied with the impossibility of a prag-

---

[1] Note, e.g., in Prag, 192: "On pragmatistic principles, if the hypothesis of God works satisfactorily in the widest sense of the word, it is true. ... I firmly disbelieve, myself, that our human experience is the highest form of experience extant in the universe." Also, cf. Royce's doctrine of the Absolute with the characteristics with which James, in "The Will to Believe," claims a genuine option is endowed, viz., that it be forced, living and momentous. Another pertinent remark of James in this regard occurs in a letter to Mrs. Glendower Evans, from Cambridge, Dec. 11, 1906, quoted in Perry, *The Thought...*, Vol. II, 474: "There may *be* an Absolute, of course; and its pragmatic use to us is to make us optimistic."

[2] William James, *The Varieties of Religious Experience* (New York: Random House, Inc., 1929), p. 515.

matism without an absolute, Royce insists that the two notions are perfectly compatible. His absolute pragmatism is an effort to demonstrate their compatibility. The Absolute he thereby postulates becomes for Royce a more pragmatic god than that of James.

A. *The Absolute, filling our need for Truth, Reality, and a Cause*

In his own estimation, Royce's theory readily and wholly accords with the pragmatists' assertion that truth means "the fulfilment of a need."[3] In fact, he claims, absolute idealism "meets at once an ethical and a logical need."[4] It does this precisely because God, as pragmatic postulate, is Absolute Truth, Absolute Reality, and Absolute Cause.

As Absolute Truth, God satisfies a logical need of man. In *The Sources of Religious Insight*, absolute truth is defined as

the sort of truth that belongs to those opinions which, for a given purpose, counsel individual deeds, when the deeds in fact meet the purpose for which they were intended.[5]

Whether we admit it or not, Royce maintains, we all use the concept of absolute truth in the ordinary judgments and decisions of our daily lives, as well as in scientific inquiry and in the pursuit of ethical, metaphysical and religious interests.[6] To consider anything at all as true means to consider it absolutely so, since there is really "only one sort of truth."[7] When certain pragmatists claim that all truth is relative they are merely affirming a fact upon which the absolutist insists, viz., that all truths known to man are partial aspects of the eternal Truth which is their not-yet-fully realized End.[8] All our references to a temporal future necessarily imply a finally fulfilling future Experience. That man's grasp of the infinite absolute Truth is limited and relative is admittedly a matter of experience and, at the same time, a principal motivation for Royce's absolutism. Hence, the terms "absolute truth" and "truth" are actually redundant expressions. To call something "absolutely true," he says, "really means no more than ought to be meant by calling it 'true.'"[9] It is true through its participation in the Absolute.

[3] PL, 346.
[4] PL, 376.
[5] SRI, 157. Note the attribution of the term *opinions* to the content of absolute truth.
[6] Cf. Vol. 83, Philadelphia Lectures, 1910 or later, Lecture I, "The Nature and the Use of Absolute Truth" (second copy), 1.
[7] *Ibid.*, 8.
[8] Cf. WJO, 237: "We can define the truth even of relativism only by asserting that relativism is after all absolutely true."
[9] Vol. 83, Philadelphia Lecture I, "The Nature and the Use of Absolute Truth," (second copy) 8.

Royce attributes the absoluteness or irreversibility of truth to two factors, both associated with his theory of knowledge by interpretation, and therefore also with his notion of community. The first is based upon the relation between the hypothetical premises of a reasoning process. If the assertion of any hypothesis is true, it is always and irrevocably true. It is absolutely true because it is purely hypothetical, and consequently cannot be affected by changing experience or empirical facts. In mathematics, for example, deduction may lead "to an absolutely correct and irrevocably true discovery of a relation of implication between exactly stated premises and some conclusion."[10] The ideas compared suggest to the observant reasoner an interpretation which, if it applies at all, must apply universally.

The second reason that an assertion may be absolutely true is that it counsels the one who makes an interpretation to do some determinate and individual deed. Once done, the deed is irrevocable, and the truth which motivated it is therefore shown as absolute, as changeless. For

[i]f, by interpreting your ideas in a certain way, at a certain moment, you have been led to do a worthy deed, – then the interpretation remains as irrevocably true as the good deed remains irrevocably done.[11]

In this way Royce identifies irrevocability with absoluteness, claiming that the value and truth of one's acts of interpretation arise from "an insight which surveys, as from above, an unity wherein are combined various ideas."[12] The ideas themselves, defined here as "pragmatic leadings," are interpreted, verified, and synthesized in experience. The insight into unity which enables man to combine these ideas is an insight into the Roycean Absolute.

Further, Royce contends that actual verification of the ideas can take place as the future unfolds only through the experience of a community, or more specifically, through that of the community of interpretation. Since the ideas of interpreters are not verifiable unless there is an absolute, both the community and the Absolute are indispensable elements to verification through interpretation. For such a goal as Absolute Truth

is essentially the experience of a community; and the success, – the salvation, the final truth of each idea, or of each individual person, that enters into this community, is due (when the goal is reached) neither to its "works" nor to its workings, but to its essential spiritual unity in and with the community.[13]

[10] PC, 311.
[11] Ibid.
[12] Ibid.
[13] PC, 329.

The essential spiritual unity of which Royce speaks is thus a fundamentally social and absolute reality. Only as such can it meet the requirements of his absolute pragmatism.

As Absolute Reality, God satisfies an ethical need in man. In *The Sources of Religious Insight* Royce describes absolute reality as "the sort of reality that belongs to irrevocable deeds."[14] As with Truth, man comes to an awareness of the absoluteness of reality only with the aid of interpretation and community. Through that process, one first must recognize that his own existence is inseparably bound up with that of others as community:

> My life means nothing, either theoretically or practically, unless I am a member of a community. This community, then, is real whatever is real. And in that community my life is interpreted.[15]

Then, looking at his neighbor, man postulates the neighbor's existence, because he knows him as another mind which interprets. "You are a real being," he says, knowing him as such only because he has experienced a genuine communal relationship with the neighbor.[16] Next, looking at the world, man exclaims to it: "I know that you are real, because my life needs and finds its interpreter. You, O World, are the interpretation of my existence."[17] Finally, the ultimate interpretation that one makes is to postulate the reality of the Absolute which Royce in the end identifies with Community. "This essentially social universe," he writes, "this community which we have now declared to be real, and to be, in fact, the sole and supreme reality, – [is] the Absolute."[18] Without this Absolute, nothing else is real, and nothing is true. Hence, without the community of interpretation which we experience as a fact of existence, we could know neither the truth nor the reality of the Absolute.

With an infinite God as its pragmatic postulate, Royce's idealism merges Absolute Truth and Absolute Reality into the God of his absolute pragmatism. The usefulness and even the necessity of postulating the Absolute arises from Royce's conviction that "absolute reality and absolute truth are the most concrete and practical and familiar of matters."[19] Such a Being must be

---

[14] SRI, 157.
[15] PC, 357.
[16] Cf. PC, 358.
[17] PC, 358.
[18] PC, 350.
[19] SRI, 157. Cf. WJO, vi: "As to the defense of the concept of "absolute truth"... I may at once say that "the absolute" seems to me personally not something remote, impractical, inhuman, but the most pervasive and omnipresent and practical, as it is also the most inclusive of beings. "Absolute truth" has therefore a distinctly and intensely practical import."

infinite in order to accommodate man's need for a total final Unity of all Thought and Experience.

As Absolute Cause, God satisfies another of man's ethical needs, viz., his need of acting with direction. Because of its relationship to the Absolute as both Thinker and Doer, Truth and reality, "Cause" is perhaps the most appropriate designation for the Roycean Absolute in his later thought. Moreover, since it is as Cause that the Absolute evokes man's practical response, it is here that Royce most clearly illustrates that his notion of God is a pragmatic postulate. From anticipation of the total final fulfilment towards which they are directed, present actions derive their value and validity. The relevance of their orientation towards an immediate future practice arises from that final reference to the Absolute as final Cause.

The practical posture through which men relate to the Absolute as Cause is loyalty. Actually, the two notions are inseparable in their reality as well as in idea. Loyalty ultimately implies an Absolute Cause, even as that Cause implies loyalty. Together, the point of relevance that they stress is man's necessary relatedness to God and God's to man. It is as the final and universal Cause of loyalty that God makes a difference in the day to day living of individuals and groups, eliciting the active gestures that contribute to the final fulfilment of his Will. A single directedness on the part of many or all individuals is possible only through the existence of one absolute Cause. Because he exists as their ultimate End, men can, through their own loyal acts of will, actually constitute the unity of the world. Human loyalty is their "will to manifest, so far as is possible, the Eternal, that is the conscious and superhuman unity of life, in the form of the acts of an individual Self."[20] Through this practical loyalty, the Roycean Absolute is taken from a plane of abstraction and touched to the concrete reality of life.

Summarily, Royce claims that the pragmatic value to be derived from his conception of God as absolute Truth, absolute Reality, and absolute Cause consists of the following facts:

First, the rational unity and goodness of the world – life; next, its true but invisible nearness to us, despite our ignorance; further, its fulness of meaning despite our barrenness of present experience; and yet more, its interest in our personal destiny as moral beings; and finally, the certainty that, through our actual human loyalty, we come, like Moses, face to face with the true will of the world, as a man speaks to his friend.[21]

Admittedly, our conception of the Absolute can be a mere abstraction, to-

---

[20] PL, 357. (Italics omitted.)
[21] PL, 390. (Italics omitted.)

tally impractical and unrelated to life. If we befriend him through loyalty, however, so that he is no longer an abstraction but a living personal Cause of our own being and the being of the world, guiding our present judgments through a reference to future experience, such loyalty makes it practically possible to fill up what is wanting of truth and reality – for ourselves and others. Such loyalty is the only adequate practical response to the Roycean Absolute.

B. Solving the religious paradox

As propadeutic to this study of Royce his notion of religion was described as one involving man's general awareness of his need to be saved.[22] It seems obvious that the awareness of one's need for salvation necessarily entails the consciousness of an ideal to be reached. Concurrence of need and ideal in turn provoke the hope for some assistance in translating the need situation into a realized ideal. Man's basic optimism is his hope for such deliverance. Thus the three objects of man's religious awareness are his need, his ideal, and his deliverer. In every different type of religion, all three objects are in some way expressed. The diversity of those expressions illustrates the means that men employ in their efforts to solve the "religious paradox."

To Royce the religious paradox, a paradox that every man must face in life, is the "Paradox of Revelation."[23] In keeping with his intent to remain on a philosophical rather than a theological level, he defines revelation quite generally as "whatever intercourse there may be between the divine and the human."[24] Presumably, revelation points the way to bridge the gap between religious need (as human) and religious ideal (as divine). For man's ultimate ideal is indeed divine, in the sense of "superhuman" or "supernatural," i.e., in the sense in which its being must transcend what is merely human and natural in order that it might meet needs arising from man's inevitable limitedness.[25]

But how can revelation do this? Or how can man with his finite intelligence ever relate to the divine? According to Royce, the paradox that arises whenever man becomes conscious of his need and his ideal is

that a being who is so ignorant of his duty and of his destiny as to need guidance at every point, so weak as to need saving, should still hope, in his fallible experience, to get into touch with anything divine. The question is, how is this possible?[26]

[22] See Chapter I, section B *supra*.
[23] SRI, 20.
[24] SRI, 19.
[25] Cf. SRI, 266-8.
[26] SRI, 25.

Clearly, the paradoxicalness of the paradox hinges upon the two prior considerations of need and ideal. It presupposes that man's principal religious motives are so perfectly natural and human that they require no mysterious movings from another world to explain their presence in our lives. Moreover, these very motives "force us to seek for relief from spiritual sources that cannot satisfy unless they are far above our natural human level of life – that is, unless they are in some definable sense superhuman."[27] As Royce views them, both considerations, i.e., religious need and religious ideal, bear the testimony of experience in support of their reality. Together they comprise the paradox which is "one of the deepest facts in all religious history and experience, ...the paradox of being thoughtfully alive in any sense whatever."[28] Once we accept this religious paradox as a fact, however, the fundamental questions it entails persists: How can mere man obtain the power to transcend himself, i.e., "to get into a genuine touch with a real life that is above his own level?"[29]

The simple answer to Royce's question is that no mere man can do it. In fact no group of men can do it. That revelation itself is a form of individual religious experience is a point in which Royce concurs with William James. Unlike his colleague, however, Royce insists that the religious experience is also social. Although the social element offers some criterion for judging the veracity of revelation, social experience alone is not finally enough. If we are ever actually to engage in intercourse with the divine in such a way as to be empowered thereby to realize our religious ideals, we cannot do this apart from divine assistance. In some way, then, we must "come into touch with a Power or a Spirit that is in some true sense not-Ourselves."[30] Through contact with him, we can transcend the boundaries of experience that is merely individual or merely human. This Other, Royce writes,

must be in some sense the Master of Life, the Might that overcometh the world, the revealer of final truth.[31]

Without ceasing to be personal and intimate, our experience must in some way come into "direct touch" with this Other, who is the absolute and total fulfilment of all our finite experiences.[32] We must be able to anticipate that future fulfilment even as we form our present judgments in the light of their

[27] SRI, 41-2.
[28] SRI, 21.
[29] SRI, 43.
[30] SRI, 32.
[31] *Ibid.*
[32] *Ibid.* Note again the pantheistic strain of thought in Royce.

orientation towards a temporal future. To Royce, a sense of transcendence is grounded in such anticipation.

When he asserts the possibility of men coming into "direct touch" with the divine, Royce necessarily implies that revelation – at least some form or forms of it – is grounded in experience, i.e., in religious experience. As a man becomes experientially aware of his need and ideal of salvation he may similarly become conscious of the reality of divine assistance, i.e., the presence of a deliverer. In fact, Royce contends, were a person never to have such a religious experience, his path to salvation would be seriously impeded.

[U]nless, in moments of peace, of illumination, of hope, of devotion, of inward vision, you have seemed to feel the presence of your Deliverer, unless it has sometimes *seemed* to you as if the way to the home land of the spirit were opened to your sight by a revelation as from the divine, unless this privilege has been yours, the way to a higher growth in insight will be slow and uncertain to you.[33]

For our absolute idealist, then, all genuine religious progress must be rooted in religious experience.

Ultimately, the entire history of man involves the solving of the religious paradox. As finite and as temporal, human solutions never adequately bridge the gap between the ideal and the real. Life itself in its unfolding is the solving, and the End of life is the final Solution. Interpretation is again the means through which men approach the Answer to the paradox, an answer whose adequateness lies in the fact that it is the very Being of the Absolute as Interpreter. If, then,

we aim to conceive the divine nature, how better can we conceive it than in the form of the Community of Interpretation, and above all in the form of the Interpreter, who interprets all to all, and each individual to the world. . ..[34]

Through such an Interpreter all the paradoxes of life find their solution.

C. Christianity as interpretation of man's experience

As awareness of the religious paradox is based upon experience, so also in the course of history man finds ways of interpreting that experience. The various religions of the world result from the differing interpretations. In surveying their diversity, however, Royce finds several characteristics held in common. These, he claims, are essential to their vitality, and to the validity of any interpretation of man's religious experience.

[33] SRI, 33-4.
[34] PC, 318.

In the more primitive religions, Royce observes that religious practices are regarded as paramount. Cults and rituals take precedence over any kind of religious theorizing or indoctrination. As a result, if and whenever a group's religious practices die out, "the nation in question either dwindles, or is conquered, or passes over into some new form of social order."[35] Higher religions, on the other hand, rate belief and doctrine as more essential than religious practices, thereby placing the greater emphasis upon the inner life of the believer. Practices are not ignored, but they follow upon faith as a necessary expression of belief. The frequent consequence of such procedure, however, is that the practices multiply and gradually lose contact with the religious doctrine that initially provoked them. The conflict that then arises is the old familiar one between faith and merely external works.

As a rule, the higher religions endeavor to settle the conflict between formal observance and genuine faith rather pragmatically, drawing the differing emphases together through a broader interpretation of religion in general. Hence,

[t]he proposed solution which is most familiar, most promising, if it can be won, and most difficult to be won, is the solution which consists in asserting and of showing, if possible, in life, that what is most vital to religion is not practice apart from faith, nor faith apart from practice, but a complete spiritual reaction of the entire man... In a word, what this solution supposes to be most vital to the highest religion is the union of faith and works through a completed spirituality.[36]

Christianity is obviously one of those higher religions which has proposed its own solution to the conflict. Since the Christian tradition is at very least an impressive historical interpretation of man's religious experience, it deserves serious philosophical consideration.[37]

According to Royce, there are three possible attitudes with which one might consider Christianity, viz., that of an apologist, that of an adversary, and that of a questioner.[38] Following his own proclivity towards mediation, Royce chooses the last of the three, hoping thereby to preserve the positive elements of the other two attitudes. The position that emerges is his approach to a "problem." Since all religions are "problematic" in the sense that their content is not fully understood, the adequacy of their interpretive solutions to the religious paradox not only can but should be questioned. The proper task of the philosopher of religion is to direct such questioning in the

---

[35] Josiah Royce, "What is Vital in Christianity?" *Harvard Theological Review* 2 (1909), 418. Hereafter, WVC.
[36] WVC, 419.
[37] Cf. PC, 64.
[38] Cf. PC, 59-61.

interest of clarifying and extending man's understanding of religious experience. In particular, because the Christian religion represents a major historical interpretation of man's solution to the religious paradox, Royce addresses his attention to the problem of Christianity.

Basically, the problem is what it has always been in regard to all religions, viz., to examine what is most essential to religious doctrine and religious practice in order to synthesize the two in applying them effectively to the entire life of man. While the Founder of Christianity is a historical figure, the life of Christians is an ongoing process. Religious truths are transmitted to each successive age only through this living process. Whatever is vital in Christianity, therefore, must be more than a set body of doctrine. If it is truly to influence the lives of Christians in a changing world, theory must affect practice in the here and now. More precisely, Royce puts the problem in the form of a question:

> When we consider what are the most essential features of Christianity, is the acceptance of a creed that embodies these features consistent with the lessons that, so far as we can yet learn, the growth of human wisdom and the course of the ages have taught man regarding religious truth?[39]

In other words, the problem of Christianity is to discern what is essentially vital within it, so that it will be neither mere theory nor mere practice but a total way of living for people who are themselves both theoretical and practical. Its task is to orientate its theory towards future experience.

In attempting an answer to the problem, Royce observes that Christianity has always had two principal and contrasting characteristics. The first is that it was initially taught and lived out by an individual person, "a man who dwelt among men, who counselled a mode of living, who aroused and expressed a certain spirit, and who taught that in this spirit, and in this life, the way of salvation is to be found for all men."[40] The second characteristic is that the teachings and life of this man have always been the subject of interpretation by those who were (and are) his followers (as also by those who were and are not). Royce remarks that

> [w]hatever the reason why the Master and the interpretation of his person and of his teaching have come to be thus contrasted, it is necessary at once to call attention to the historical fact that such an interpretation of the Master, of his person, and of his mission, always has existed ever since there was any Christian religion at all.[41]

---

[39] PC, 65.
[40] *Ibid.*
[41] PC, 66.

Historically, then, Christian traditions have consistently held to a distinction between their interpretation of the Master and the Master himself. What Jesus said and did has never been construed as identical with any one Christian interpretation.

In examining which of the two characteristics is more vital to the Christian religion Royce notes that Jesus himself lived his own interpretation of his mission, and that Christianity itself would never have survived till now except through Christians' interpretation of that interpretation. Thus the historical Founder is not so essential to our understanding of the problem of Christianity as are the communities of interpretation through whom his teachings have been transmitted to successive generations. Revelation, as whatever intercourse exists between the divine and human, continues only through such communities of interpretation.

Included in all the Christian interpretations of the ages are three ideas which Royce considers the essence of Christianity. Summarily, these three – that of the Community, of the Lost Individual, and of the Atonement – represent man's effort to explain his felt religious need, his religious ideal, and his hope for assistance in bridging the gap between the two.[42] Together they comprise the Christian explanation of the objects of any man's religious experience.

1. *The Community*

Since this topic is treated rather extensively in the next chapter, it is sufficient here merely to mention that there are several notions of community that the mature thought of Royce encompasses. As an essentially Christian idea, community refers primarily to "the spiritual community in union with which man is to win salvation."[43] Without membership in such a community salvation is impossible. The motivation and power for relating individual Christians to one another so that a community is actually formed is their love or loyalty for the Cause who is Christ. Hence, while "the Christian community is itself something visible," it can only be realized through the presence of Christ in the midst of its members.[44] In God's becoming man, for Christians, man, through community, becomes God in the sense that he is thereby directed and empowered towards final union with the Absolute, i.e., with a God who is himself a Community of persons. Community thus becomes the Christian interpretation of mankind's basic religious ideal.

[42] PC, 50.
[43] PC, 74.
[44] Cf. PC, 94, 95.

2. *The Lost Individual*

The second essentially Christian idea which Royce considers is expressed as follows:

The individual human being is by nature subject to some overwhelming moral burden from which, if unaided, he cannot escape. Both because of what has technically been called original sin, and because of the sins that he himself has committed, the individual is doomed to a spiritual ruin from which only a divine intervention can save him.[45]

In other words, the Christian interpretation of the religious need of man takes the form of its doctrine of original sin and its teaching on human sinfulness in general. Because man recognizes his own proneness to sin, because he realizes that salvation is inaccessible to him as a mere individual (i.e., unaided by the "divine intervention" that Christians call "grace"[46]), he is subject to the moral burden that arises from such self-awareness. It is an awareness, however, that has both empirical and social roots, as well as a directedness towards future experience.

In explaining what he means by the moral burden of the individual Royce repeatedly refers to the seventh chapter of Paul's Letter to the Romans, where the apostle describes the moral experience of struggle between the "inner" and the "outer" man. "My inner being delights in the law of God," writes Paul. "But I see a different law at work in my body – a law that fights against the law that my mind approves of."[47] Royce points out that what Paul depicts here is the common lot of humankind, whether they are believers or not. For all men, as their social consciousness develops, are influenced by the society in which they live. A moral conscience is always formed through social contrast: one hears or reads of laws or rules of conduct that other men or groups of men have advocated; one feels inclined at times to go against such laws. Eventually, one becomes so socially cultivated through his environment that he cannot merely ignore or repudiate the rules of society without experiencing a certain moral tension. As a matter of fact, the more a person is involved in this process of social formation, the more sensitive he will be to its precisions and prescriptions, the more responsible he will feel, and possibly the more tension he will be required to sustain.[48]

---

[45] PC, 100. Royce's mention here of original sin portends what was suggested earlier, that although he intends to keep his reflections within the realm of philosophy he does not succeed in doing so.

[46] Royce uses both of these terms in describing the Christian idea of redemption in PC, Ch. IV. It is apparently another indication of departure from philosophy into theology.

[47] Rom. 7:22, 23.

[48] Cf. PC, 111 and 113.

The truth which man's experience of moral tension discloses is that of our inevitable limitation as individuals. While Royce often claims empirical grounding for human limitation in regard to knowledge, he here asserts it with equal force in regard to the moral life of individuals. An encouraging factor present in the real situation, however, is that the moral burden, while felt by each individual as individual, is also a universally felt need. As long as there are finite conscious selves in the world, no individual man is alone in feeling and in being so burdened. Moreover, the universality of the condition is precisely what motivates the hope by which men live. For faced with the bare fact that the individual by himself is unable to achieve salvation, men must find ways to transcend their limitation. In the Christian interpretation of their religious ideal as divine, the means to be discovered must be adequate to their ultimate End which is the Absolute.

3. *The Atonement*

According to Royce the third leading idea of Christianity is the one that many modern minds regard as hardest to accept. This idea is expressed in the assertion that

[t]he only escape for the individual, the only union with the divine spiritual community which he can obtain, is provided by the divine plan for the redemption of mankind. And this plan is one which includes an Atonement for the sins and for the guilt of mankind.[49]

The "hard" and unpopular elements included in the doctrine are the notions of sin and guilt. Despite their unattractiveness, however, man's consciousness of their reality is so universal an experience that if there were no Christian idea of atonement, something like it "would have to be invented, before the higher levels of our moral existence could be fairly understood."[50] As a matter of fact, in ordinary human life, frequent instances of atonement occur, in which one does experience the meaning of "deliverance." According to Royce, in order truly to appreciate such instances we must first understand what he means by "treason."[51]

Actually, an act of treason is what constitutes "sin." The act is necessarily not that of a mere individual, but of a social being who realizes his social-

---

[49] PC, 73.
[50] PC, 165. Actually the empirical rooting of the idea stems not from moral conduct in itself but from man's consciousness about that conduct. Cf. PC, 110: "Paul's main thesis about our moral burden relates not to our conduct, but to our consciousness about our conduct."
[51] For a more extended treatment than that given here, see PC, Chapter V.

ness. It is an act freely performed by one who has established ties with other persons, and then deliberately broken them, anticipating the consequences. No one who has not at one time recognized the value of fidelity can subsequently be unfaithful. No one who has not first been loyal can be disloyal. Consequently, no one ever perceives as clearly as the traitor the horrendousness of his own infidelity. This perception is at the same time his awareness of the need for atonement. Any experience in life (infidelity in marriage may be the most common example) in which one knows himself to have deliberately betrayed the trust of another or others – is a situation that calls for atonement.

The atonement itself is a triumph over treason. It is not mere penal satisfaction, or forgiveness, or repentance. Neither can it be identified with the love which often prompts it and accompanies it. For atonement is a positive creative act in its own right, unique in that it effects a righting which is in fact a new being. This new being could never have existed at all had a betrayal not taken place. Hence, through the atoning act

[t]he world, as transformed by this creative deed, is better than it would have been had all else remained the same, but had that deed of treason not been done at all.[52]

Retrospectively, one learns through treason that freedom is essential to human fidelity. If faith were never broken, the individual might not realize this. So, writes Royce, all men are free, frail and capable of loyalty – but unless the individual recognizes all three traits within himself, he cannot meaningfully be faithful. One must know his freedom to be freely faithful. "And especially," he adds, "must those who are freely loyal possess a certain freedom to become faithless if they choose."[53]

Certainly, the Christian idea of atonement comprises all the notes of human atoning experiences. In positing Christ, a God-man, as the redeemer, Christianity purports to explain the connection between the treason of humankind which the sin of Adam represents and the new being of man and his world which was made possible through the atoning work of Christ. Christian redemption is more, then, than an illustration of reconciliation between God and humanity; it is the birth of a new kind of life for man, a life brought into being through the power of divine love.

That Christ as God and man performs the work of atonement for men is a central doctrine of Christianity. Through his redemption, men can overcome their own moral limitation as individuals and achieve their ultimate communal End. Because Christ is God and therefore Absolute, however,

---

[52] PC, 180. (Italics omitted.)
[53] PC, 177.

men cannot precisely define the function of his divinity in regard to the redemptive act. Under this aspect, the Christian idea of atonement is best expressed through symbol. On the other hand, the human aspect of redemption is best expressed through the practical postulate that adequate atonement is possible and hoped for. The motivation for our present striving is the expectation of a future at-oneness with God. Coupling both the symbol and the practical postulate, we have an apt description of the role of Christ as deliverer.

As a Christian idea, the atonement is expressed in a symbol, whose divine interpretation is merely felt, and is viewed as a mystery. As a human idea, atonement is expressed by a peculiarly noble and practically efficacious type of human deeds... The Christian symbol and the practical postulate are two sides of the same life, – at once human and divine.[54]

Christ as God and man is the perfect mediator. The Absolute, through its Christian interpretation of Christ as Deliverer, becomes an extremely practical postulate for the life of man, providing a present means for obtaining final future fulfilment.

Even from this brief discussion of the essential ideas of Christianity it is evident that the three are interrelated. Royce formulates their interrelatedness and suggests a synthesizing view through his principle of loyalty.[55] The "Community" (ultimately, the Absolute), he asserts, is the object to which loyalty is due. The "Lost State" of the individual is the condition of those who have never discovered or who have broken the ties to others (or Other) which loyalty establishes. "Atonement" may be considered the process through which men seek to form (or to reestablish) an at-oneness with others (or the Other). Thus loyalty becomes the key to our understanding of Christianity as a valid and useful interpretation of human experience.

The title of this chapter now deserves further elucidation. In an effort to discern the development of a Roycean pragmatism, his doctrine has necessarily been interpreted to suit that purpose. Consequently, in treating Royce's mature notion of the Absolute the practical use to which he put that concept has been stressed. References to God as "postulate" are not intended to suggest that Royce himself considered God's existence merely hypothetical. His early claim to having adequately demonstrated the existence of the Absolute continued (although differently expressed) through the middle and late writings. On the other hand, leaving aside the question of whether Royce

[54] PC, 186.
[55] Cf. PC, 50.

actually succeeded in demonstrating the existence of God, his notion of the Absolute can surely be accepted as a postulate. As such it performed for Royce himself several practical functions in regard to man. For the Absolute, as interpreted by our idealist, is the Truth because of which all other truths work, the Reality which satisfies man's present needs, and the Cause which grounds his hope. God – as Royce interprets him through Christianity, i.e., as also man in Christ, – is the mediator par excellence, who makes it practically possible for man to bridge the gap between his needs and his ideals. In all these ways – whether or not his existence has satisfactorily been "proved," the God who is the Roycean Absolute can most certainly be accepted as pragmatic postulate, i.e., as a notion which involves an essential emphasis on future experience.

CHAPTER XI

COMMUNITY AS PERFECTIVE OF THE INDIVIDUAL

We have come now to that notion in Royce's later philosophy which he himself regarded as his main metaphysical tenet. Even a cursory reading of the early, middle and mature works indicates that his later considerations of the individual self and the Absolute gradually diminish by contrast with an increasing emphasis upon the community and the spirit of community. In the autobiographical remarks delivered after a dinner in his honor in 1915, Royce expressed the judgment that his entire life, although he had not always realized it, had gravitated around the notion of community.

When I review this whole process, I strongly feel that my deepest motives and problems have centred about the Idea of the Community, although this idea has only come gradually to my clear consciousness.[1]

The claim is as applicable to Royce's personal life as it is to his philosophical pursuit. From the early days in San Francisco where he was first introduced to "the majesty of the community" through the pranks and teasings of his school friends, on through the rest of his life, Royce retained a natural reticence in regard to mixing with others, along with a very real moral and intellectual appreciation for community. In his own experience, then, he knew the tension between inner and outer man resulting from a dispositional shyness and even an inborn "non-conformism."[2] As a matter of fact, Royce confesses himself rather a poor contributor in communal efforts such as team play, politics, and committee work. "Over against this natural ineffectiveness in serving the community," however,

and over against this rebellion there has always stood the interest which has taught me what I nowadays try to express by teaching that we are saved through the community.[3]

[1] HGC, 129. Cf. Moses Judah Aronson, *La philosophie morale de Josiah Royce* (Paris: Librairie Félix Alcan, 1927), xiii: "La philosophie de Josiah Royce gravite autour de l'idée de la communauté." Note also John Smith, *The Spirit of American Philosophy*, 84.
[2] Cf. HGC, 124: "I was a born non-conformist."
[3] HGC, 130-1.

In his own estimation, at least part of the motivation for the philosophical interests in which community eventually came to figure so centrally was his natural propensity towards filling up what seemed lacking in his own experience and personality.

The motivation was certainly not only dispositional, however. It was equally in keeping with Royce's consistent awareness of human fallibleness and limitation, and with his idealistic desire to find ways of achieving intellectual and moral progress. "No individual," he contended, "can set his personal ideals too high."[4] But neither can those ideals be achieved by the individual alone: one needs others to facilitate their attainment. Moreover, in regard to groups of individuals, no community can set its ideals too high: achievement of any communal ideal depends upon the individual cooperative efforts of those who form the community. In order practically to effect the transition between human needs and human ideals, community and individuality are both necessary.

Another motivational factor for Royce's emphasis on community was his desire to acquire objectivity in regard to truth and values. Here our idealist draws upon the Peircean notion that such objectivity can only be reached through a community of minds working to achieve it.[5] Individual judgments cannot be objective unless they are made within a social context, a context which may exist even when our judgments seem most private or subjective. Thus, regarding a possible conflict of values, Royce writes the following:

> My valuation is subjective; it depends upon my personal point of view. My opponent's valuation is subjective; it depends upon his personality and his plans. But the fact that both are valuations determines values which whether we personally recognize them or no are as real in the world of one of us, as they are in the world of the other; and the truth that these valuations of ours are facts in the same world of values: this truth, I say is objective, it exists apart from either of us, apart from both of us.[6]

In other words, subjectivity can be transcended through the intersubjective relationships which constitute community. Only through such social ties can the difficulties inherent in a Jamesian individualism be overcome.

Related to Royce's concern for objectivity is the voluntaristic element

---

[4] "Provincialism," *Putnam's Magazine* (November, 1909), 239.

[5] Cf. Vol. 84, "An untitled paper," 1915?, 56a: "Some of you who hear this account may ask how this doctrine of Charles Peirce's differs from what William James taught as Pragmatism. ... I can say at once that in so far as I understand James, his theory of truth was in its essence very highly individualistic."

[6] Vol. 76, Urbana Lectures 1907, Lecture I, "The Problem of Ethics," 36.

which is woven through his entire philosophy. In the first of his Urbana Lectures on ethics, Royce defines the individual person as "a being with a will of his own."[7] It is precisely because of will that objective values exist at all, whether for individuals or for communities. For

[t]he world of values and the world of wills are logically inseparable. . . . Facts without persons are empty of significance, as the dark room is empty of visible meaning.[8]

Moreover, in manifesting the voluntarism so essential to his personality, the individual necessarily expresses a certain dissatisfaction with himself which points towards the possibility of fulfilment. "This very discontent," Royce writes, "I myself am."[9] Ultimately, the discontent that all of humankind experiences is directed towards the Absolute as the only Being that can adequately fulfill all wants. Whether advertently or not, then, human will acts always indicate the reality of some relationship with God. Each decision of the individual necessarily entails the assertion: "This is my link with God, that now I am discontent with the expression of my personality."[10] In all of our finite selves the Absolute is discontented with his own temporal manifestation. In each self also, insofar as he acknowledges the existence of the Absolute, lies a fundamental trust or optimism that the finite will which reaches towards infinity will one day be completely satisfied. This basic hope is the grounding for our notion of community.

A. Community in general

In the fall semester of a class in metaphysics at Harvard in 1910, Royce developed the following tentative definition of a community: "An expression of Ideas whose being consists in the conscious cooperation of many selves whose cooperation and mutual distinction are both marked and important."[11] Here he expresses two of the requisites for genuine community which he elaborated upon in the (1913) Oxford lectures: communication (conscious cooperation) and distinctness of selves. However, what is not spelled out in the definition (but perhaps presupposed) is actually the most important factor of all, and one which he had written much about already, viz., the

---

[7] *Ibid.*, 9-10.
[8] *Ibid.*, 10.
[9] "Immortality," *Hibbert Journal*, 'July, 1907) 741.
[10] *Ibid.*
[11] From the notebook of E. W. Friend for his metaphysics course taught by Royce, 1913-14, preserved at Harvard University Archives. The entry cited is dated Dec. 9, and titled "Tentative Definition of a Community."

principle of union among the various selves who compose a community.[12]

Because of his appreciation for community as an ultimate goal, i.e., as a not-yet existing reality, Royce refrains from enunciating a precise definition of "community." Nonetheless, his later attempt to explicate the term (in *The Problem of Christianity*) serves to clarify the first formulation. There he names three conditions as essential to the existence of any real community, anytime and anywhere. The first requisite is an integrated individuality, or rather two or more such integrated individualities. Community is founded upon "the power of an individual self to extend his life, in ideal fashion, so as to regard it as including past and future events which lie far away in time, and which he does not now personally remember."[13] Each self is the present reality of a particular past and a particular future, the interpreter of what has been and will be in his own unique regard. It is precisely from his own unrepeatable individuality that a man contributes to the greater wealth that is community.

The second condition for true community is communication among the various selves. This is not something that happens automatically, for "a community does *not* become one . . . by virtue of any reduction or melting of these various selves into a single merely present self, or into a mass of passing experience."[14] Rather the existence of community depends upon the fact that there are in the social world a number of distinct selves who are not only capable of social communication, but also generally engaged in such communication.

The last requisite is a principle of unity through which the individuals involved share a common past and/or a common future. In regard to their past, the group constitutes a community of memory; in regard to the future, a community of hope. To Royce,

[t]his third condition is the one which furnishes both [sic] the most exact, the most widely variable, and the most important of the motives which warrant us in calling a community a real unit.[15]

Insofar as they are conscious of their unity, the members are empowered to act as a community as well as individuals. In so acting they achieve a personal reality over and above their isolated individualities. Thus community is always greater than the mere summation of its parts.

---

[12] In *The Philosophy of Loyalty* (1908) Royce devoted the whole volume to a consideration of that which he construed as the unifying principle of all genuine communal relationships.
[13] PC, 253.
[14] PC, 255-6. (Italics in text.)
[15] PC, 256.

Collecting the conditions stipulated for genuine community we can formulate the following general Roycean notion: community is a reality constituted by unique individual selves who share a common history and/or aim.[16] As we will subsequently see, all the instances of community which Royce describes in some way fit this formulation.

To facilitate a clearer understanding of the community principle in Royce, the writer here employs the Roycean prerogative of interpretation (Royce would claim any explanation is interpretation). Accordingly, in the next two sections, Community is construed as end to be achieved, and communities as means of attaining that end. Such an interpretation is amply justified in view of the centrality of the community notion in the later philosophy of Royce.

First, then, a consideration of that community which Royce calls Universal or Beloved. This is the paradigm community, the ideal to which all other communities can only approximate.

B. *Community as end: the Beloved Community*

As an idealist Royce would certainly agree with the lines of Browning:

Ah, but a man's reach should exceed his grasp, Or what's a heaven for?[17]

Inevitably, the aim of the idealist remains unattainably beyond the real situation. Yet, he generally persists not only in reaching for his impossible goal, but in trying to show others the worthwhileness of his reaching. The heaven of Browning is the ideal of the idealist; man's idealism is his effort to transcend himself by grasping that ideal despite the limitedness of his human nature.

But what precisely is the ideal of the idealist Josiah Royce? Actually, the ideal which he speaks of in terms of "Beloved Community" is the Kingdom of Heaven.[18] Moreover, Royce does not consider that he has stepped out

---

[16] Cf. PC, 316.
[17] Robert Browning, "Andrea del Sarto," *Men and Women* (1891). The pertinence of Browning's lines is not surprising. Royce devoted two excellent studies to *Paracelsus* and to Browning's Theism, both found in the *Anthology of Boston Society Papers* (Macmillan, 1897). Marcel remarks that we ought to give much weight to the poets who influenced Royce, and above all to Browning. Cf. *La métaphysique de Royce*, 9: "[I]l faudrait faire une très grande place aux poetes dont il médita ou revécut profondément l'expérience intime, et avant tout à Browning. Ce que Dante, Shelley ou Keats purent être pour un Bosanquet, c'est incontestablement Browning qui le fut pour Royce."
[18] Cf. PC, 197, 199. In both places Royce identifies the Beloved Community with the Kingdom of Heaven. Some Roycean commentators, however, suggest that the Beloved Community of Royce is an earthly rather than heavenly reality. See, e.g., Marcel in *op. cit.*, 194, and John Smith in *Royce's Social Infinite* (New York: The Liberal Arts Press, 1950),

of the realm of philosophy through his use of "heaven" terminology. "Heaven" is an appropriate designation for his ideal, suggesting the beyondness and sublimity which are characteristic of the Beloved Community. To pursue that ideal, he claims, is to progress towards its own realization in future experience.[19]

Ultimately Royce acknowledges that in order for the ideal of the Beloved Community to become a reality there must be present within it some real principle which constitutes its unity and life. This principle is love, personified in the divine Spirit, the Spirit of the Universal and Beloved Community.[20] According to Royce, when Saint John identifies the Logos of his Gospel with the spirit of the community, he is making a distinct and positive contribution to philosophy.[21] For without the doctrine of the Spirit as its lifegiving principle, the Logos-doctrine of the fourth Gospel is a "mere following of Greek metaphysics."[22]

Since love is the principle of unity in the Beloved Community, our best approach to an understanding of Royce's ideal is through the experience of human love. In a beautiful passage of *The Problem of Christianity* Royce invites us to recall our own dearest friendships, realizing that the meaning derived from their experience applies validly although inadequately to the Kingdom of the beloved:

> Think of the *closest* unity of human souls that you know. Then conceive of the Kingdom in terms of such love. When friends really join hands and hearts and lives, it is not the mere collection of sundered organisms and of divided feelings and will that these friends view as their life. Their life, as friends, is the unity which, while above their own level, wins them to itself and gives them meaning. . .
> Now of such unity is the Kingdom of Heaven,. . . the Beloved Community.[23]

127 ff. Both Marcel and Smith equate Royce's notion of Church with that of the ideal Beloved Community. Admitting that the invisible Church is not in any sense an institutionalized church in Royce's thought, the writer would nonetheless maintain that this invisible Church is itself a presently existing *reality*, while the Beloved Community remains the *ideal* of the Church – an ideal not yet realized, viz., the Kingdom of Heaven.

[19] Cf. John Wright Buckham, "The Contribution of Professor Royce to Christian Thought," 230: "It is never the Community in its empirical nature or its mass aspect, that Professor Royce presents to us as divine and worthy of devoted loyalty, but always the Community as an Ideal in process of realization."

[20] Cf. PC, 234 and 403-4.

[21] Use of the terms *spirit* and *Spirit* follows the text of Royce (cf., e.g., PC, 234). Evidently, Royce sees a relation between the Spirit in the Community and the Holy Spirit in the traditional Christian doctrine of the Trinity. Nonetheless, when he identifies the second person of the Trinity, the Logos, with the spirit or Spirit, basing this interpretation on the gospel of John, he seems to be departing from the traditional trinitarian doctrine. This appears to be another instance in which Royce steps from philosophy into theology.

[22] PC, 234.

[23] PC, 197. In general the terms "love" and "loyalty" are used by Royce inter-

Of such unity also, i.e., a unity effected by love, are all the lesser but genuine communities established by men in their quest for the sublime ideal described by Royce.

Because the ideal remains ideal, however, one can never describe in detail the meaning of Royce's Beloved Community. What can be done, however (and will be in what follows) is to sharpen an appreciation for the inexhaustible wealth of the Roycean ideal through a consideration of those lesser communities which are means to the end.

C. Communities as means

The end of Community requires community or communities as means to its achievement. Moreover, Royce claims that man's very efforts to reach the heaven which he calls the Beloved Community gives him a present participation in the life of that Community, even while leading him towards the fulness of its enjoyment. The present participation is itself a communal experience. In other words, the communities which man establishes and experiences here and now on earth serve a mediating function between him and the Absolute, between his limitation as an individual and the limitlessness of the Beloved Community.

In general Royce considers three types of communities as means to his ideal end. Small communities such as families and groups of friends, the Great Community, and the Church are means by which individuals, civil and religious society effectively approach a common goal. Fundamental to all of these, however, is the community of interpretation which we have already discussed. According to Royce, without interpretation there can be no type of communal existence, whether familial, civil or religious.

1. *Small communities*

Although Royce never dwells at length upon the family and friends as instances of community, he says enough to reinforce what we would expect from his overall orientation. In general his point of view is that the establishment of genuine communal ties in the family and among one's friends accomplishes practical functions in regard to individuals. First of all, such ties

changeably, although he prefers the latter term. Cf. Vol. 78, Smith College Lectures (1910), "Present Problems of Philosophy," 42-3: "To that word love, in well known Christian context, I have of course no objection to offer. But my present purpose requires the use of another term. My own common name for both these motives [i.e., love of God and love of man] to which the higher life of man whatever his religion or his notion has been due, is the term Loyalty." E. A. Singer supports this interpretation in his "Love and Loyalty," *Philosophical Review* 25 (May, 1916), 456-65.

enable the individual to transcend the limits of individuality and thereby become a fuller human being. Secondly, they empower him to overcome the false individualism to which finite selves are always inclined. And thirdly, such ties set up an atmosphere in which the pain of estrangement with which so many modern men are afflicted can be prevented or at least alleviated.

In regard to individualism Royce was consistently concerned about the damage done to individuals who confuse uniqueness with independence, using the former as an excuse for a "false individualism."[24] His purpose in stressing loyalty as the relational factor in forming communities is to avoid that type of individualism which in reality forgets or ignores what each unique individual truly is, i.e., a socially responsible being. Loyalty to loyalty, i.e., loyalty to a cause which is universal rather than individualistic, is the only remedy against the destruction of unique selves through false individualism. For "loyalty to loyalty" means "that my individual service, although unique, is not the foe of the equally unique service of other men."[25] Communities, established through loyalty, are the safeguard of genuine uniqueness.

All communal situations provide a climate suitable for mediation, but this function is most felt by us in the small communities in which we live and work. In general, as Royce observes, there are three kinds of estrangement with which most individuals are acquainted through experience, whether directly or vicariously. The first is the estrangement of friends or lovers, the second is the estrangement of brothers and/or sisters, and the third is the estrangement of successive generations, e.g., parents and their children. In all three cases, the experience, while regrettable in itself, points to an awareness of love or loyalty as necessarily involving a synthesis of three ethical ideas: the idea of independence, the idea of the good, and the idea of duty. Where the pain of estrangement is felt it is because one or other of the ideas is emphasized to the near or total exclusion of the other or others. In other words, the genuine loyalty which forms community by synthesizing the three is not present. As a consequence, no real mediation as a resolution of the estranged situation can take place.[26] Our experience of estrangement are always indicative of our need for community, so that the unique individuals who comprise our families and our friends, sharing a common background and/or a common hope, may truly live in harmony.

---

[24] Vol. 76, Lecture IV: "Loyalty as a Factor in American Life" (incomplete), 27.
[25] Vol. 76, Lecture III; "Loyalty as a Personal and as a Social Virtue," 34.
[26] Cf. Vol. 95, "Comments upon the Problem of the Mid-Year Examinations," 18 ff.

2. The Great Community

The idealistic political projection of Royce's notion of community is the Great Community. The term "political" is used here not in any limiting sense, but to suggest a broader one, viz., that the concerns of the nations encompass all of the concerns of the individuals who compose them, and that therefore, within a Roycean context, world "politics" ought to be concerned with serving the various needs of the nations, whether the needs be labeled social, economic or political.

Royce expressed his ideas on the Great Community at a time when war in Europe was instancing the kind of severance in international relations that would prevent his Great Community from ever becoming actualized. Attempting to analyze the issues posed by the war, he called it "a conflict between the community of mankind and the particular interests of individual nations,"[27] maintaining that no single nation engaged in such a conflict could be right in pursuing its cause unless that cause were the community of all mankind, or the Great Community. Such a cause, Royce claimed, must be based upon interests that surpass distinctions of nation or of race; it must be firmly rooted in the unified interests of humanity. Only then could a nation's engagement in conflict be morally justified.[28]

In other words, Royce's Great Community was intended as a means to be actualized "for the healing of the nations."[29] To its membership, all mankind, as individuals and as communities, were invited. In fact, only insofar as all nations and men responsibly accepted this membership could the Great Community, as a community of communities be effected and effective.

Unlike the Beloved Community, the Great Community contains within itself the possibility of its own realization, prior to the arrival of the heavenly Kingdom. The already existing grounds for this realization is the "modern institution called insurance."[30] The insurance principle was first suggested by Royce in a small but significant work entitled *War and Insurance*, written three years before the United States entered World War I, and four years before President Wilson's proposal for the establishment of a league of nations.[31] In 1916, when Royce wrote the essays contained in *The Hope of the*

---

[27] HGC, 31.

[28] Cf. Smith, *Royce's Social Infinite*, 162.

[29] HGC, 37.

[30] Josiah Royce, *War and Insurance* (New York: The Macmillan Company, 1914), ix. Hereafter, *War*.

[31] Recall April 6, 1917 as the date of U.S. entry into World War I, and January 8, 1918 as the date when President Wilson issued his Fourteen Points stressing the need for a League of Nations.

Great Community, he was still convinced that the principle could and ought to be applied on a larger scale. Consequently, he

stated and defended the thesis that the cause of the world's peace would be aided if in future the principle of insurance were gradually and progressively introduced into international business.[32]

For "[i]nsurance has already proved to be," he claimed,

in the modern life of individual nations, a cause of no little growth in social organization, in human solidarity, in reasonableness, and in peace.[33]

Like his concept of the Great Community, Royce's notion of insurance is extremely broad in scope. Viewing it as both mode of business and as social institution, he considered insurance "one of the most momentous instances of the union of very highly theoretical enterprises with very concrete social applications."[34] Thus convinced of its efficacy, he urged the specific application of the principle of insurance to international affairs through the organization of a group of nations that would comprise a world community, mutually insuring its members against any kind of risks.[35]

The proposal of Royce is deliberately tentative. His aim is to attract the attention of someone else or some group of persons who might effectively specify and execute his suggestion. At a moment of "unprecedented crisis in the world's history" (his estimate of the world situation in 1914), he maintained that the new mode of international cooperation which he advocated was worthy of careful study.[36]

Nonetheless, despite his reticence about specifics, Royce himself had studied insurance sufficiently to be qualified in the general claims he made about it. To him the principle of insurance could serve a mediating, reconciling, unifying function between the diverse interests of the member nations in the world community.[37] As individual members multiply, insurance becomes the basis for whatever interrelatedness exists among the nations, forming them into a communal reality.

Only if this Great Community is international in scope can it realize the ideal which Royce envisions. For only then can it utilize all the positive contributions of member nations for their mutual advantage. Nevertheless, even were it not to extend its influence to all the nations but only to some,

[32] HGC, 71.
[33] *Ibid.*
[34] War, x, xi.
[35] Cf. *Ibid.*
[36] Cf. War, xi.
[37] HGC, 62.

Royce contends that the principle of insurance could be effectively applied.

If the principle of insurance were introduced into international affairs, even in a very small degree, it would involve, first the creation of an entirely new sort of international body – namely, an "international board of trustees.". . . [A] beginning would be made in a process that would, from the very first, tend to make the unity of the various nations of mankind something practical and obvious, as well as certain to possess, as time went on, more and more significance for all concerned in such a process.[38]

From the present vantage point of history and experience we can safely say that Royce's prediction in the above passage was proved true: as time went on, the process of forming a world community did become an increasingly significant concern among men.

Through his own study of history and his observation of the world situation, Royce had clearly become convinced that the world can be saved from the disruption and corruption of false individualism and collectivism only by uniting the already existing communities of men into higher communities. Political institutions, he claimed, cannot secure the well-being of their people merely by freeing them from oppression or giving a greater voice in government – unless those institutions form a government "by the united community, through the united community, and for the united community."[39] Hence, when the Great Community becomes actualized, it shall structure its own institution to serve its communal end.

Royce was surprisingly optimistic about the realization of his hope of the Great Community. Reflecting on recent advances in science and in the humane arts, particularly in communication and in preventive medicine, he judged that perfectly human conditions could become the basis for a charity which might transform society into a social order worthy "of a new heaven and a new earth."[40] Such progress meant increased means of strengthening and extending the universal brotherhood of men.

In brief, the last two centuries have given us a right to hope for the unity of mankind, a right of which we had only mythical glimpses and mystical visions before. This right we gained through the recent development both of our natural sciences and of our modern humanities. The idea of the human community has tended of late to win a certain clearness which it never could possess until now.[41]

In the fifty-three years since Royce's death we have come to view yet more

---

[38] HGC, 65, 66-7.
[39] HGC, 49, 50.
[40] Cf. HGC, 39.
[41] Ibid.

clearly the idea and the ideal of human community which he called "great" – even as we continue struggling to achieve it.

3. *The Church*

Royce's notion of the invisible church is the closest he comes to being specific in his philosophy of religion – specific in the sense of doctrinal.[42] This is the notion of an ideal kingdom whose present reality (insofar as it has any present reality) consists in the closest possible human approximation to the perfect community which bears the label of "beloved." As means for approaching this ideal, the Church is seen by Royce as the instrument through which he hopes ultimately to solve the religious paradox. For the religious paradox, as we have already seen, cannot be solved by any individual alone. Man's basic communalness is the key to its solution.

More precisely, the only way to solve the religious paradox is through the loyalty that constitutes community. The cause which elicits this loyalty, thus rendering man capable of satisfying his own most basic religious need, is the "common cause of all the loyal," i.e., the very invisible Church which Royce calls "the community of all who have sought for salvation through loyalty."[43] As instrument for solving the religious paradox of all individuals, the church which Royce envisions must be considered as a reality that extends to all of mankind, a church that is the universal community of those who seek salvation. The following passage is particularly pertinent in regard to the universal extension that is requisite for the invisible church:

Any brotherhood of men who thus loyally live in the Spirit is, from my point of view, a brotherhood essentially religious in its nature, precisely in proportion as it is practically moved by an effort to serve – not merely the special cause to which its members, because of their training and their traditions, happen to be devoted, but also the common cause of all the loyal... They are a source of insight to all who know of their life, and who rightly appreciate its meaning. And of such is the kingdom of loyalty. And the communities which such men form and serve are essentially religious communities. Each one is an example of the unity of the Spirit. Each one stands for a reality that belongs to the superhuman world.[44]

---

[42] Smith remarks that Royce dared here to undertake a task that could only have been attempted within the framework of American religious pluralism and freedom of religious thought. Regarding his enterprise as a "metaphysical analysis of experience,' Royce sought to show the philosophically minded that there is a logical and experiential content in many classical theological doctrines. It is not surprising, then, that there seems to be much theological content included in Royce's philosophizing, but this is not the equivalent of claiming that Royce is "doing" theology. Cf. *The Spirit of American Philosophy*, 112-3.

[43] SRI, 280.

[44] SRI, 273.

The entire superhuman world is what constitutes church. According to Royce, without membership in this spiritual or religious community, a community which in its inmost nature is also divine, the salvation of an individual man is impossible.[45] The Church differs from the Great Community because of its superhuman or divine element; it differs from the Beloved Community precisely because it is (although invisible) a temporal reality.

In addition to mediating for its individual members the solution to the religious paradox, the Church furnishes each individual member with the supernatural assistance of grace which makes it possible for him to reach his ideal end. For

the principal means of grace – that is, the principal means of attaining instruction in the spirit of loyalty, encouragment in its toils, solace in its sorrows, and power to endure and to triumph – the principal means of grace, I say, which is open to any man lies in such communion with the faithful and with the unity of the spirit which they express in their lives.[46]

In other words, a man is empowered to transcend his own individuality by the unity of spirit which is the Church. His power is the power of the "new being" of the universal Christian community.[47] This spirit is the very life of Royce's communitarian man, the spirit which animates all his efforts to achieve an ideal that lies beyond him. It is the only spirit which gives a man hope of obtaining his ultimate ideal in the Beloved Community, a spirit that becomes Spirit in the eternal Community of the divine nature.

As love is the underlying principle of community, where love is perfect, there is perfect community. The Christian Church is to Royce the closest approximation to perfection of love, arising as it does out of the Pauline charity of the first Christian communities. It is in this context that the religious paradox is nearest to its perfect resolution: the individual need and the communal ideal tend to fuse into one living personal reality, the new being effected through the presence of an integrating love. Royce goes so far as to assert that Saint Paul's famous hymn of charity "is also a technically true statement of how the principle of loyalty applies to a brotherhood fully conscious of its common aim."[48] What Paul said about charity, he claims,

---

[45] Cf. PC, 72: "Membership in that community [i.e., the Christian Church] is necessary to the salvation of man."

[46] SRI, 291.

[47] Cf. PC, 118. Also cf. "Comment by Prof. Royce to Miss Mary Whiton Calkins" in *Philosophical Review* 25, 3 (May, 1916), 295: "For me, at present, genuinely and loyally united community which lives a coherent life, is, in a perfectly literal sense, a person. Such a person, for Paul, the Church of Christ was." To which one might add: Such a person or new being, for Royce, the Church of Christ is.

[48] SRI, 295. Paul's "hymn of charity" is in II Cor. 13.

must be universalized if it is true. But when we universalize the Pauline charity it becomes once more the loyalty which is the grounding for Royce's metaphysical principle of community.[49]

In the first section of this chapter an interpretation was proposed, viz., that community is both end and means in Roycean philosophy. The Beloved Community remains for Royce the ideal end, whose attainment is rendered possible by the existence of communities which approximate the ideal and facilitate its ultimate achievement. The general means to this end takes the form of a Community of Interpretation. But this general notion may be further specified as the means for small communities such as families and groups of friends, as the means for civil society which is Royce's Great Community, and as the invisible Church which provides the religious means for reaching the ideal.

Overlapping of individual members and of member communities among all three means is not only inevitable but desirable. For no one, and no group, belongs to any one community exclusively. The uniqueness that individual members can contribute to community is enhanced by involvement in other communities. Were an individual to refuse such involvement he would thereby surrender the very individuality which is the first requisite for genuine community.

Despite the diversity of various kinds of community described by Royce and despite the overlapping in their memberships and functions, the mediating role of community is served in every genuine communal situation. By offering the individual a means of supplementing his inevitably limited knowledge, communities mediate in the service of truth; by giving to each needy individual the life-power shared by many members, communities mediate in the service of life. The ideal of Royce's communitarian man, the end which is participation in the truth and life of the Beloved Community, can be accomplished in no other way than through such mediation.

In all the instances of community described, the underlying principle of union or mediation is love. Although Royce generally speaks of this love in terms of loyalty, it is love which gathers individuals into genuine communities; it is love which is the basis for our hope in a world community; it is love which makes existent the communal reality of Church. Finally, it is Love personified which founds the reality of the Beloved Community. Without love, then, or its universal form of loyalty, there is no community – whether as end or means.

[49] Cf. SRI, 296: "[W]hat Paul said about charity must be universalized if it is true. When we universalize the Pauline Charity, it becomes once more the loyalty that, as a fact, is now justified in seeking her loyal own; but that still, like charity, rejoices in the truth."

The conclusion to be drawn from this study of the notion of community in Royce is a simple one: communities exist for the sake of Community. In this lies the pragmatic relevance of Royce's thought. Man's practical thrust towards the ideal which is Community is grounded in his experience of individual need filled-up through his fellowship with others. That thrust is energized by the very relatedness which is community.

CONCLUSION

CHAPTER XII*

THE ROYCEAN PRAGMATIC

Since the purpose of this interpretive study of Roycean philosophy was to convey certain of his views as clearly and objectively as possible, his own texts have been employed rather liberally, and no attempt has been made to subject those views to a close developmental or consistent criticism. The aim in such an approach was to afford the ideas of Royce as sympathetic a hearing as possible, so that those which are of worth might not be sloughed aside because others are judged unacceptable. At this point, however, some sifting is in order, so that we may gather together those notions in Royce that are presently most pertinent. Accordingly, our final chapter shall include some form of summary and critique before specifying the result of the preceding considerations.

A. Recapitulation

In the interest of clarity and conciseness the development of Royce's philosophy may be summarized according to our three leading topics: knowledge, the Absolute, and the individual.

In regard to knowing, Royce's early theory saw a stress on the practical that remained with him throughout his life (FE; Vol. 60, 79). This is the factor that marked his idealism as distinct from that of Hegel, a distinction Royce himself esteemed significant precisely because it pointed up the practical element in his thought (RAP). Later on, in the middle period, Royce's general voluntaristic stress was specified in his synthetic view of reality, wherein he defined ideas as conscious embodiments of purpose (WI). Later still, Royce used his theory of knowledge as a practical means for settling the age old philosophical dispute concerning human cognition, and offered

* N.B. Specific references in this chapter are given within the text itself, using the abbreviations employed in the Notes. The intent is thus to avoid excessive documentation, while indicating, through a comparison of the sources, the progress of the pragmatic element in Royce's thought.

the same theory as a means by which men presently might settle similar disputes (PC).

What is lacking in the early works, present theoretically in the middle period, and applied in the mature writings, is the social dimension of the knowing process. Cognition would legitimately be construed as a rather individual affair if we look only to RAP and FE for our sources. But as soon as we turn to some parts of WI, and particularly to certain of the unpublished manuscripts (68, 69, 70), it is clear that it is essentially a social process. In PC the social element of Royce's idealism is embodied in the community of interpretation, as a metaphysical as well as epistemological principle.

While Royce remains an absolutist in regard to knowing, he is never loathe to admit that man's grasp of truth is always relative (RAP). The relativity and absoluteness are reconciled through his construing the former as "partialness," the latter as "wholeness" (WI). To Royce, "relative" truth is a portion of the fulness of truth which is the Absolute (CG). In this sense, relative truth is understood as actually Absolute. Again, because of his idealism, the being of that Absolute Truth is ontological as well as logical (PC).

Moreover, while Royce remains an absolutist, he never loses sight of the usefulness of postulation in philosophizing (Cf. RAP and SRI). Although in the early works he does more "talking" on this point (FE), in the later writings he practices what he had previously "preached," in particular by applying the postulate of the Absolute on a moral as well as cognitive level (WI and PC). In other words, he uses the idea of God, tracing its practical implications in experience, so that we might judge the worth of the notion through its consequences, without having to have been certainly convinced that God's existence is actual rather than hypothetical. Part of the reason for this development in Royce's thought is his growing interest in community, which carried with it a concern to make his absolute idealism socially relevant.

When Royce details his theory of interpretation in PC he shows the way through which he has come to see that the inadequacies of James's theory are best remedied through the Peircean approach. In following Peirce, Royce departs from James but not from pragmatism. He retains the pragmatic emphasis on experiential verification but insists that such verification is more practically efficacious if it is communal rather than individual. In adhering to the definition of idea which he had enunciated in WI, he joins the Peircean notion to his absolute idealism. The result is his absolute pragmatism, wherein he combines idealism with an emphasis on future experience.

In regard to the Absolute, the sequence of Royce's writings indicates that the pertinent considerations shift their emphasis from Thought and Experience (RAP), to Experience and Will (CG), to Cause (PL), and then to Community (PC). All of these terms are used to describe a Being who is the source of whatever practical significance there is in life. The progression of emphasis is clearly orientated towards showing that the Absolute is no lifeless abstraction, no lone speculation, no impersonal idea or impossible ideal, but a living personal Being whose thinking, willing and experiencing makes a difference in the here and now. As ultimate Cause he draws forth from finite beings whatever practical responses are theirs to give. As Community he supports their present efforts and crowns their achievements. Each designation of the Absolute which Royce employs, while retaining all the practical force of preceding appellations, points to an added awareness of his Absolute's concrete relevance.

Another indication of the general pragmatic directedness of Royce's notion of the Absolute is his use of the term "God." In RAP and WI, the term "Absolute" is used frequently, while references to "God" are quite infrequent. In CG, the two terms are employed a fairly equal number of times. In PC "Absolute" occurs less and "God" more often. The sequence suggests that in using the term God Royce wanted to impress upon his readers that the Absolute is no mere metaphysical abstraction, a being whose existence is confined to the realm of philosophical speculation, but the very God that ordinary people talk about, a real being with whom man is presently and practically involved. God is the final future Experience who gives meaning to all our temporal futures.

Although Royce treats the topic of belief more at length in his early works (FE), we find the implications of that treatment later on in his discussions of the relationship between will and the Absolute (CG). People are responsible for what they believe, he had claimed (FE), precisely because their believing assertions are freely willed. Through their willing, they live out the life of the Absolute who can act temporally only through finite individuals. As the human will is capable of integrating the various thoughts and experiences that fill the life of individuals, so the divine Will integrates perfectly fulfilled Thought and Experience in the unity of the Absolute (CG). Ultimately, our finite wills, which remain inseparable from whatever we believe or know, are fulfilled in the Will to interpret, the Cause of loyalty, a God who is Love (PL and PC).

Generally speaking, Royce's considerations on the Absolute are more speculative in RAP, and more intent upon showing God's relatedness to men in CG. Not until PC does Royce specifically address himself to the

Christian religion's interpretation of the Absolute. Having remained in previous works religiously "universal," the focus here seems a rather practical precision on the part of Royce. Actually, his aim in discussing the Christian ideas is to indicate their applicability in solving the religious paradox which in some way all men experience.

In regard to the individual, Royce never relinquishes his early claim that each finite self derives his worth and meaning from the Absolute. In general the blurring of any real distinction between the individual and the Absolute is more pronounced in RAP than in CG, where Royce considers love as the principle of individuation and in OP where he emphasizes the freedom and responsibility of the individual. Despite the effort to justify individuality in WI, Royce never succeeds in establishing that the self is other than a part of the divine Whole. The entire explanation and fulfilment of his being is determined by the Absolute who is the source of all future fulfilment in experience.

Actually, Royce's failure to justify individuality has its practical point, one similar to the position taken by Peirce in contrast with James. For Royce is so intent on remedying the practical evil of false individualism, and on diminishing and supplementing individual limitation – both intellectual and moral – that when he eventually arrives at the notion of community as the means best suited to assist man in reaching his communal ideal (PC), this idea becomes the focus for his philosophical consideration. As individuality had earlier been explained as a partial manifestation of the life of the Absolute (RAP and WI), it can only be understood thereafter as the unique contribution of a self to the life of a community (PC).

Although Royce claims that his philosophy was always orientated towards the notion of community, when we examine the texts of the early and middle periods we find that the subject is scarcely treated. Instead, the emphasis (in RAP) is upon the individual as an instrument of the Absolute, and then (in WI) upon the social aspect of human cognition. The latter factor logically led to Royce's mature (and Peircean) theory of knowledge (PC), and that in turn, because of his idealism, resulted in the metaphysical application of interpretation to community. Such a development indicates that the pragmatic "instrumentalism" of Royce's early theory of the individual was best served through his later theory of mediation through the community of interpretation. In applying that notion to the community of nations and to the invisible church as well as to individuals, Royce extended the practical usefulness of his principle universally (HGC and PC).

Certainly the increasing specificity of Royce's early abstract ideas is evident as one reads his works. The specificity is directed towards the practical application of the idealist's views, and towards showing that the ideas themselves are rooted in and directed towards experience. In regard to the Great Community, for example, Royce chose a principle with which modern man has had much experience (insurance) and pointed to this as the specific means through which the practical end of world community might be achieved (HGC and War). It is clear then that Royce's overall orientation was always towards the practical. While he readily accepted designations such as "absolutist" and "idealist," he would never have allowed the label of "abstractionist."

One of the needs of the individual, which, according to Royce, classical pragmatism fails to satisfy, is his need for an ideal. No man, he claims, can live without a basic optimism (FE), i.e., without reaching towards something or someone beyond himself, greater than himself. That man is inevitably discontent is the very grounds for his free will acts (Im). It is also the experiential grounding for ideals as anticipations of the future. Community furnishes the individual with a description of his ultimate ideal fulfilment (PC), while communities offer him the means for attaining that Ideal.

Summarily, the notion of community in the thought of Royce marks the culmination of the pragmatic progress of his thought in regard to the individual. It was because he wished to emphasize future experience that the earlier stress on the individual diminished in support of his notion of community.

B. Critique

A detailed critique of the entire philosophy of Royce is not here intended. Nonetheless, some criticism is in order so that the conclusions at which the author has arrived concerning the development of a Roycean pragmatism might be understood within their context. Again it will be useful to follow the division of the study.

In regard to knowledge, Royce approaches the formulation of his synthetic idealistic view (WI) after a critique of realism that is inadequate and inconclusive. It is inadequate because he fails to distinguish between the realist's conception of being and his theory of cognition. It is inconclusive because, had he made that distinction, the inherent contradiction which realism supposedly contains would thereby have been dissolved. In other words, Royce seems to read the realist as an idealist: he equates the existence of a thing with the knowing of an object, claiming that since the realist asserts the absolute independence of the thing known he therefore renders himself incapable of knowing it. Actually, the realist can quite compatibly hold (1) that the existence of a thing remains unalterably independent of the knower (and he of it), and (2) that the cognitive process always implies mutual dependence between the knower and known object. Although Royce seems to miss this significant point, the existential and cognitive levels are quite distinct to any genuine realist.

To this writer, the point is particularly pertinent because it offers solid grounding for an approach other than Royce's idealism. Further, it opens the way to a realist's appreciation for his idealism. In other words, one need not be an idealist to see and utilize the value of Royce's thought. One might well reject his idealism itself while accepting some of his fundamental insights. A key instance would be his definition of ideas as embodiments of conscious purpose (WI). Certainly it is agreed that ideas involve purposes and that Royce's insistence on the point is well placed. Nonetheless, the knower's approach to reality always and inevitably includes the whole of his being – not only intellect and will but feelings also. Hence, were Royce to formulate his definition so as to indicate that all of a man is involved in cognition – the definition would be yet more satisfactory. While allowing that purpose is practically inseparable from ideas, one may also (quite validly) maintain that cognition *quâ* cognition is theoretically separable from other human acts involved in knowing. Moreover, Royce's extremely broad usage of the terms idea and purpose cannot explain the difference between our knowledge of the good as an end to be pursued through action and our knowledge of being (i.e., the good as object). In the Roycean texts, idea and concept are used interchangeably, as are purpose and intention. Had Royce admitted and explained a distinction between these terms – intention always attending concept (i.e., our knowledge of being), purpose attending idea (our knowledge of good) – the precision would be consonant with realism as well as with idealism. In both cases, ideas and/or concepts presuppose the existence of the things we know.

In regard to the Absolute, there are two main criticisms. The first concerns Royce's demonstration of the existence of the Absolute in RAP, his argument from "the possibility of error." Generally speaking, Royce reasons from man's actual experience of error to the existence of God as absolute Truth. While this reasoning justifies the inference that absolute truth necessarily exists as the measure against which error is actual, the absolute whose existence it demonstrates is not necessarily infinite or eternal. The absolute fact of error is a temporal event which implies an equally temporal (although absolute) truth. As facts of finite experience, neither truth nor error offer adequate grounds for claiming the actual existence of an eternal infinite God. From Royce's argument one might validly infer only the possible existence of such an Absolute.

The second criticism relates to Royce's pantheism. Although he explicitly denies that his absolute idealism is pantheistic (WI), his failure to provide any qualitative principle of distinction greatly diminishes the weight of his denial. Since finite wills, finite experiences and finite (relative) truths are defined as neither more nor less than partial manifestations of the Absolute Will, Absolute Experience and Absolute Truth, these are all in reality conceived as parts of the Absolute who is God. Within Royce's idealistic system, the world itself, as constituting partial fulfilment of the divine purpose, becomes for all its finitude divine. In the end, no being exists or can be thought to exist apart from this Absolute, whose *all-inclusiveness* is intended by Royce to be taken quite literally.

In regard to the individual, a critique of the Roycean position is closely related to his notion of the Absolute. For the consequence of his pantheism is the destruction of genuine individuality or uniqueness. While Royce insists upon the importance of real distinction among the various selves who form community (PC), his idealism cannot ultimately support this. At most he leaves us with a quantitative basis for distinguishing among individuals: each self is unique as an unrepeatable aspect or part of the Whole who is the Absolute. Such a basis is inadequate to explain qualitative differences that exist among persons.

Royce seems nearest to a qualitative distinction when he deals with love as the principle of individuation (CG). But since love is translated into loyalty, and all forms of genuine loyalty are directed towards the Absolute as Cause, the discernment of uniqueness which we arrive at through love is in reality no more than our consciousness of a specific aspect of the divine Whole. The specificity is therefore merely quantitative.

Perhaps the key factor here is the notion of freedom. If Royce were to explore this notion more adequately we might then discover a principle of distinction within his thought. This would enable us to agree that his system is not pantheistic and that individuals are truly unique. But he doesn't. Where he refers to freedom, its meaning is for the most part presupposed (WI), or he treats it only on a psychological level (OP); in neither case does he explain or justify its reality. To have done so would certainly have lent more force to his ideas concerning the Absolute and the individual, possibly even to the extent of rendering them acceptable to a realist.

C. Result

Chapter II treated of the possibilities for a Roycean pragmatism. The influences of Charles Sanders Peirce and William James, two great American pragmatists, on the life and thought of Royce were therein noted. Royce's notion of a pragmatism consistent with his absolute idealism was also discussed. Now that we have examined the development of Royce's philosophy with a view to discerning whatever pragmatic element may be found within his thought, we are in a position to draw some conclusions.

Recalling the general notion of pragmatism described in Chapter II we return for the last time to our three main topics.

In regard to his theory of knowledge, the philosophy of Royce definitely discloses an increasing emphasis upon future experience. A comparison of SRI with any of the early or middle works clearly indicates that experience is a more predominant theme in Royce's later writings. A comparison between his mature notion of interpretation (PC) and his earlier conception of cognition illustrates the development of the theoretical voluntarism, which he held throughout his life, into an active principle of mediation – to be applied in all of life. This progression in Royce's thought is certainly a reflection of the influence of Peirce.

In regard to the Absolute, although the proofs Royce offers for his existence in RAP and CG are both empirically grounded, the latter work gives more weight to moral than to intellectual experience, while in PC Royce's treatment of the Absolute turns into a description of man's practical experience of community. It is clear that purely speculative considerations diminish in importance as the thought of Royce develops. As this happens, the concept of God becomes more and more a pragmatic postulate, i.e., a notion which even to someone who does not accept Royce's idealistic proof for God's existence, is a practically workable hypothesis, a truth which is true because it works or makes a difference in the here and now. This progression in the thought of Royce reflects in part at least the influence of James, who refused to accept a God who would make no difference.

In regard to the individual, it is the notion of experience which forwards Royce's reflections on the meaning of uniqueness, individualism and human limitation. Through that empirical impetus Royce eventually arrives at his mature conception of community as the principle through which he expects to settle all the practical problems of the world. That man's consciousness of himself can only take place within a social context is an idea not found in the early works, precisely because the stress there is more speculative than experiential. But by the time Royce wrote SRI he had come to consider not only self-awareness but individuality as inseparable from the social situation. The progress of Royce's thought from a concern for the evil of intellectual limitation to a concern for moral limitation to the means for supplementing these limitations through community is certainly indicative of an increasing emphasis on future experience. The development clearly shows the influence of Peirce, for whom community was essential in man's quest for truth.

Although the influence of Peirce and James are evident in the development of Roycean philosophy, the "Roycean pragmatic" is itself neither Peircean nor Jamesian. As James's pragmatism was different from Peirce's, so Royce's was different from both. Some similarity to James's pragmatism lies in Royce's use of his theory of knowledge as a mediating principle, in his insistence that knowing is more than a speculative process, and in his claim that belief in an absolute is a useful postulate. Because of his notion of interpretation and community, however, the mature philosophy of Royce bears a closer resemblance to Peirce than to James. Without the Peircean doctrines one could scarcely appreciate the later thought of Royce, or discern a pragmatic development culminating therein.

For all the positive pragmatic influences exerted upon Royce by James and Peirce, his philosophy remains unique because he preserves both his absolutism and his idealism. His refusal to "let go" of the Absolute is admittedly motivated by his desire to have a theory which works in both the near and final future. Hence he claims that without an Absolute, pragmatism is not pragmatic enough. Further, his idealism remains compatible with an increasingly pragmatic theory of truth. An apt description for the resulting reconciliation is pragmatic idealism, an approach quite distinct from that of either James or Peirce.

In the second chapter pragmatism was described as a method for finding the clarity we need to live by, a way of philosophizing which emphasizes future experience as the guide for achieving that clarity. Thus the essential query of the pragmatist becomes "What practical difference would this idea make?" According to our understanding of pragmatism and according to our interpretation of the pertinent texts, Royce's entire philosophy develops as an effort to answer this question. The clarification of his ideas of the Absolute, of knowing and of the individual is governed by an orientation towards future experience. Because of this essential practical emphasis, Royce's mature theory of knowledge and of the individual requires a community of interpretation in order to fill the experienced intellectual and moral needs of men, so that their future may be richer than the present. Similarly, his idea of the Absolute is clarified through a progressively greater stress on the difference that this concept makes in terms of experience. Other pragmatists are less pragmatic than Royce precisely because they reject the absolute grounding which makes their pragmatism work. In short, our study of the texts of Royce has brought us to a twofold conclusion: (1) that there is a genuinely pragmatic element in his philosophy, and (2) that that element increases as his thought develops.

Throughout this study we have used the term "idealism" to describe a philosophical conception of being and knowledge. Were we to use the term in a less technical sense, however, the fact that Royce is an American idealist would make him a rather lone representative of an aspect of American experience which is largely neglected by the classical American pragmatists. That aspect might properly be called American idealism. For Americans are on the whole a people with an amazingly idealistic bent. All through their history, a practical orientation and appreciation for immediate experience has been joined with a hopeful thrust towards high ideals and expectation of the realization of those ideals. In other words Americans seem to stress both relative and absolute future experience. Through that dual emphasis the American spirit appears to combine – now as truly as at the turn of the century – a pragmatism and an idealism.

Perhaps, then, our best description of the Roycean pragmatic, suggesting a synthesis of his idealism with the empirical and practical directedness of his thought, is to label that synthesis the Idealistic Pragmatism of Josiah Royce. The same label could designate the pragmatic position of a realist who interprets "idealistic" in its less technical sense, and that of an idealist who interprets the term in a stricter philosophical sense. In this way one might utilize the Roycean pragmatic to mediate between realism and idealism, so that the pragmatic element in Royce's thought would be acceptable to both positions. From either perspective, "Idealistic Pragmatism" aptly describes the spirit of American philosophy.

BIBLIOGRAPHY

Hernandez, Victoria *et al. Index to the Josiah Royce Papers.* An Unpublished Guide to the Roycean MSS Folios (98 vols.) and Boxes (14). Widener Library Archives, Harvard University.
Oppenheim, Frank M., S.J. "Bibliography of the Published Works of Josiah Royce," *Revue internationale de philosophie,* Numéro 79-80 (1967), fascicule 1-2.
Rand, Benjamin. "A Bibliography of the Writings of Josiah Royce," *The Philosophical Review* 25 (1916), 515-23.
Skrupkelıs, Ignas K. "Annotated Bibliography of the Publications of Josiah Royce," *The Basic Writings of Josiah Royce* (Vol. 2), edited by John J. McDermott (Chicago: University of Chicago Press, 1969), Part IX, 1167-1226.

PRIMARY SOURCES

THE EARLY ROYCE (c. 1875-90)

Books

The Feud of Oakfield Creek; a Novel of California Life. Boston: Houghton, Mifflin and Company, 1887.
Fugitive Essays by Josiah Royce, ed. by J. Loewenberg. Cambridge: Harvard University Press, 1920.
Primer of Logical Analysis for the Use of Composition Students. San Francisco: A. L. Bancroft, 1881.
The Religious Aspect of Philosophy. Boston: Houghton Mifflin and Company, 1885.

Articles

"Dr. Abbot's 'Way Out of Agnosticism,'" *International Journal of Ethics* 1 (1890), 98-115.
"The Intention of the Prometheus Bound of Aeschylus: Being an Introduction in the Department of Greek Theology," *California University Bulletin* 16 (June, 1875).
"Kant's Relation to Modern Philosophic Progress," *Journal of Speculative Philosophy* 15 (1881), 360-81.
"Mind and Reality," *Mind* 7 (1882), 30-54.
"'Mind-stuff' and Reality," *Mind* 6 (1881), 365-77.

Unpublished Material

"Of the interdependence of the principles of knowledge; an investigation of the problems of elementary epistemology." Ph. D. Thesis, Johns Hopkins University, 1878.
Primer of Logical Analysis... (the original MS). Houghton Library, Harvard University.
Roycean Manuscript Folios. Widener Library Archives, Harvard University, Vols. 1-4, 40, 53-61, 79-80.

THE MIDDLE PERIOD (c. 1890-1906)

Books

The Conception of God (by Royce et al.). New York: The Macmillan Company, 1897.
The Conception of Immortality. Boston: Houghton Mifflin Company, 1900.
Herbert Spencer: An Estimate and a Review. New York: Fox, Duffield, 1904.
Outlines of Psychology. New York: The Macmillan Company, 1903.
The Spirit of Modern Philosophy. Boston: Houghton Mifflin Company, 1892.
Studies of Good and Evil. New York: D. Appleton and Company, 1898.
The World and the Individual, 2 vols. New York: Dover Publications, Inc., 1959. An unabridged and unaltered republication of the First Edition (with Introduction by John E. Smith) which was originally published by The Macmillan Company, 1899 (I) and 1901 (II).

Articles

"Browning's Theism," *The Boston Browning Society Papers*, 1886-97. New York: The Macmillan Company, 1897.
"The Concept of the Infinite," *Hibbert Journal* 1 (1902), 21-45.
"The Eternal and the Practical," *Philosophical Review* 13 (1904), 113-42.
"The External World and the Social Consciousness," *Philosophical Review* 3 (1894), 513-45.
"Hegel's Terminology," *Dictionary of Philosophy and Psychology*. Ed. by J. Mark Baldwin. Vol. I. New York: Macmillan, 1901.
"The Implications of Self-Consciousness," *New World* 1 (1892), 289-310.
Introduction to *Dialogues of Plato*. Ed. by Benjamin Jowett. New York: Appleton, 1898, vii-xix.
"The Problem of Natural Religion," *International Quarterly* 7 (1903), 85-107.
"The Problem of Paracelsus," *The Boston Browning Society Papers*, 1886-1897. New York: The Macmillan Company, 1897.
Review of J. McTaggart's *Studies in the Hegelian Dialectic, Philosophical Review* 6 (1897), 69-76.
"What Should be the Attitude of Teachers of Philosophy towards Religion?" *International Journal of Ethics* 13 (1903), 280-85.

Unpublished Material

Roycean Manuscript Folios. Widener Library Archives, Harvard University, Vols. 5-26, 43-47, 50, 52, 62-75, 81, 89-95.

THE MATURE ROYCE (c. 1906-16)

Books

The Hope of the Great Community. New York: The Macmillan Company, 1916.
Lectures on Modern Idealism. Ed. by J. Loewenberg. New Haven: Yale University Press, 1919.
The Philosophy of Loyalty. New York: The Macmillan Company, 1908.
The Problem of Christianity. Original edition published in 2 vols. by Macmillan, New York, 1913. Two 1968 editions: one a two-volumed edition with foreword by Jesse A. Mann (Chicago: Henry Regnery Company, Gateway Books), the other a single volume introduced by John E. Smith (Chicago: University of Chicago Press). The latter was first published of a series on Royce by University of Chicago Press. With its remaining volumes, viz. *The Basic Writings of Josiah Royce* (2 vol.), edited with Introduction by John J. McDermott, 1969, and *The Letters of Josiah Royce,* edited with Introduction by John Clendenning, 1970, this series is the most complete collection of Royce's writings presently available. The selections are drawn from all three periods of his philosophical development.
Race Questions, Provincialism, and Other American Problems. New York: The Macmillan Company, 1908.
Royce's Logical Essays. Ed. by Daniel S. Robinson. Dubuque: William C. Brown Company, 1951.
The Sources of Religious Insight. New York: Scribner and Sons, Inc., 1912.
War and Insurance. New York: The Macmillan Company, 1914.
William James and Other Essays on the Philosophy of Life. New York: The Macmillan Company, 1911.

Articles

"Charles Sanders Peirce," *Journal of Philosophy* 13 (1916), 701-9.
"The duties of Americans in the present war," address delivered at Tremont Temple, Jan. 30, 1916. Boston: 1916.
"Immortality," *Hibbert Journal* 5 (1907), 724-44.
"Monotheism," *Encyclopedia of Religion and Ethics* 8, 817-21.
"The Present State of the Question Regarding the First Principles of Theoretical Science," *Proceedings of the American Philosophical Society* 45 (1906), 82-102.
"Provincialism," *Putnam's Magazine,* (Nov., 1909) 239.
"The Reality of the Temporal," *International Journal of Ethics* 20 (1910), 257-70.
"Some Psychological Problems Emphasized by Pragmatism," *Popular Science Monthly,* 83 (1913) 394-411.
"What is Vital in Christianity," *Harvard Theological Review* 2 (1909), 408-45.

Unpublished Material

Notebook of E. W. Friend for his metaphysics course taught by Royce, 1913-14. Widener Library Archives, Harvard University.
"The Mechanical, the Historical and the Statistical," a paper read at Harvard Club of Boston, March 1, 1914. Houghton Library, Harvard University.

Letter to Reginald Chauncey Robbins, November 8, 1914. Houghton Library, Harvard University.
Roycean Manuscript Folios. Widener Library Archives, Harvard University, Vols. 27-39, 41-2, 48, 49, 51, 76-8, 82-4, 86-88, 98.

UNDATED MANUSCRIPTS

Roycean Manuscript Folios. Widener Library Archives, Harvard University, Vols. 85, 96-97.

SECONDARY SOURCES

Books

Aronson, Moses Judah. *La philosophie morale de Josiah Royce.* Paris: Librairie Felix Alcan, 1927.
Bergson, Henri. *A Study in Metaphysics: the Creative Mind.* Trans. by Mabelle L. Andison. Totowa, New Jersey: Littlefield, Adams and Company, 1965.
Buranelli, Vincent. *Josiah Royce.* New York: Twayne Publishers, Inc., 1964.
Brown, Stuart Gerry (ed.). *The Religious Philosophy of Josiah Royce.* Syracuse, N.Y.: Syracuse University Press, 1952.
Browning, Robert. *Men and Women.* Boston: Houghton Mifflin, 1891.
Costello, Harry T. *Josiah Royce's Seminar, 1913-1914.* Ed. by Grover Smith. New Brunswick, N.J.: Rutgers University Press, 1963.
Cotton, James Harry. *Royce on the Human Self.* Cambridge: Harvard University Press, 1954.
Dewey, John. *Philosophy and Civilization.* New York: G. P. Putnam's Sons, 1931.
—. *Reconstruction in Philosophy.* Boston: Beacon Press, 1957.
DiPasquale, Ralph, O. F. M. *The Social Dimensions of the Philosophy of Josiah Royce.* Rome: Pontificium Athenaeum Antonianum, 1961.
Fisch, Max H. (ed.) *Classic American Philosophers.* New York: Appleton-Century-Crofts, Inc., 1951.
Fuss, Peter. *The Moral Philosophy of Josiah Royce.* Cambridge: Harvard University Press, 1965.
Hegel, Georg W. F. *The Phenomenology of Mind.* Trans. by J. B. Baillie. New York: Harper Torchbooks (The Academy Library), 1967.
Humbach, Karl-Theo. *Das Verhältnis von Einzelperson und Gemeinschaft nach Josiah Royce.* Heidelberg: Carl Winter Universitätsverlag, 1962.
James, William. *A Pluralistic Universe.* New York: Longmans, Green, 1909.
—. *Pragmatism and Four Essays from The Meaning of Truth.* New York: The World Publishing Company 1955.
—. *Principles of Psychology.* New York: Henry Holt and Company, 1927.
—. *The Varieties of Religious Experience.* New York: Random House, 1929.
Kant, Immanuel. *Foundations of the Metaphysics of Morals.* Trans. by Lewis Beck. New York: Bobbs-Merrill Company, 1959.
Marcel, Gabriel. *La metaphysique de Royce.* Aubier: Editions Montaigne, 1945. Translated by Virginia and Gordon Ringer as *Royce's Metaphysics* (Chicago: Henry Regnery Company, 1956.
Moore, Edward. *American Pragmatism: Peirce, James and Dewey.* New York: Columbia University Press, 1961.

Peirce, Charles Sanders. *Collected Papers of Charles Sanders Peirce.* Ed. by Charles Hartshorne and Paul Weiss. Cambridge: The Belknap Press of Harvard University 1965.
—. *The Philosophy of Peirce Selected Writings.* Ed. by Justus Buchler. London: Routledge and Kegan Paul LTD, 1940.
Perry, Ralph Barton. *In the Spirit of William James.* New Haven: Yale University Press, 1938.
—. *Philosophy of the Recent Past.* New York: Charles Scribners Sons, 1926.
—. *The Thought and Character of William James.* Boston: Little, Brown and Company, 1936.
Powell, Thomas F. *Josiah Royce.* New York: Washington Square Press, 1967.
Rogers, Arthur Kenyon. *English and American Philosophy since 1800.* New York: Macmillan, 1923.
Roth, Robert, S. J. *American Religious Philosophy.* New York: Harcourt, Brace and World, Inc., 1967.
Santayana, George. *Character and Opinion in the United States.* New York: George Braziller, 1955.
Schneider, Herbert W. *A History of American Philosophy.* New York: Columbia University Press, 1963.
Smith, John E. *Royce's Social Infinite.* New York: The Liberal Arts Press, 1950.
—. *The Spirit of American Philosophy.* New York: Oxford University Press, 1963.
Thayer, H. S. *Meaning and Action, A Critical History of Pragmatism.* New York: Bobbs-Merrill Company, 1968.
Wahl, Jean. *The Pluralist Philosophies of England and America.* Trans. by Fred Rothwell. London: The Open Court Company, 1925.
Whittemore, Robert C. *Makers of the American Mind.* New York: William Morrow and Company, 1964.
Winn, Ralph B. (ed.) *American Philosophy.* New York: Philosophical Library, Inc., 1955.

Articles and Unpublished Papers

Bakewell, Charles M. "Novum Itinerarium Mentis in Deum," *Philosophical Review* 25, 3 (May, 1916), 255-264.
Bixler, Julius. "Josiah Royce – Twenty Years after," *Harvard Theological Review* 29 (July, 1936).
Buckham, John Wright "Contribution of Professor Royce to Christian Thought," *Harvard Theological Review* 8 (1915), 219-37.
Calkins, Mary Whiton. "The Foundation in Royce's Philosophy for Christian Theism," *Philosophical Review* 25 (May, 1916), 282-93.
Farley, Gerard C. "The pragmatic element in the philosophy of Royce." Unpublished MA Thesis for Department of Philosophy, Fordham University, 1957.
Fontinell, Eugene. "The participation theory of being in the philosophy of Josiah Royce. Unpublished Ph.D. dissertation, Department of Philosophy, Fordham University, 1957.
Fuss, Peter. "Royce's Urbana Lectures," *Journal of the History of Philosophy* 5 (Jan., 1967), 60-78.
Johnson, Paul E. "Josiah Royce: Theist or Pantheist," *Harvard Theological Review* 21 (July, 1928).

Lovejoy, Arthur O. "The Thirteen Pragmatisms," *Journal of Philosophy* 5 (1908), 5-12, 29-39.
Oppenheim, Frank M., S. J. "Royce's mature idea of general metaphysics." Unpublished PH.D. dissertation Department of Philosophy, St. Louis University, 1962.
Papini, Giovanni. "What Pragmatism is Like," *Popular Science Monthly* 71 (1907).
Rothman, Walter. "Josiah Royces versuch einer synthese von pragmatismus und objektivität." Inaugural dissertation, Jena. G. Neuenhahn, 1926.
Schiller, C. S. "William James and the Making of Pragmatism," *The Personalist* 8 (1927).
Singer, E. A. "Love and Loyalty," *Philosophical Review* 25 (May, 1916), 456-465.

INDEX

Absolute, ch. IV, VII, X; 5, 6, 18, 19, 25-6, 31, 41-2, 57, 59, 60, 61, 63-5, 67-8, 71, 82, 84, 103-4, 107, 112-3, 119, 149, 151, 155, 168-70, 172-5; see also God
– Cause, 137; see also Cause
– Consciousness, 97, 98, 108
– Experience, 87-96
– Individual, 97, 112
– pragmatism, 25, 128, 133, 134, 136, 168
– Reality, 136-7
– Thought, 48; see also Thought
– Truth, 25, 41-2, 60, 91, 134-7, 172-3
– voluntarism, 6
– Will, 108, 173; see also Universal Will
absolutist, 18, 25-6, 48 n., 134, 168, 171
action, 25, 27, 34, 37, 42, 52, 72, 76, 106, 172
adversity, 13
Alter, 81-2
American philosophy, 176
Aristotle, 72, 104
Aronson, Moses, 149 n.
assertions, 38, 45, 135
atheism, 53 n.
Atman, 74
atonement, 145-7
attention, 44, 93, 95, 96, 109

being, conceptions of, 72-78
belief, 21, 34, 36-7, 43 ff., 52, 63, 65-7, 71, 76, 78-9, 133, 169, 175
Beloved Community, 153 ff., 161, 162
Bergson, Henri, 119 n., 120-1, 124, 126
Berkeley, George, 10
Berkeley, University of California at, 17, 18, 92 n.
Browning, Robert, 153
Buckham, John Wright, 8, 154 n., 158
Buddhists, 74
Buranelli, Vincent, 17 n.

Calkins, Mary W., 161 n.
Cause, 12-3, 137-8, 143, 148, 160, 169, 173
charity, 161-2
choice, 92, 106-7, 109
Christ, 14, 143, 146-8
Christianity, 140 ff., 170
church, 10, 11, 13-4, 155, 160 ff., 170
cognition, 41, 119, 124-5, 128, 131, 167-8, 170-2, 174; see also knowledge
communication, 59, 80-1, 114, 125-6, 151-6, 159
Community, ch. VIII, XI; 19-20, 28, 52, 84, 110, 119, 125, 128-31, 135-6, 143, 147, 159, 168-71, 174
– as End, 136, 153-5, 163
– of interpretation, 18, 124-8, 130, 135-6, 140, 143, 162, 168, 175
– as means, 153, 155-63
conception, 119 ff., 125, 129
conditional idealism, 22 n.
consciousness, 32, 48, 50-1, 57-9, 81, 98, 145, 149
conservatism, 65-7
contemplation, 74
creation, accounts of, 79
creed, 44, 47-8
critical rationalism, 74-5, 77-8

Dante, 153 n.
death, 97-99
deliverer, 9, 10, 138, 140; see also mediator
Design argument, 54, n.
desire, 92-3
Dewey, John, 15, 17, 27, 64, 68, 71 n.
dialectical method, 18, 25, 91
dogma, 8
dogmatism, 40
doubt, 21, 34 ff., 51
dualism, 54 n., 121, 129

Eckhardt, Meister, 74
Ego, 32, 81-3, 102
Eleatic One, 72
empirical grounding, 10 ff., 27, 61, 65, 67, 71, 102, 144-5, 171, 174
empiricism, 27, 119
End, 48, 52, 107, 134, 137, 140, 145-6
epistemology, 27, 31-2, 77, 123, 168; see also knowledge
error, 41-2, 48 n., 172
estrangement, 130, 156
Eternal, need for, 84, 99, 119
evil, 53 ff., 174
evolution, 64
experience, 11 ff., 26-7, 34, 38-40, 58, 63, 65, 73-4, 80, 83-4, 87 ff., 95, 103, 135, 139-40, 154, 156, 160 n., 168-9, 174

faith, 34, 36-7, 46-8, 52, 141; see also belief
falsity, 41 n.
Feeling, 58, 73
Fichte, Johann, 3, 7
fidelity, 146
freedom, 47, 96, 107 ff., 146, 160 n., 169-71, 173
Friend, E. W., 151 n.
Fuss, Peter, 53 n., 108, 109 n.
future experience, 16 n., 21, 23-4, 26-8, 31, 42, 45, 49, 53, 68, 72 n., 83-4, 86, 92, 98, 101, 110, 125, 130, 132, 134, 138, 142, 144, 168, 171, 174-5

God, 45, 48, 53-5, 62, 75, 79, 86-7, 104, 106, 110, 112, 114, 119, 132 ff., 143, 151, 168-9, 172-4; see also Absolute
Good, 40, 54, 59, 63-4, 156
grace, 144, 161
Great Community, 155, 157 ff., 162, 171
guilt, 145

harmony, 47, 52, 131, 156
Harvard University, 18, 79, 151
Heaven, 153-5, 157; see also Beloved Community
Hegel, Georg, 3, 7, 18, 22, 167-8
historical method, 129-30
hope, 65, 138, 145, 148, 152, 156, 159; see also optimism
Howison, George, 92
hypothesis, 4, 34-5, 41, 94, 133 n., 174

idea, 6, 14, 32, 72-3, 76 ff., 89, 95, 113, 127-9, 131, 135, 167-8, 172

ideal, 9, 41, 47, 52-3, 61-2, 68, 82, 89, 107-8, 128, 138-40, 143, 148, 150, 153-5, 161, 170-1, 176
idealism, 3 ff., 22, 75-8, 98, 127, 167-8, 170, 172-6
idealist, 4, 25, 57, 59, 63, 76, 153, 171
idealistic pragmatism, ch. XII
immortality, 99
individual, ch. V, VIII, XI; 31, 143-5, 170-1, 173-5
individualism, 61-4, 156, 159, 170, 174
individuality, 57, 60-1, 68, 97 ff., 102-3, 105-7, 112, 150, 152, 156, 170, 173-4
individuation, 104-7, 170, 173
insight, 9, 11, 36, 40, 73, 135, 160
instrumentalism, 68, 170
insularity, 40
insurance, 157-8, 171
interpretation, ch. IX; 18, 22, 84, 135, 140, 143, 155, 168, 170, 175
- Christianity as, 140-8
- community of, 124-8, 143, 155, 162
- conceptions of being as, 72 ff.

James, William, 15 ff., 38, 40, 59, 65, 68, 71 n., 101, 121-4, 126, 128, 132-4, 139, 150 n., 168, 170, 173-5
Jesus, 143; see Christ
John, St., 154
Johns Hopkins University, 8 n., 17, 18, 35
Judge, 55, 56
judgments, 32, 34, 38-9, 41, 45, 83, 125, 150

Kant, Immanuel, 20, 72, 110, 119
Keats, John, 153 n.
Kingdom of Heaven, 153-4, 157
knowledge, ch. III, VI, IX; 18, 44-5, 50, 58, 67, 88, 135, 167-8, 170-2, 174

LeConte, Joseph, 92
Lewis, C. I., 16
life, 48, 52, 61, 63, 67, 112, 136
limitation, 35, 40, 42, 52, 54, 56, 63, 98, 109-10, 145, 150, 153, 170, 174
literary works, 8
logic, 7, 17-8, 127
Logos, 154
love, 67, 104 ff., 113, 115, 131-2, 137, 143, 146, 154-6, 161-2, 169, 173
Lovejoy, Arthur, 15
loyalty, 13, 115, 137-8, 146-7, 154, 156, 160-2, 169, 173

INDEX

Mann, Jesse, 119 n.
Marcel, Gabriel, 16 n., 17, 109 n., 153-4
materialism, 129
Mead, George H., 15
means, communities as, 155-63
mechanical method, 129-30
mediation, 39, 128, 130-1, 141, 145 ff., 155-6, 162, 170, 174
mediating principle, interpretation as, ch. IX, 27, 175
mediator, 125, 128-32, 148
memory, 59, 112, 152
Mezes, Sidney, 92
Mill, J. S., 3
monism, 3, 18, 25 n., 43, 54 n., 92
Moore, Edward C., 22 n.
moral burden, 144-5
moral insight, 10, 39, 40, 51, 54-5
mystery, 51, 82, 104, 113, 147
mysticism, 73-5, 77-8, 120-1

naturalism, 8
nature, 103
need, religious, 9, 138-40, 143-5, 148, 160

objective idealism, 6, 14
objectivity, 150
Omniscient Being, 87-9, 106
Oppenheim, Frank M., 16 n., 17 n., 28
optimism, 63, 65, 110, 133 n., 138, 151, 171

pantheism, 50, 55 n., 60, 99, 173
Papini, Giovanni, 15
paradox, 138-40
Paul, St., 144, 161-2
Pauline Christians, 14
Peirce, Charles Sanders, 15 ff., 33 n., 34-6, 45, 65, 125-8, 130 n., 132, 150 n., 168, 170, 173-5
perception, 119 ff., 125, 129
Perry, Ralph Barton, 18, 19 n., 20, 122 n., 133
person, 59, 97, 114, 151, 173; see also individual, self
personality, 58, 60, 97, 108, 111, 150-1
pessimism, 63-5
philosophy, 108, 114
philosophy of religion, 7-8, 11, 14, 52 n., 87, 141, 160
Platonic ideas, 72
pluralism, 3, 18, 25 n., 43, 92, 160 n.
possible, 4, 41, 49, 95

possible experience, 5, 34-5, 49, 75, 77, 83, 89
possibility of error, 4, 41, 172
postulate, 4, 8-9, 34, 36-7, 41, 49, 106, 147-8, 168, 172, 175
Powell, Joseph, 17 n.
Power, 48, 53, 60, 139
practical, 6, 16, 22-3, 31 ff., 37, 55, 71, 84, 100, 124, 130, 147, 155, 167, 171, 175
practicalism, 15, 20
pragmaticism, 22
pragmatic postulate, God as, ch. X; 28, 174
pragmatism, ch. II, VI, XII; 3, 15 ff., 31, 43, 68, 101, 120-4, 132
process philosophy, 24 n.
Prometheus, heresy of, 62
purpose, 7, 14, 27, 33, 67, 76-7, 84, 102-3, 123, 167, 172

radical empiricism, 27
radicals, 65
rationalism, 71, 119
real, 48 n., 72-3, 89-90, 121
realism, 4, 22, 27, 72 ff., 102, 171-2, 176
reason, 11, 12, 80 ff., 103
redemption, 144 n., 145 ff.
relativity, 25-6, 40 ff., 55, 64, 75, 110, 123, 134, 168
religion, 8, 37, 45, 52 n., 86, 138, 140 ff.
religious element in Royce's philosophy, 7 ff.
religious experience, objects of, 11 ff., 138, 143
religious insight, 9-14, 39-40
religious paradox, 138 ff., 160
Renouvier, Charles, 3
responsibility, 10, 35, 44, 47-8, 107 ff., 169-70
revelation, 14, 138-40, 143
Robbins, Reginald C., 126 n., 127
Roth, Robert, 8
Russell, Bertrand, 119 n.

salvation, 9, 11, 138, 140, 143-5, 160-1
Schiller, F. C. S., 15, 22, 71 n.
Schopenhauer, Arthur, 3
self, 32, 36, 58, 64, 99, 101 ff., 110-5, 131, 137, 145, 151-2, 170, 173; see also individual
Shelley, Percy, 153 n.
signs, 18, 125-9
sin, 36, 110, 144-5

Singer, E. A., 155 n.
Smith, John E. 15, 149 n., 153-4, 160 n.
social character of knowledge, 58-9, 78-85, 168
social plasticity, 111
society, 11, 13, 80, 84, 114, 144, 159
Socrates, 19
sorrow, 11, 13
soul-substance, 102
speculation, 31 ff., 169, 174-5
Spinoza, Benedict, 72
Spirit, 10, 51, 67, 130, 139, 154, 160-1
statistics, 129-30
subjective idealism, 6
subjectivity, 150
superhuman, 13, 137-9, 160-1; see supernatural
supernatural, 13, 46, 138, 161
symbol, 147
synthetic view of reality, 75-8, 167, 171

Thayer, H. S., 15-6, 21 n., 27 n., 33 n., 49 n.
theological usage, 14
theoretical idealism, 6-7, 14
thinking, 36, 88
Thomas Aquinas, 75
Thought, 4, 48, 50-1, 53, 55-6, 60, 63, 65, 67, 74-5, 86, 89, 93-6, 137, 169
Titanism, 62
treason, 145-6

triadic process, 18, 22, 127·09, 131
Trinity, 154 n.
true, 47, 72, 74-5, 79, 83, 91, 94, 134 ff.
truth, 23, 25 ff., 32-6, 38-42, 45, 47-8, 50, 63-4, 67-8, 72-7, 79-80, 84, 90-1, 95, 101, 120, 122, 133 ff., 138-9, 145, 148, 150, 168, 172, 174-5

unity of community, 126, 152, 154
Universal Community, 153 ff., see also Beloved Community
Universal will, 51 ff., 60, 65-6, 68, 94, 169

validity, 31, 72, 74-7
value, 59, 68, 128, 137, 150-1
verifiability, 23, 38
verification, 23-4, 26, 37-8, 42, 47, 64, 67, 77, 79, 83-4, 89-90, 101, 125, 133, 135, 168
vitalism, 129-30
voluntarism, 6-7, 14, 32-3, 42, 51, 65-8, 77-8, 103, 123, 151, 167, 174

war, 157
Whitehead, Alfred N., 24 n.
Wholeness, 25, 40, 65, 89, 96
will, 11, 12, 27, 32-3, 39, 44, 52-5, 63-4, 71, 92 ff., 99, 104, 110, 123, 137, 168-9; see also voluntarism
Wilson, Woodrow, 157
world, 3-4, 25, 80, 136-7